Measurement in
PERSONALITY
AND COGNITION

edited by

SAMUEL MESSICK
Educational Testing Service

and

JOHN ROSS
University of Western Australia

Measurement in
PERSONALITY
AND COGNITION

John Wiley and Sons, Inc.
New York   •   London

Preface

This book attempts to preserve the essence of a conference on personality measurement sponsored by Educational
Testing Service at Princeton, New Jersey, in October 1960.
One purpose of the conference was to bring together for con-
structive interaction research specialists in personality
measurement who had diverse backgrounds and interests,
ranging from factor analysis to psychoanalysis and including
clinical, social, psychometric, and cognitive emphases.

The conference was divided into five sessions, which
correspond to the five sections of the present volume. The
papers formally delivered at each session were followed by
active and provocative interchanges which together constituted one of the most important and rewarding aspects of
the entire enterprise. Although these discussions were
carefully transcribed, much of the vigor and some of the
sense originally carried by gestures and inflections were
lost. The transcription, being a faithful reproduction of the
spoken version with all its natural repetitions and interrup-
tions, did not appear to be a sufficiently concise or coherent
account of the discussions to warrant publication. Since the
alternative of simply eliminating these comments from the
present volume would have simultaneously disregarded one
of the major functions of the conference, it was instead decided to rewrite some of the remarks for more concise pre-

v

sentation. Accordingly, a special commentary chapter was solicited for each set of papers, which would serve to summarize most of the major arguments and interchanges, while also offering some of the discussants an opportunity to expand their views. The editors are especially grateful to the discussants who undertook this task, since their chapters contribute materially to this volume as a conference report by helping to capture an important aspect of the general proceedings: W. Grant Dahlstrom of the University of North Carolina, Michael A. Wallach of Massachusetts Institute of Technology, Robert P. Abelson of Yale University, and Silvan S. Tomkins of Princeton University.

Although from one point of view the conference was deliberately conceived rather broadly in terms of the backgrounds of the participants and the attendant range of topics likely to be discussed, the formal papers were organized ostensibly in terms of five general topics to provide a structured context for discussion. The first section contains three papers by Andrew L. Comrey, George G. Stern, and John Ross, respectively, which discuss questionnaire measures of personality dimensions and the application of factor analysis for developing inventory scales and appraising their interrelationships. In the second section three papers by Allen L. Edwards, by Jerry S. Wiggins, and by Douglas N. Jackson and Samuel Messick stress the role of stylistic factors in personality assessment and attack the dual problem of measuring response styles as personality variables and of controlling their influence on content scales. In the third section, Hanna F. Faterson and Riley W. Gardner discuss the measurement of stylistic consistencies in cognition and consider the intricate way in which such cognitive styles are linked to and illuminate the organization of personality. The fourth section includes papers by Edward E. Jones and by James Bieri emphasizing the roles of social influences and situational or stimulus determinants in assessing personality and social variables. Commentaries for these four sections were provided by Ross and Messick, Dahlstrom, Wallach, and Abelson, respectively.

The first four sections consider personality measurement in terms of response consistencies in endorsing the content of items and in terms of stylistic consistencies in response to formal item properties, to adaptive task requirements in cognitive performance, and to situational and social influences. Implicit in the discussions of relationships among these types of variables were strong preferences for different modes of approaching the research problem, ranging from reliance upon clinical interpretation through developmental description and experimental manipulation to psychometric analysis. In the fifth section these differences in research strategy are treated explicitly first from a multivariate-statistical point of view by Raymond B. Cattell and then from a clinical-experimental standpoint by Robert R. Holt. Some philosophical perspectives upon research orientations in psychology are provided in the concluding commentary by Silvan S. Tomkins.

This brief outline of the formal papers presented at the conference is intended to provide a summary impression of the focus around which the subsequent discussions evolved. As already indicated, the ensuing provocative interchanges of viewpoints fulfilled one of the major aims of the conference, and special thanks are due to the other discussants and participants for their many thoughtful contributions:

Irving E. Alexander, National Institute of
   Mental Health
Donald Campbell, Northwestern University
Henry Chauncey, Educational Testing Service
Lee J. Cronbach, University of Illinois
Fred L. Damarin, Educational Testing Service
Henry P. David, New Jersey Department of
   Institutions and Agencies
Edward Engel, State University of New York,
   Syracuse
Cyril M. Franks, New Jersey Neuropsychiatric
   Institute
Norman Frederiksen, Educational Testing
   Service

Charles Hanley, Michigan State University
E. Lowell Kelly, University of Michigan
Nathan Kogan, Educational Testing Service
Jane Loevinger, Washington University
    Medical School
Warren T. Norman, University of Michigan
Jerry Osterweil, University of Pennsylvania
    Hospital
Milton Rokeach, Michigan State University
David R. Saunders, Princeton, New Jersey
Harold Schroder, Princeton University
Lee Sechrest, Northwestern University
Lawrence J. Stricker, Educational Testing
    Service
Ernest C. Tupes, Personnel Laboratory,
    Lackland AFB, Texas
William W. Turnbull, Educational Testing
    Service

A major acknowledgment is also due to Educational Testing Service for its encouragement in financing both the conference and the preparation of this manuscript and to Henry Chauncey, its President, for his many helpful comments and suggestions about the selection of topics and the organization of the program.

The editors also gratefully acknowledge the assistance of Gerri Asbury and Miriam Kiss in making the conference arrangements and of Jean Herman, Dannie Kennedy, Ann King, and Sally Matlack in preparing the manuscript for publication. Because of the pressures of research and teaching duties, some of the time required for editing this volume was in effect donated by our wives and families, and this contribution by Betty Messick and Jill Ross is explicitly and gratefully acknowledged.

                                        Samuel Messick
Princeton, N. J., 1962   John Ross

Contents

ix

Samuel Messick
Educational Testing Service
and
John Ross
University of Western Australia

1

Introduction:
Psychological Structure
and Measurement Models
in Personality Assessment

This book reports the proceedings of a conference on personality measurement held under the auspices of Educational Testing Service at Princeton, New Jersey, in October 1960. In addition to the papers formally delivered as part of the conference program, this volume also includes five specially prepared commentary chapters that serve to summarize and expand upon discussions which developed from the formal presentations.

Since the scope of the conference was deliberately broad, participants were invited to represent a wide range of interests from the psychoanalytic to the factor analytic. At the same time, however, the intent of the conference was to focus the participants' attention upon some central issues in personality assessment to provide a common basis for interaction. The major foci were (1) the complementary constructs of content and style in human assessment, and (2) a concern with the fit between substantive theories and measurement models in personality.

In connection with the problem of content and style, the papers taken as a whole stress both (a) dimensions of content consistency in response to items and stimulus properties; and (b) stylistic consistencies in response to item form, to adaptive task requirements in cognitive performance, to situational and social influences, and even to choice

1

of preferred research strategy. The conference did not
pretend to treat this theme exhaustively, but rather to
examine it with respect to some salient contemporary problems in personality assessment and research. In addition,
the general issue of content and style--with its intimate
relation to both theoretical and methodological problems
(cf. Jackson and Messick, 1958)--provided both a stimulus
and a context for the second major focus of discussion:
the fit between substantive theories and measurement
models in personality. It is the contribution of the conference papers to this latter topic to which we now turn.

Although the terms theory and model are often used
interchangeably, systematic distinctions are sometimes
made between them (cf. Davidson, Suppes, and Siegel,
1957; Lachman, 1960; Suppes, 1957). A theory, for example, may refer to a set of assertions about interrelationships among processes or constructs presumed to
underlie and account for observed phenomena in some
domain. The term "model," on the other hand, may be
restricted in reference to a separate system of symbolic
representation which is thought to correspond to a substantive system of central interest. For our purposes,
the term "model" will be used arbitrarily only in connection with measurement, and "measurement model" will be
taken to refer to the elements, properties, and relationships represented in a separate symbolic or mathematical
system that are to be coordinated with properties of empirical phenomena. The elements of the model are usually
real numbers and the properties usually reflect ordinal,
interval, and ratio relationships (Stevens, 1951; Torgerson,
1958), but measurement models vary greatly beyond this
point in the complexity of their technical machinery. Some
models may include rules of inference, possible interpretations, geometric or topological representations, and much
of the calculus of logic and mathematics for deriving testable consequences and relationships (Lachman, 1960;
Gulliksen, 1959). At the more complex levels, a model
may not only provide a system for measuring particular

attributes, but also a basis for statistical analysis or dimensional resolution, as in the factor analytic model.

The term "measurement theory" will be used to refer to the linking of a measurement model to an empirical domain in such a way that properties of the model are isomorphic to properties of the domain (Luce, 1959; Suppes, 1957). There are thus different types of theories which differ widely in their intended inclusiveness and ultimate generality. Whereas one type may apply only to the measurement of particular attributes, another may integrate a complicated network of substantive relationships. At the level of measurement, a theory tells how to assign numbers and some of their properties (aspects of the model) to the properties of objects or events (aspects of the domain) in such a way that the numerical operations and relations are isomorphic to certain specified empirical operations and relations (Luce, 1959; Torgerson, 1958). A substantive theory, by way of contrast, may be considered to be at a higher level of discourse in the sense that it usually involves relationships among several variables, each assessed in terms of its own measurement theory (Luce, 1959).

One problem in personality measurement, as we see it, is that personality theorists and measurement theorists are out of touch. By and large they do not speak the same language, and the effect may be serious. On the one hand, there appears to be considerable lag on the part of measurement specialists in taking account of the psychological theorists' requirements, such as in developing models that would handle moderator effects and other curvilinear relations, a problem discussed in more detail later by Ross (Chapter 4), Ross and Messick (Chapter 5), Wallach (Chapter 12), and Abelson (Chapter 15). On the other hand, many personality theorists do not seem to appreciate all the strictures inherent in the adoption of a model as a basis for measurement or statistical analysis. In the latter connection, Loevinger (1957), in her discussion of structural validity in measurement as a component of con-

struct validity (Cronbach and Meehl, 1955), has emphasized the need to evaluate the extent to which structural
relations between items resulting from the application of
a particular measurement model parallel structural relations occurring in other manifestations of the trait being
measured.

Since substantive structure is difficult to determine
without measurement of some kind, the problem is somewhat circular and will probably need to be approached
iteratively by successive evaluations of substantive structure and subsequent changes in measurement models as
the science progresses. However, the application of
several different measurement approaches in assessing
a particular set of substantive relationships and, conversely, the application of a given measurement technique
to several different variables should provide insights into
the nature of both the substantive relationships and the
models' restrictions in a multitrait-multimethod design
(Campbell and Fiske, 1959). The point to be emphasized
here is that at the stage of experimental implementation
and measurement of the personality theorist's constructs,
measurement models are ubiquitously introduced, and
systematic attempts should be made to relate the assumptions and requirements of the model to properties of observed behavioral consistencies.

The present conference represented nothing so ambi-
tious as a full-scale attack on this problem of matching
personality theories and measurement models, nor even
an attempt to explore its implications fully. We chose
instead to look at a few related problem areas in personality measurement in the presence of psychologists with
varying degrees of commitment to particular substantive
theories and measurement approaches. Many of the papers
bore more or less directly upon the issue of structural
validity in measurement, in that they discussed attempts
to measure personality variables with techniques that
reflect the nature and complexity of the domain without
artificially restricting possible substantive relations.

Since the conference audience covered a broad range of interests and skills, the discussions following the formal presentations tended to focus upon this problem in a context that permitted the differential emphases of both personality theorists and measurement specialists. As a result, the five commentary chapters in the present volume reflect this concern fairly directly; they discuss some of the problems involved in formulating and utilizing measurement approaches whose structural assumptions appropriately reflect structural relations in an empirical domain.

The present volume is divided into five parts. The first section--comprised of papers by Comrey, Stern, and Ross--considers the measurement of personality dimensions using inventory scales, an enterprise heavily involved with both substantive theories and measurement models. The involvement with personality theories is a general one, since inventories are usually built either to measure constructs thought to be significant in terms of some theory or to provide a source of response consistency to help determine the number and nature of important variables requiring theoretical integration. The involvement with measurement models is a more intimate one, since the techniques used to derive measures from responses to a test depend, implicitly or explicitly, upon models of the relationship between the respondent and his test responses. Comrey (Chapter 2), employing the model of factor analysis (which is perhaps not so much a model as a set of mathematical restrictions upon possible psychological relationships), deals with the problems of identifying the variables measured by a test and of providing a consistent, reliable basis for inferences from scale scores to underlying trait dimensions. Stern (Chapter 3) also applies factor analysis to ascertain the number of dimensions underlying scores on his need scales and to describe the structure of their interrelationships, using the vector language of the analytic model directly in discussing the psychological system. Ross (Chapter 4) proposes to use factor analytic results somewhat differently--primarily as a basis for inference about the structure of the underlying domain, arguing that if empirical relationships are adequately described by the factor model, then certain other incompatible models do not apply.

In the second section, Edwards (Chapter 6), Wiggins (Chapter 7), and Jackson and Messick (Chapter 8) discuss the role of response styles in personality measurement--a topic requiring attention both to psychological conceptualizations and to measurement models, but in particular to the restrictions upon one which are inherent in the adoption of the other. For example, if one wished to measure certain content dimensions, the confounding influence of stylistic variance should be controlled in the total content scores. However, if the stylistic consistencies are considered to reflect personality variables in their own right, the form of the control is critical--in particular, it should not bias estimates of relationships between content traits and response styles. For example, one statistical approach to the control problem--that of administering independent measures of response sets to be regressed out of content scores (Webster, 1958, 1959)--seems inappropriate for investigating the structure of the domain, since the partial correlation approach produces corrected content scales which are uncorrelated with the response styles in question. This may be a desirable feature for control purposes, but it severely interferes with the evaluation of possible content-style interrelationships (Messick, 1962). In addition to demonstrating massive stylistic effects in the questionnaire measurement of personality, the three papers in this section approach the problems of measurement and control in a manner which highlights the properties of both response styles and content consistencies and which underscores the need for procedures that maintain the substantive integrity of both.

The third section considers similar problems in the measurement of stylistic consistencies, this time in the area of cognition, and faces similar pitfalls in the assessment of content-style relationships. Faterson (Chapter 10) and Gardner (Chapter 11) discuss the measurement of cognitive controls and cognitive styles as regulatory tendencies which are reflected in a person's typical modes of perceiving, remembering, thinking, and problem solving. This is a difficult area in terms of both the substantive theories and the measurement models, since the conceptions and measures of stylistic consistencies should both distinguish them from, and appropriately relate them to, specific cognitive content and relevant intellectual abilities. The possibility of different stylistic propensities and even of different cognitive structures for the two sexes (and for subjects high or low on other moderating variables, such as particular defenses, abilities, or temperaments) greatly multiplies the conceptual and measurement difficulties, since multivariate procedures for uncovering and analyzing such moderator effects have not evolved very far.

In the fourth section, Jones (Chapter 13) and Bieri (Chapter 14) report research findings bearing upon the measurement of situational and stimulus influences in social judgment and interpersonal relations. As in the previous section, the possible influence of moderating variables or conditions is also emphasized, particularly the role of the situation in moderating relationships between personality variables and interpersonal behavior.

As pointed out previously, the commentary chapters for each of the first four sections--by Ross and Messick (Chapter 5), Dahlstrom (Chapter 9), Wallach (Chapter 12), and Abelson (Chapter 15)--tend to focus upon relationships and interactions between psychological theories and measurement models in each area. Apart from the question of whether or not measurement models appropriately reflect substantive structure, however, there seemed to be a constant interplay running through the conference between two points of view: on the one hand, a preference for assessment procedures that involve little mathematical restriction but presumably offer more opportunity for substantive relations to emerge unfettered, and on the other hand, a preference for measurement approaches whose admittedly restrictive mathematical assumptions nevertheless form the basis for powerful analytic techniques. These relative preferences reflect different research strategies in the study of personality which are discussed explicitly in the final section of the volume, the multivariate-statistical point of view being favored by Cattell (Chapter 16) and the clinical-experimental position being endorsed by Holt (Chapter 17). In the final commentary chapter (Chapter 18), Tomkins suggests that the preferences in question reflect different value systems which consistently polarize ideological commitments and urges us not to be too dogmatic in our insistence that either one or the other is the royal road for psychological inquiry.

PART I

Questionnaire Measures
of Personality Dimensions

2

Andrew L. Comrey

University of California,
Los Angeles

Factored Homogeneous Item Dimensions: A Strategy for Personality Research

Even a casual glance at reviews of personality research reveals that there is as yet little agreement about which variables should be studied. Even when consideration is limited to research involving paper-and-pencil personality tests and inventories in which factor-analytic methods have played an important part, there is still an evident lack of general agreement for many possible reasons. If we consider two investigators studying the personality factors identifiable by means of questionnaires and inventories, we might find them differing significantly with respect to one or more of the following procedures: kind of sample studied, type of item written, factor complexity of the variables introduced into analysis, size of sample, size of correlation

This study was supported by a grant from the University of California. The author is indebted to Alladin Soufi who wrote the first draft of most of the items used in this study and helped with the data collection. All computations were carried out on SWAC, an electronic computer located on the campus of the University of California at Los Angeles and supported by the Office of Naval Research.

Permission to reproduce this paper, which appeared in Educational and Psychological Measurement, 21, No. 2, Summer, 1961, has been granted through the courtesy of G. Frederic Kuder, Editor.

matrix analyzed, method of correlation used, method of
factor extraction, number of factors extracted, and method
of rotation. With so many degrees of freedom, perhaps one
should be surprised to find any agreement whatsoever between two independent investigators.

It will not be possible, and probably would be unwise,
to force complete standardization of practice upon different
investigators in order to achieve a greater degree of agreement among them. It is important to explore what can be
achieved with different methods. Sources of disagreement
which fulfill no useful function, however, should be sought
out and eliminated. It is the author's belief that one such
source of disagreement is the improper use of personality
items as variables in factor-analytic work. Contrary to the
general practice in work with ability tests, personality
factor-analytic research has tended to use the single item
as the unit. Instead of factor analyzing total scores over
collections of relatively homogeneous items, as with ability
test research, the tendency in personality research has been
rather to factor analyze collections of heterogeneous single
items.

It has long been known that an individual item, particularly a true-false personality item, tends to be unreliable.
When a matrix of considerable size is obtained, particularly
with relatively small samples, certain correlations may be
seriously in error. These effects are very apt to be aggra-
vated further if tetrachoric coefficients or phi-over-phi-max
coefficients are used with items which depart from an even
split between the alternatives (Comrey and Levonian, 1958).
To the extent that the correlations obtained are in error, we
may expect the factor structure obtained to be distorted.

An obvious way of increasing stability of results is to
increase the reliability of the variables intercorrelated.
An improvement in stability could therefore be obtained by
correlating total scores from several items with the same
factor content, rather than single items. Factor results
based upon such correlations would be less subject to
chance fluctuation from one analysis to another.

The first problem is to establish that a group of items is homogeneous in factor content. If we are to be objective, we are forced back to an analysis of items, but the distortion due to chance errors will be much less pronounced in subsequent analyses of total score variables than it is likely to be for analyses based upon unpooled single items. One suggested procedure starts with definitions of the particular variables which one wishes to investigate. Next, several items are written with the intent to provide a homogeneous, internally consistent pool for measuring each defined variable. Then a factor analysis of the items is carried out. A factor should appear for each variable defined, provided these variables are not too highly correlated. If the variable defined is a reasonably definite and independent one, and if the items written are good ones, a strong factor should emerge with high loadings for most of the items written to measure the factor. The items with highest loadings may be picked as the pool of items over which a total score is obtained. This will be called a factored homogeneous item dimension. The procedure automatically eliminates items with low factor loadings, e.g., less than .4. Items with satisfactorily high loadings which were designed for some other dimension are also usually eliminated.

The procedure outlined here is designed to obtain greater consistency of results through the joint agreement of both logical and statistical criteria. Certain items are conceived logically to measure a particular defined variable. Empirical results are obtained to determine which of these items actually do seem to go together. These results are then independently verified by further work. By rejecting items with substantial loadings when they were not written for the given factor, we may be rejecting good items, along with items measuring logically different but substantially correlated variables, and items high by chance. But if only items which meet both logical and empirical criteria of acceptability are used to measure a particular factored homogeneous item dimension, there is less chance that we will erect an elaborate superstructure upon a foundation of error variance.

Once the items are chosen to define a total score on a factor dimension, the variable is ready for use. Total scores may be obtained in the same way for other dimensions. Some of the dimensions will come from the same factor analysis of items, while others will be derived from different analyses. The total dimension scores obtained in this way may be intercorrelated, using the Pearson correlation coefficient, and the resulting matrix may then be factor analyzed. The intercorrelations between such factored homogeneous item dimensions will be considerably more stable under most conditions than intercorrelations between single items. As a consequence, greater stability of factor analytic results should be obtained. This, in turn, should contribute to improved consistency among the results of independent investigations in the same domain. To illustrate the application of these procedures, the results of an empirical investigation using them will be described.

Two Factor-Analytic Studies

Over forty dimensions of personality were selected for investigation. Some of these were suggested by factors found by the author in his studies of MMPI items (Comrey, 1957a, 1957b, 1957c, 1958a, 1958b, 1958c, 1958d, 1958e, 1958f, 1959); others were based upon factors described by previous investigators (Cattell, 1957; Guilford, 1959); and still others, mostly background variables, were introduced for their possible role in clarifying the meaning of the factors obtained. Multiple-choice items were written to measure each of these defined dimensions, usually four or six items per dimension. A booklet containing all these items was part of a packet which also included three answer sheets and a set of instructions explaining the study and promising a later report on the respondent's test results if he would fill out the test and mail the answer sheet to the investigator. These packets were distributed to virtually every third dwelling unit in Culver City, California, an upper middle class community on the western edge of Los Angeles. About 1,000 of these packets were distributed to the doorstep and about 300 completed answer sheets were returned. The sample selected for analysis included the first 100 answer sheets received from male subjects and the first 152 answer sheets received from female subjects.

The dimensions studied were divided into four groups for purposes of analysis. Within each group, all the items written to measure those dimensions were intercorrelated using the Pearson coefficient, and the obtained matrix was subjected to a factor analysis. The centroid factors obtained in each case were rotated analytically to orthogonal simple structure using the Varimax method (Kaiser, 1958). The first three of these analyses, dealing principally with factor dimensions suggested by previous research, have been described elsewhere (Comrey and Soufi, 1960, 1961). The fourth analysis will be described here, together with the results of an over-all analysis of total dimension scores obtained from the principal factors isolated in the first four analyses.

The 13 dimensions analyzed in the fourth study and the 55 items written to measure them will be described below. Each item employed one of the following three sets of response alternatives:

(X) A. very frequently, B. frequently,
     C. occasionally, D. rarely, E. never
(Y) A. always, B. usually, C. occasionally,
     D. rarely, E. never
(Z) A. definitely, B. probably, C. possibly,
     D. probably not, E. definitely not

Each dimension will be named below and followed with the items written to measure it. For each item, the booklet number of the item will be followed by a letter, X, Y, or Z, to indicate which set of the possible response alternatives given above was used with that item. Following each item for most dimensions will be given, in parentheses, the factor loading on the obtained factor which most closely approximated the hypothesized factor dimension. Loadings will not be shown for the items in the dimensions Hostility and Attitude toward School Authorities because no factor emerged which could be identified with either of these dimensions.

Hostility

64Y.   When I become angry I feel like smashing things.

71Y.   When someone causes me a lot of trouble, I imagine myself hurting or killing him.

191Z. I would like to see an execution.

200Z. I wish someone would put all the people I hate in one room and set fire to it.

Psychopathic Personality

154Z. I think if a person is stupid enough to be cheated, then he deserves to be cheated. (.56)

167Z. If a thief can outsmart the police, he deserves to keep what he steals. (.58)

173Z. I think it would be fun to get away with cheating certain people. (.10)

181Z. The important thing is to get what you want. How you get it is less important. (.30)

229Z. I think it is wrong to take anything, even from someone who can afford it. (-.17)

Aggression

52Y.   When I get mad I break things. (.70)

192Z. I would avoid physical violence if I possibly could. (-.07)

197Z. I could easily lose control of myself and hurt someone badly. (.31)

231Z. I can become so angry that I might hit someone. (.57)

Discipline

5X.   As a child I used to be whipped. (.63)

14X.   As a child I was punished severely for little things. (.72)

33X.   As a child I received severe physical punishment at home. (.73)

158Z. I believe I was more frequently punished than most other children. (.60)

Personal Appearance
134Z. I have been considered to be good looking. (.73)
171Z. I have always wished that I was better looking.
         (-.19)
205Z. My acquaintances consider me physically attrac-
         tive. (.71)
216Z. I have been very attractive to the opposite sex. (.59)

History of Illness
8X.   As an adult (16 or over) I have been seriously ill.
         (.11)
32X.   During childhood I was seriously ill. (.60)
87Y.   I was physically a normal and healthy child. (-.72)
141Z. As a child I was physically weak. (.57)

Socio-economic Level
190Z. My mother was (is) a highly educated woman. (.66)
195Z. My father was (is) a highly educated man. (.78)
207Z. During my childhood we were well off financially.
         (.45)
211Z. My father was (is) an important man in the commu-
         nity. (.53)

Delinquency
3X.   My teen-age friends got into trouble with the law.
         (.37)
12X.   I was kicked out of school or transferred for
         getting into trouble. (.49)
17X.   During my teens I was picked up or questioned by
         the police. (.64)
37X.   As a teenager I engaged in gang fights. (.44)
182Z. My parent(s) (or guardian) liked my teen-age
         friends. (-.07)
193Z. School authorities regarded me as a discipline
         problem. (.59)

Academic Standing
29X.   I received poor grades at school. (-.75)
56Y.   I passed my school subjects with better than
         average grades. (.81)

Academic Standing (contd)
67Y.   My teachers thought I was a good student. (.75)
162Z.   I received failing grades at school rather frequently.
        (-.61)

Attitude toward School Authorities
24X.   I was punished at school.
55Y.   I was happy at school.
131Z.   At school I disliked most of the teachers.
144Z.   Most of my teachers were interested in me and my
        work.

Status in Child Peer Group
53Y.   When I was a child the other kids considered me to
        be a leader. (.77)
70Y.   I was active in school affairs such as sports, clubs,
        and so on. (.54)
89Y.   As a kid I was a leader among my friends. (.80)
150Z.   I was popular among my schoolmates. (.61)

Closeness to Father
59Y.   As a child I felt free to go to my father and ask him
        to help me. (.68)
106Y.   My father was indifferent toward me. (-.58)
194Z.   My father loved me when I was a child. (.60)
232Z.   I was (am) close to my father. (.74)

Closeness to Mother
26X.   As a child I had the feeling that my mother didn't
        want me. (-.55)
91Y.   My mother helped me with my problems when she
        could. (.72)
187Z.   My mother did the best she could to make me happy.
        (.71)
202Z.   I was (am) close to my mother. (.60)

Fifteen factors were extracted and rotated in this
analysis. Eleven of these were identified with corresponding factor dimensions hypothesized prior to the collection
of data. Of the four remaining factors, two had no loadings

over .34 and another had only one loading over .3, a loading of .55 for item 200. The remaining factor had only
three moderate loadings over .33: .41 for item 191, .44
for item 173, and -.39 for item 192. Small loadings about
.3 also occurred on this factor for items 181, 197, and
231. None of these extra factors could be described as
prominent.

Hostility and Aggression were included as separate
dimensions to test a hypothesis that there might be distinct factors for covert and overt aggression. Items for
the Hostility dimension were written therefore to omit
references to action based on the hostile feelings. Aggression, on the other hand, included items mentioning direct
action based on the hostile feelings. Only one major factor
emerged in this area, taking items from both these dimensions. This factor included loadings of .81 for item 84 and
.34 for item 71 from the Hostility dimension as well as
those listed above for the Aggression dimension.

Attitude toward School Authorities failed to achieve
independent factor status, merging with the factor of Delinquency. Items 24 and 55 from Attitude toward School
Authorities had loadings on the Delinquency factor of .47
and -.36, respectively. Neither of the remaining items,
131 or 144, had a loading as large as .35 on any factor.

Aside from those mentioned above, only two items had
loadings over .35 on factors other than the one for which
they were written. Item 3 from Delinquency had a loading
of .46 on the Personal Appearance factor and item 55 from
Attitude toward School Authorities had a loading of .38 on
Status in Child Peer Group.

The four factor analyses of these items, including that
just described and those previously reported, yielded 36
factor dimensions over which total scores were obtained.
Two validation scales and six personal data items were
added to make 44 variables for an over-all factor analysis.
These 44 variables and the numbers of the items used to
measure them will be given below. The specific items defining the factors from the first three analyses have been

presented elsewhere (Comrey and Soufi, 1960, 1961) and therefore will not be repeated here.

(1)   Depression: 36, 51, 96, 101, 125, 133, 221
(2)   Shyness: 60, 75, 95, 118, 186
(3)   Poor Physical Health: 42, 76, 110, 127
(4)   Sensitivity: 73, 161, 199
(5)   Sex Drive: 149, 172
(6)   Poor Concentration: 10, 99, 105, 219
(7)   Cynicism: 135, 136, 137, 138, 142, 163
(8)   Sex Concern: 13, 23, 39, 97
(9)   Satisfaction with Life: 63, 111, 119, 148, 183
(10) Agitation: 2, 20, 43
(11) Restraint: 82, 108
(12) Paranoia: 206, 210
(13) Poor Reality Contact: 25, 30
(14) Psychopathic Personality: 154, 167
(15) Aggression: 52, 64, 231
(16) Rhathymia: 143, 153, 174
(17) Taciturnity: 49, 81, 222, 224
(18) Alertness: 1, 146
(19) Friendliness: 98, 126
(20) Lie Scale: 8 items
(21) Validity Scale: 7 items
(22) Discipline: 5, 14, 33, 158
(23) Succorance: 21, 83, 115
(24) Nervousness: 113, 164
(25) Stability: 145, 176, 225, 234
(26) Poise: 129, 220
(27) Ascendance: 58, 114, 116, 147, 226
(28) Socialization: 92, 151, 178, 212
(29) Social Initiative: 50, 74
(30) Hostility: 160, 223
(31) Personal Appearance: 134, 205, 216
(32) Childhood Illness: 32, 87, 141
(33) Socio-economic Level: 190, 195, 207, 211
(34) Delinquency: 12, 17, 24, 37, 193
(35) Academic Standing: 29, 56, 67, 162
(36) Status in Peer Group: 53, 70, 89, 150

(37)   Closeness to Father: 59, 106, 194, 232
(38)   Closeness to Mother: 26, 91, 187, 202
(39)   Sex: female vs. male
(40)   Age: by decades
(41)   Educational Level: completed college, some col-
        lege, completed high school, some high school,
        grade school
(42)   Marital Status: married vs. not married
(43)   Religion: Protestant vs. not Protestant
(44)   Politics: Republican, no preference, Democrat

The higher scores were assigned to the first mentioned
categories in variables 39 to 44.

Variable 20 was designed to give a high score to the
individual deliberately or unconsciously trying to present a
favorable picture of himself. Variable 21 was designed to
give a high score to the person who was marking the answer
sheet in an irrational manner. Variables 39 through 44
were single-item variables based on personal data re-
quested on the test answer sheet. The remaining variables
were total factored homogeneous item dimension scores
derived from factors isolated in the analysis described
above or in one of the two previously reported studies.

These 44 variables were intercorrelated using the
Pearson correlation coefficient. Fourteen centroid factors
were extracted and rotated analytically to approximate
orthogonal simple structure using Kaiser's Varimax
method. In presenting the factors obtained, only those
variables with loadings over .35 will be mentioned.

Factor I seems best described as a Neuroticism factor.
Variables with important loadings were Agitation .64,
Stability -.62, Nervousness .62, Sensitivity .55, Taciturnity -.47, Succorance .41, Depression .41, Sex .39, and
Sex Concern .38. Because of the orientation of the sex
dichotomy, the positive loading for Sex indicates that
females were higher on this factor than males.

Factor II will be named Hostility. Variables on this
factor were Hostility .61, Cynicism .50, and Friendliness
-.39. The two items included in this Hostility score were

160Z, "I believe that most people are stupid jerks," and
223Z, "I have no use for most people." The correlation
between this dimension and Aggression was .05. This
implies that there is perhaps a definite distinction between
covert and overt hostility (aggression) despite the fact
that the items written to highlight this distinction in analysis IV failed to do so. Cynicism, which had the highest
loading on this factor, has been prominently identified in
several previous factor analyses.

Factor III is the Shyness factor found in several previous analyses. The Shyness and Poise dimensions are
virtually alternate forms of the same thing, although both
place more emphasis upon reactions to being before an
audience than in the previously identified Shyness factors.
Loadings were Shyness .91, Poise -.83, Social Initiative
-.53, and Status in Peer Group -.41.

Factor V was a Closeness to Parents factor with the
following loadings: Closeness to Father .55, Closeness to
Mother .55, Discipline -.43, and Satisfaction with Life .37.

Factor VII was called Poor Concentration. The important loadings were Poor Concentration .50, Alertness -.49,
and Succorance .37.

Factor IX was labeled Psychopathic Personality. The
important factor loadings were Delinquency .65, Sex -.56,
Sex Drive .45, Lie Scale -.44, Aggression .37, and Discipline .36. The person with a high score on this factor
would tend to be a male with a previous record of trouble
with authority. He has a strong sex impulse and a tendency
to violence.

Factor X had loadings as follows: Cheerfulness vs.
Depression .67, Poor Physical Health .60, and Satisfaction
with Life -.58. It is perhaps best described as a Depression factor, one which seems to have a foundation in dete-
riorated circumstances.

Factor XI had only two important loadings, Psychopathic Personality -.56 and Academic Standing .47. One
might wonder why the first of these variables did not have
a substantial loading on the Psychopathic Personality factor

described above. Perusal of the items on the dimension of Psychopathic Personality reveals that both items concern the individual's abstract attitude about dishonest behavior of other people. This dimension, therefore, reveals anti-social attitudes, whereas the Psychopathic Personality factor described above is based to a greater extent on overt psychopathic behavior by the respondent.

Those loadings greater than .35 will be listed for the remaining factors without comment or interpretation since none of them was prominent. Factor IV, Socialization .58; Factor VI, Socio-economic Level .50; Factor VIII, Poor Reality Contact .38, Ascendance -.38, Validity Scale .49; Factor XII, Education .62, Age -.39; Factor XIII, Religion .52, Rhathymia -.44, Politics .38; Factor XIV, Personal Appearance .55, Lie Scale -.38.

Discussion

The results of the first factor analysis reported in this paper show clearly that it is not difficult to write items which will define a factor in some prescribed area. It is merely necessary to write several homogeneous items all measuring the same variable, combine them with other collections of homogeneous items which are uncorrelated with each other and the first set, and factor analyze the items. Each homogeneous subset of items will ordinarily produce a factor, unless the items are not really homo-geneous or have substantial correlations with items in some other subset. These facts suggest that a factor produced by analyzing collections of homogeneous subsets of items does not necessarily represent a phenomenon of deep underlying significance for the understanding of personality dynamics. On the other hand, each factored homogeneous item dimen-sion does represent a well-defined variable which may be useful in describing personality and predicting behavior.

Each investigator working with personality tests of the paper-and-pencil type believes certain variables to be important. Applying the principles followed in the factor studies discussed here, it should be possible for him to

develop a factored homogeneous item dimension for each
of his personality variables. Where two variables are correlated, it may be necessary to include them in separate
analyses to prevent their merging into the same factor.
Item analysis and refactoring will be necessary in most
cases to provide a collection of items all of which have
adequately high loadings on the obtained factor. If these
factored homogeneous item dimensions and the actual items
which have been empirically demonstrated to measure them
are published, it will be possible to integrate the findings
from different investigators by carrying out comprehensive
investigations in which the factors from several different
workers are combined in the same analysis. Such analyses
will inevitably show a great deal of overlap among the
factors contributed by different investigators. This phenomenon was revealed in the present study with the dimensions of Shyness and Poise as well as with Cheerfulness vs.
Depression and Satisfaction with Life. Applying the analogy
of n-dimensional hyperspace to this case, test vectors will
crowd in upon one another in some areas of the hyperspace,
whereas in other areas the test vectors stand alone.

    Analysis of the intercorrelations found among factored
homogeneous item dimensions will provide the means of
establishing a more stable picture of the factor structure
of personality in the domain of inventories. For example,
in the second factor analysis reported in this paper, it was
found that Agitation, Stability, Nervousness, and Sensitivity were sufficiently interrelated to produce a major
factor, which was described as a second-order factor of
Neuroticism. Several other factors indicated significant
overlap among some of the remaining dimensions analyzed.
Other dimensions, however, such as Sex Drive, Restraint,
Poor Reality Contact, and so on, failed to be sufficiently
related to the other dimensions included in this analysis to
define any major common factor. As other dimensions are
added to those studied here, it is to be expected that the
number of well-defined common factors will increase.
Some of these second-order factors will be broad in content,

like the Neuroticism factor here, whereas others will be
so narrow as to be considered virtual artifacts introduced
by the inclusion of highly similar dimensions in the same
analysis. An example of the second kind of factor is that
defined mainly by Poise and Shyness in the present investigation. It should be emphasized, however, that even if a
factored homogeneous item dimension seems to have no
substantial correlation with any other dimensions except
those which are virtually alternate forms, and hence has
no large loadings on any important second-order factor, it
still may be measuring a variable no less important than
those which do have high loadings on second-order factors.

Proliferation of dimensions in the same hyperspace
sector is wasteful duplication of effort, both in test development and in testing time. At the same time, to ignore areas
of the personality hyperspace which are relatively unexplored is to omit variance which must be considered in
order to obtain the best possible personality description
and prediction of personal adjustment. What is needed,
therefore, is some way to discourage investigators from
developing new personality scales which merely account for
variance that is already being measured by dimensions
proposed by others, and at the same time to encourage them
to develop dimensions which will bring in new variance not
yet adequately covered. Progress toward these objectives
would be made if each investigator who proposes a new
variable would develop a factored homogeneous item dimension to measure that variable and then determine its relationship to other published dimensions.

The factored homogeneous item dimensions presented
here were based upon the work of many different investigators and may serve as a possible starting point for building up a collection to cover the entire personality domain
which can be measured by such methods. It should be
added quickly, however, that most of the dimensions described here are based upon too few items and have yet to
be verified adequately. Further research, therefore, will
be needed to (1) verify and increase the reliability of the

dimensions reported here, by finding more items with
higher factor loadings; (2) develop additional factored
homogeneous item dimensions which will contribute something new; (3) investigate the relationships among these
dimensions in several kinds of samples; and (4) relate
these dimensions to external criteria of practical interest.
A vigorous implementation of such a program of research
should help to bring about more order and agreement than
is now evident in the field of personality measurement.

3 ‖ George G. Stern
Syracuse University

The Measurement of
Psychological Characteristics
of Students and
Learning Environments

Although behavior is generally regarded as a product of environmental as well as personalistic variables, predictions of behavior from psychometric data have been limited to measures of the individual to the exclusion of the situation. Despite the proliferation of instruments intended to measure personality processes, there has been no comparable development in regard to the environment. Murray (1938) is one of the few theorists to attempt a systematic elaboration of environmental forces, at least insofar as they are perceived by and have meaning for the acting person. The present paper describes a conceptual scheme and objective measuring devices based on Murray's need-press formulations which have as their purpose the study of behavioral outcomes as a function of relationships between

A composite of papers read in August, 1960, at the Annual Meeting of the American Sociological Association in New York City and at the Educational Testing Service Conference on Personality at Princeton in October, 1960. The paper is based in part on materials adapted from other sources (Stern, 1958, 1960, 1961). The opportunity to undertake the research described in this paper has been greatly facilitated by grants from the U. S. Air Force, the U. S. Office of Education, and the Carnegie Corporation. The supervision of data processing and the preparation of materials for this paper was undertaken by Dagny Henderson, ably assisted by Janice Marsden, Barbara Sisskin, Harriet Dorn, Elizabeth Schwenderman, Joanne Garcia, and Alice Mahan.

quantified characteristics of the person and corresponding
characteristics of the environment.

The Need-Press Model

Needs refer to organizational tendencies which appear
to give unity and direction to personality. They were defined originally by Murray as "a force (the physico-chemical
nature of which is unknown) in the brain region, a force
which organizes perception, apperception, intellection,
conation, and action in such a way as to transform in a certain direction an existing, unsatisfying situation." (Murray,
1938, p. 124.) The presumed biological and architectonic
aspects of psychogenic needs have never been given serious
consideration, but there are two further characteristics to
be noted in this definition which have been made even more
explicit by Murray in his more recent writings (1952).

On the one hand needs are functional in character, being
identified with the goals or purposes which an interaction
serves for the individual. In this sense a listing of needs
is essentially a taxonomy of the objectives which individuals
characteristically strive to achieve for themselves. Teleo-
logical constructs of this kind, whether in classical mechan-
ics or in clinical psychology, refer to entities which are not
in themselves directly observable even though given a hypothetical locus in a physical body; they must be inferred from
observations of an interaction. Thus, the second characteristic of a need is that it is revealed in the modes of behavior
employed by the individual. In this sense a listing of needs
is a taxonomy of interaction processes.

In either case a need is something inferred from behavior. A person's actions may be quite diversified, and
lend themselves individually to many different explanations
in various contexts, but they are given a unified theme in
the interpretation we place on them. We may impute a
variety of meanings to the fact that someone seems to "enjoy
taking the blame for something done by a friend," for example, but when we also discover that this person "likes
telling others about his mistakes and failures," "tries to

figure out how he was to blame whenever he gets involved in
an argument," and "dislikes making a fuss when someone
deliberately takes advantage of him," we may begin to suspect that a strong tendency towards self-depreciation and
devaluation is characteristic of this person.

All actions undertaken by the individual which are relevant to this tendency may be classified under the general
title of abasement. Inferences may also be made concerning the purpose which these characteristic interpersonal
actions serve for the individual; i.e., we may say of such
a person that he has a need to abase himself, but it is important to note that the imputation of purpose or motive is
not as essential a requirement for the prediction of behavior
as is the systematic description of the potential interactions
an individual is most likely to sustain. In either event, however, the determination of needs characterizing an individual
can only be made from an examination of the interactions in
which he engages; needs may therefore be defined as a taxonomic classification of the characteristic behaviors manifested by individuals in their life transactions.

The concept of environmental press provides an external
situational counterpart of the internal personality needs. In
the ultimate sense of the term, press refers to the phenom-
enological world of the individual, the unique and inevitably
private view which each person has of the events in which
he takes part (Murray, 1938). But there is a point at which
this private world merges with that of others; people who
share a common ideology--whether theological, political, or
professional--also tend to share common interpretations of
the events in which they participate, although these interpretations may be quite different from those which might
occur to a more detached observer (Stern, Stein, and Bloom,
1956).

Both the private and the mutually shared press are of
interest in their own right, but, in the final analysis, the
inferences we make as observers about the events in which
others participate are the ultimate source of a taxonomy of
situational variables. It is the observer who can describe

the situational climate, the permissible roles and relationships, the sanctions, etc., by his interpretations of events
to which the participant qua participant can only respond in
terms of action and/or ideological evaluation. The participants themselves may consider these events to have a different significance or may fail to give them any formal
recognition, reflecting a distinction, discussed more fully
elsewhere (Stern et al., 1956, pp. 39-45), between explicit
objectives, representing the stated purposes for which given
institutional events are organized, and the implicit objectives
which are in fact served by institutional events regardless of
the official interpretations. This distinction has its direct
parallel in individual behavioral acts which may be interpreted differently by the observer than by the actor, who
may also ignore or deny their significance.

As in the case of needs, descriptions of press are based
on inferred continuities and consistencies in otherwise discrete events. Thus, there may be several implications
which follow from the fact that "resident students at a given
college must get written permission to be away from campus
overnight." If we also discover, however, that "students
are often kept waiting when they have appointments with
faculty members," "freshmen have to take orders from
upperclassmen for a period of time," and "the school administration will not tolerate student complaints or pro-
tests," we may feel justified in assuming that the press at
this school emphasizes the development of abasement responses on the part of the student. Press then, like needs,
are taxonomic classifications of characteristic behaviors
manifested by aggregates of individuals in their mutual
interpersonal transactions.

The Measurement of Need and Press

Although our own behavior is based to a large extent on
our implicit categorization of the immediately experienced
actions of others, direct observation of ordinary life transactions is an impractical source of information for research
purposes. R. G. Barker, M. F. Schoggen, and L. S. Barker

(1955) have provided an extended behavioral description of one child throughout one day, but even this extraordinary effort fails to provide an adequate sample of the range of interactions this subject was undoubtedly capable of sustaining. A broader range of opportunities for interaction may be presented as test stimuli in a controlled environment, as in the case of the OSS assessment program (OSS, 1948), but this too must be limited in scope and high in cost.

Of the various indirect sources from which estimates of typical interaction characteristics have been attempted-- autobiographical data, interviews, projective tests, meas- ures of physical and intellectual qualities, inventories of attitudes and values, etc. --the simplest is based on the preferences an individual expresses in response to verbal descriptions of various possible activities. Although the relationship between these choices and actual behavior will be less than perfect, the procedure provides a useful ap- proximation and has been the rationale behind many widely used psychological instruments, including the Strong Voca- tional Interest Blank, the Kuder Preference Record, and the Edwards Personal Preference Schedule, as well as the Activities Index[1] to be considered here.

The Activities Index was developed originally for use in studies of student personality assessment at the University of Chicago (Stern et al., 1956). It has since gone through several revisions, the current form being based on items derived from analyses of preceding adult and juvenile forms and used effectively with persons from 12 to 63 years of age in various social and educational strata.

Both needs and press are inferred from characteristic activities and events. Unlike needs, however, it is diffi- cult to describe characteristic press in terms which can be

---

[1] Devised initially in collaboration with Benjamin S. Bloom, Morris I. Stein, Hugh Lane, Mary Tyler, Sharon Goldberg, Paul Baer, James Sachs, Dorothy Whitman, and James Abegglan. Subsequent revisions have been contributed to by Charles Van Buskirk, Fred Carleton, Walter Stellwagen, John Scanlon, Louis DiAngelo, and others.

generalized beyond a specific type of setting. The instrument employed in the studies to be reported below, the College Characteristics Index,[2] is restricted to the description of activities, policies, procedures, attitudes, and impressions which might be characteristic of various types of
undergraduate college settings. Other versions applicable
to high schools[3] and evening colleges[4] have recently been
completed.

Each of these needs and press instruments consists of
300 items of the kind used as examples before, distributed
among 30 scales of 10 items each. These are listed in
Table 3-1, which also presents relevant data regarding the
psychometric properties of the Activities Index and the College Characteristics Index.[5] It will be noted that the scales
have an average reliability (Kuder-Richardson) of .67,
which is close to the practical maximum for scales of such
short length. They are also characterized by a high degree
of internal consistency, as reflected in the average item
discrimination index (Ebel) of .54.

The intercorrelation matrices for these scales, as
shown in Table 3-2, are characterized by large positive correlations next to the main diagonal, becoming increasingly
negative away from the diagonal except at the corner which
is positive again. The data are consistent with a quasi-
circumplex, a law of order postulated by Guttman (1954,
pp. 258-348) for scales similar in complexity but differing
in the kind of abilities they define. Such an order has neither
beginning nor end, being characterized by a continuous circular relationship between the variables involved.

This relationship is limited to the first nine clusters
indicated in Table 3-2, ending with the Rejection scale in

[2]Developed in collaboration with C. Robert Pace, with the assistance of Anne McFee, Dagny Henderson, Barnett Denton, Sally
Donovan, Harriet Dorn, Eugene Farber, and others.
[3]Prepared with the aid of John Dopyera, Vernon L. Woolston,
James Lyons, and Eva K. Woolfolk.
[4]An adaptation by Sidney Archer, Clifford Winters, and Donald
Meyer.
[5]Further psychometric data may be found in the manual for these
tests (Stern, 1958a).

TABLE 3-1. ACTIVITIES INDEX AND COLLEGE
CHARACTERISTICS INDEX SCALE CHARACTERISTICS

| Scale | Forms AI-CCI, 1158[a] | | | | | | | |
| | Mean | | Sigma | | Reliability[b] | | Item Index[c] | |
	AI	CCI	AI	CCI	AI	CCI	AI	CCI
Abasement	4.07	2.99	1.88	1.93	.51	.67	.42	.51
Achievement	6.33	6.23	2.24	2.56	.73	.81	.60	.66
Adaptiveness	5.23	4.54	2.33	1.98	.64	.58	.58	.48
Affiliation-Rejection	6.70	6.95	2.72	1.93	.81	.69	.66	.47
Aggression-Blameavoidance	4.09	3.99	2.37	2.37	.69	.72	.59	.56
Change-Sameness	5.34	6.41	2.33	2.02	.67	.44	.57	.47
Conjunctivity-Disjunctivity	5.81	7.09	2.35	2.37	.70	.72	.58	.54
Counteraction-Infavoidance	6.24	5.31	2.53	1.84	.66	.50	.57	.45
Deference	6.63	4.87	2.03	1.97	.56	.60	.50	.50
Dominance	6.04	4.50	2.51	2.12	.77	.57	.62	.49
Ego Achievement	5.54	5.70	2.88	1.98	.80	.58	.70	.50
Emotionality-Placidity	4.20	6.18	2.18	2.01	.64	.56	.53	.48
Energy-Passivity	6.74	5.74	1.73	2.28	.40	.70	.41	.54
Exhibitionism-Infavoidance	3.83	5.55	2.56	2.01	.75	.57	.65	.49
Fantasied Achievement	3.34	4.72	2.06	1.74	.72	.40	.57	.43
Harmavoidance	4.93	5.66	2.40	2.11	.67	.70	.62	.51
Humanism	6.64	6.21	2.79	2.42	.83	.77	.65	.60
Impulsion-Deliberation	5.61	5.62	2.06	1.86	.64	.50	.50	.45
Narcissism	4.61	4.98	2.37	2.31	.71	.74	.58	.58
Nurturance-Rejection	6.50	5.78	2.38	2.19	.73	.70	.57	.54
Objectivity	8.90	7.40	1.43	2.14	.56	.70	.27	.51
Order	5.20	6.50	2.96	1.86	.82	.59	.74	.45
Play	5.00	5.26	2.40	2.33	.71	.75	.56	.58
Pragmatism	6.17	5.20	2.42	2.16	.74	.69	.59	.53
Reflectiveness	6.70	5.96	2.16	2.43	.68	.76	.54	.60
Scientism	5.34	6.14	3.18	2.48	.88	.77	.81	.58
Sentience	4.76	4.85	1.86	2.51	.53	.80	.43	.62
Sex-Prudery	4.84	5.95	2.58	2.18	.78	.71	.64	.53
Succorance-Autonomy	6.24	6.14	2.12	1.78	.67	.34	.52	.43
Understanding	6.98	6.55	2.34	2.21	.74	.75	.58	.54
MEAN	5.62	5.63	2.33	2.14	.69	.65	.57	.52

[a]Based on 1993 CCI, 1078 AI from undergraduates in 32 schools

[b]Kuder-Richardson formula no. 20

[c]Average Ebel Item Discrimination Index per scale

Measurement in Personality

TABLE 3-2. COMBINED TABLE OF INTERCORRELATIONS OF ACTIVITIES INDEX (AI) SCALES AND COLLEGE CHARACTERISTICS INDEX (CCI) SCALES

(AI intercorrelations above diagonal; CCI intercorrelations below diagonal. N = 1,076 students from 23 colleges.)

	1				2				3				4		
	Rej	Aut	Dsj	Agg	Dom	Nar	F/A	E/A	Exh	Imp	Emo	Sen	Sex	Cha	Ply
Rej		37	16	12	-12	-20	-02	-20	-18	-06	-14	-12	-28	-06	-18
Aut	41		19	19	-06	-29	-01	-04	-04	07	-15	-12	-41	11	-13
Dsj	35	23		18	-02	01	02	-09	04	34	16	14	03	42	36
Agg	31	23	48		41	08	35	24	33	29	12	23	01	26	17
Dom	-08	01	07	09		14	40	59	46	20	10	17	09	14	11
Nar	-38	-28	-33	-37	27		39	11	27	25	32	34	46	11	31
F/A	-12	06	-18	01	-04	-01		32	37	14	08	23	15	13	17
E/A	-30	-11	-20	-07	-09	05	35		42	11	18	19	07	12	-03
Exh	-36	-19	-25	-10	06	25	26	55		26	36	25	19	24	23
Imp	-08	-01	15	36	07	-15	21	29	27		38	29	22	36	30
Emo	-32	-17	-18	-12	06	13	20	47	41	18		31	39	24	19
Sen	-08	12	-14	-01	-22	-19	42	42	30	18	28		31	24	21
Sex	-10	-18	01	21	25	14	04	09	20	39	01	-18		10	31
Cha	08	20	-01	18	-13	-25	37	36	20	28	13	41	03		22
Ply	-32	-36	-06	-01	20	34	-06	14	35	26	06	-28	53	-12	
Eny	-16	00	-32	-14	-12	01	41	47	43	17	47	50	-14	32	-16
Pra	-19	-28	-16	-04	27	31	-14	-01	14	05	-04	-38	39	-16	50
Aff	-77	-46	-37	-27	01	33	11	28	36	11	30	11	11	-07	36
Suc	-41	-100	-23	-23	-01	28	-06	11	19	01	17	-12	18	-20	36
Nur	-77	-36	-33	-35	14	42	13	31	35	06	34	06	08	-08	29
Ada	-31	-24	-18	-11	28	40	-08	05	17	-01	12	-22	19	-20	33
Aba	19	08	36	23	35	05	-28	-26	-16	-05	-19	-42	23	-26	19
Dfr	-06	-24	-05	-18	18	35	-35	-26	-10	-26	-18	-53	20	-38	31
Ord	-22	-27	-30	-36	16	45	-17	-14	07	-27	00	-40	11	-28	28
Bla	-31	-23	-48	-100	-09	37	-01	07	10	-36	12	01	-21	-18	01
Inf	-21	04	22	03	00	-08	-32	-44	-63	-24	-32	-35	-08	-28	-12
Pas	16	00	32	14	12	-01	-41	-47	-43	-17	-47	-50	14	-32	16
Har	-24	-08	-28	-41	-14	16	02	08	02	-35	24	21	-46	-11	-30
Del	08	01	-15	-36	-07	15	-21	-29	-27	-100	-18	-18	-39	-28	-26
Plc	32	17	18	12	-06	-13	-20	-47	-41	-18	-100	-28	-01	-13	-06
Pru	10	18	-10	-21	-25	-14	-04	-09	-20	-39	-01	18	-100	-03	-53
Sam	-08	-20	01	-18	13	25	-37	-36	-20	-28	-13	-41	-03	-100	12
Rej	100	41	35	31	-08	-38	-12	-30	-36	-08	-32	-08	-10	08	-32
E/A	-30	-11	-20	-07	-09	05	35	100	55	29	47	42	09	36	14
Ctr	-07	11	-19	04	-06	-08	38	32	26	21	23	40	-05	35	-11
Eny	-16	00	-32	-14	-12	01	41	47	43	17	47	50	-14	32	-16
Und	-14	11	-42	-19	-17	02	49	36	24	07	26	53	-21	39	-27
Ach	-08	12	-38	-27	-14	11	35	20	12	-10	23	39	-27	28	-35
Cnj	-35	-23	-100	-48	-07	33	18	20	25	-15	18	14	-10	01	06
E/A	-30	-11	-20	-07	-09	05	35	100	55	29	47	42	09	36	14
Ref	-21	06	-30	-12	-17	-02	49	49	38	17	39	68	-18	40	-20
Hum	-15	07	-30	-16	-17	-02	46	46	34	13	32	66	-16	39	-23
Und	-14	11	-42	-19	-17	02	49	36	24	07	26	53	-21	39	-27
Sci	-04	12	-26	-10	-05	07	39	34	25	10	13	40	-05	41	-12
Obj	-24	-06	-39	-27	-33	01	28	26	19	10	19	38	-13	26	-03

TABLE 3-2. COMBINED TABLE OF INTERCORRELATIONS OF ACTIVITIES INDEX (AI) SCALES AND COLLEGE CHARACTERISTICS INDEX (CCI) SCALES (continued)

(AI intercorrelations above diagonal; CCI intercorrelations below diagonal. N = 1,076 students from 23 colleges.)

| | Circumplex | | Clusters | | | | | | | | | | | | |
| | 4 | | 5 | | | 6 | | | 7 | | 8 | | 9 | | |
	Eny	Pra	Aff	Suc	Nur	Ada	Aba	Dfr	Ord	Bla	Inf	Pas	Har	Del	Plc
Rej	-10	-22	-64	-37	-64	-16	-24	-29	-18	-12	-14	10	-06	06	14
Aut	09	-12	-35	-100	-39	-06	-20	-38	-20	-19	-01	-09	-25	-07	15
Dsj	-16	-30	-11	-19	-21	-19	-20	-32	-49	-18	12	16	-20	-34	-16
Agg	09	-04	-03	-19	-20	-26	-20	-39	-20	-100	-20	-09	-36	-29	-12
Dom	11	19	22	06	03	-16	-10	-16	-06	-41	-30	-11	-22	-20	-10
Nar	-08	01	23	29	17	-25	05	06	22	-08	-04	08	04	-25	-32
F/A	08	12	07	01	-03	-21	01	-13	-01	-35	-18	-08	-25	-14	-08
E/A	24	21	19	04	22	-06	06	-06	01	-24	-26	-24	-16	-11	-18
Exh	20	09	32	04	04	-09	01	-12	02	-33	-54	-20	-26	26	-36
Imp	06	-07	09	01	04	-12	-02	-17	-22	-29	-09	-06	-22	-100	-38
Emo	14	-13	16	15	12	-03	03	-05	-04	-12	-17	-14	-08	-38	-31
Sen	03	02	09	12	16	-14	02	-07	-04	-23	-10	-03	-23	-29	-31
Sex	-10	-08	32	41	24	-12	07	11	08	-01	00	10	08	-22	-39
Cha	16	-05	09	-11	02	-03	-01	-14	-26	-26	-16	-16	-25	-36	-24
Ply	-08	-13	41	13	-06	-21	-14	-10	-16	-17	02	08	-12	-30	-19
Eny		23	11	-09	09	16	07	04	10	-09	-29	-100	-27	-06	-14
Pra	-21		16	12	27	17	23	25	33	04	-17	-23	-05	07	13
Aff	15	16		35	29	06	10	23	13	03	-19	-11	02	-09	-16
Suc	00	28	46		39	06	20	38	20	19	01	09	25	07	-15
Nur	18	22	54	36		26	39	35	24	20	-10	-09	11	-04	-12
Ada	-03	40	27	24	35		39	30	13	26	-12	-16	06	12	-16
Aba	-38	26	-27	-08	-11	20		38	24	20	-08	-07	08	02	-03
Dfr	-38	45	01	24	10	29	36		31	39	00	-04	21	17	05
Ord	-13	41	19	27	26	32	14	47		20	-07	-10	20	22	04
Bla	14	04	27	23	35	27	-23	18	36		20	09	36	29	12
Inf	-45	00	-22	-04	-20	-08	26	23	04	-03		29	21	09	17
Pas	-100	21	-15	00	-18	03	38	38	13	-14	45		27	06	14
Har	22	-28	18	08	31	01	-28	-06	10	41	-06	-22		22	08
Del	-17	-05	-11	-01	-06	01	05	26	27	36	24	17	35		38
Plc	-47	04	-30	-17	-34	-12	19	18	00	-12	32	47	-24	18	
Pru	14	-39	-11	-18	-08	-19	-23	-20	-11	21	08	-14	46	39	01
Sam	-32	16	07	20	08	20	26	38	28	18	28	32	11	28	13
Rej	-16	-19	-77	-41	-77	-31	19	-06	-22	-31	-21	16	-24	08	32
E/A	47	-01	28	11	31	05	-26	-26	-14	07	-44	-47	08	-29	-47
Ctr	47	-14	08	-11	06	-01	-35	-36	-16	-04	-63	-47	09	-21	-23
Eny	100	-21	15	00	18	-03	-38	-38	-13	14	-45	-100	22	-17	-47
Und	56	-20	12	-11	16	-08	-50	-37	-14	19	-36	-56	25	-07	-26
Ach	52	-20	06	-12	10	-05	-42	-27	-04	27	-26	-52	33	10	-23
Cnj	32	16	37	23	33	18	-36	05	30	48	-22	-32	28	15	-18
E/A	47	-01	28	11	31	05	-26	-26	-14	07	-44	-47	08	-29	-47
Ref	60	-27	20	-06	22	-09	-47	-49	-26	12	-41	-60	29	-17	-39
Hum	55	-29	14	-07	16	-11	-48	-45	-20	16	-38	-55	25	-13	-32
Und	56	-20	12	-11	16	-08	-50	-37	-14	19	-36	-56	25	-07	-26
Sci	39	-03	02	-12	05	01	-31	-28	-10	10	-30	-39	01	-10	-13
Obj	35	-15	31	06	16	-16	-61	-28	-08	27	-27	-35	22	-10	-19

Measurement in Personality

TABLE 3-2. COMBINED TABLE OF INTERCORRELATIONS OF ACTIVITIES INDEX
(AI) SCALES AND COLLEGE CHARACTERISTICS INDEX (CCI) SCALES (continued)

(AI intercorrelations above diagonal; CCI intercorrelations
below diagonal. N = 1,076 students from 23 colleges.)

	9			10 (Non-Circumplex)						11					
	Pru	Sam	Rej	E/A	Ctr	Eny	Und	Ach	Cnj	E/A	Ref	Hum	Und	Sci	Obj
Rej	28	06	100	-20	-11	-10	00	-08	-16	-20	-12	-14	00	03	-01
Aut	41	-11	37	-04	06	09	07	01	-19	-04	-08	-01	07	10	03
Dsj	-03	14	16	-09	-27	-16	-17	-29	-100	-09	-01	-18	-17	-16	-03
Agg	-01	-26	12	24	06	09	19	19	-18	24	20	08	19	11	02
Dom	-09	-14	-12	59	13	11	20	27	02	59	20	16	20	15	08
Nar	-46	-11	-20	11	-19	-08	-08	-04	-01	11	24	02	-08	-15	-14
F/A	-15	-13	-02	32	-02	08	12	18	-02	32	31	03	12	19	-09
E/A	-07	-12	-20	100	11	24	26	27	09	100	30	37	26	16	09
Exh	-19	-24	-18	42	09	20	08	19	-04	42	16	08	08	02	-01
Imp	-22	-36	-06	11	-08	06	00	00	-34	11	18	06	00	-06	-05
Emo	-39	-24	-14	18	-02	14	01	01	-16	18	18	11	01	21	-06
Sen	-31	-24	-12	19	-06	03	11	07	-14	19	28	17	11	04	02
Sex	-100	-10	-28	07	-18	-10	-11	-11	-03	07	17	05	-11	-19	-13
Cha	-10	-100	-06	12	08	16	11	05	-42	12	19	10	11	00	02
Ply	-31	-22	-18	-03	-28	-08	-29	-25	-36	-03	-03	-22	-29	26	-07
Eny	10	-16	-10	24	38	100	29	38	16	24	11	15	29	19	09
Pra	08	05	-22	21	25	23	24	23	30	21	10	11	24	40	03
Aff	-32	-09	-64	19	06	11	-10	03	11	19	-01	01	-10	-14	-02
Suc	-41	11	-37	04	-06	-09	-07	-01	19	04	08	01	-07	-10	-03
Nur	-24	-02	-64	22	16	09	10	13	21	22	26	27	10	08	04
Ada	12	03	-16	-06	32	16	10	10	19	-06	01	12	10	12	06
Aba	-07	01	-24	06	16	07	09	13	20	06	12	11	09	10	-03
Dfr	-11	14	-29	-06	12	04	01	07	32	-06	02	07	01	04	-02
Ord	-08	26	-18	01	16	10	-01	12	49	01	-01	06	-01	01	-09
Bla	01	26	-12	-24	-06	-09	-19	-19	18	-24	-20	-01	-19	-11	-02
Inf	00	16	-14	-26	-54	-29	-24	-36	-12	-26	-10	-12	-24	-12	-04
Pas	-10	16	10	-24	-38	-100	-29	-38	-16	-24	-11	-15	-29	-19	-09
Har	-08	25	-06	-16	-16	-27	-19	-18	20	-16	-14	-02	-19	-23	-08
Del	22	36	06	-11	08	-06	00	00	34	-11	-18	-06	00	06	05
Plc	39	24	14	-18	02	-14	-01	-01	16	-18	-18	-11	-01	-21	06
Pru		10	28	-07	18	10	11	11	03	-07	-17	-05	11	19	13
Sam	03		06	-12	-08	-16	-11	-05	42	-12	-19	-10	-11	00	-02
Rej	10	-08		-20	-11	-10	00	-08	-16	-20	-12	-14	00	03	-01
E/A	-09	-36	-30		11	24	26	27	09	100	30	37	26	16	09
Ctr	05	-35	-07	32		38	40	52	27	11	04	17	40	23	09
Eny	14	-32	-16	47	47		29	38	16	24	11	15	29	19	09
Und	21	-39	-14	36	47	56		49	17	26	36	43	100	52	12
Ach	27	-28	-08	20	40	52	63		29	27	15	26	49	28	10
Cnj	10	-01	-35	20	19	32	42	38		09	01	18	17	16	03
E/A	-09	-36	-30	100	32	47	36	20	20		30	37	26	16	09
Ref	18	-40	-21	49	44	60	65	51	30	49		41	36	36	08
Hum	16	-39	-15	46	42	55	66	50	30	46	72		43	28	08
Und	21	-39	-14	36	47	56	100	63	42	36	65	66		52	12
Sci	05	-41	-04	34	36	39	54	46	26	34	50	59	54		08
Obj	13	-26	-24	26	35	35	50	40	39	26	44	43	50	30	

the third column of the third page of the table. The remaining columns involve two other clusters of scales which are unrelated to the circumplex.

By expanding the nine test vectors which define the needs circumplex to reflect the area of the total test hyperspace which each accounts for, individual scale scores can be graphed in the form of a polar profile. Such a graph is shown in Figure 3-1, which has superimposed on it a series of figures intended to dramatize the essential elements of the cluster configuration.[6]

Each wedge in the circle corresponds to a scale. Those close together are highly correlated; at 90° apart the relationship approaches zero, becoming extremely negative at 180°. The pattern of scales in each sub-area of the circle suggests an interesting internal structure consisting of peculiarly intrapersonal and depressed activities at the lower left of the circle which become increasingly sociable toward the top and still more outgoing and assertive toward the right.

Refactoring these clusters has yielded two independent dimensions for the circle, one of which can be represented by a diagonal from upper right to lower left which may be categorized in terms of impulse expression and control. The The second dimension is on the diagonal from upper left to lower right and may be called dependency needs versus autonomy. The grid at the bottom of the chart summarizes scores on the group of scales which yielded the third factor independent of the two in the circle, this one dealing with intellectual needs. The precise relationships shown in Figure 3-1 were based on an analysis of an earlier form of the Activities Index. Subsequent analyses, not yet complete, suggest that these basic relationships continue to hold for both instruments although not precisely as shown here.

As shown in Figure 3-2, actual scale scores are entered on each wedge from zero at the center to a maximum of 10

---

[6]Professor Fred Hauck of the Syracuse University School of Art is responsible for the graphic figures superimposed on the chart in Figure 3-1 which help dramatize the essential elements in the internal structure of these scales.

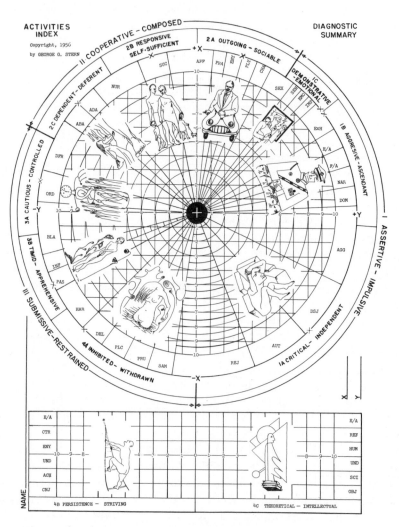

FIGURE 3-1. A Profile Summary Form for the Need and Press
Instruments Based on the Intercorrelations Between Scale Scores.

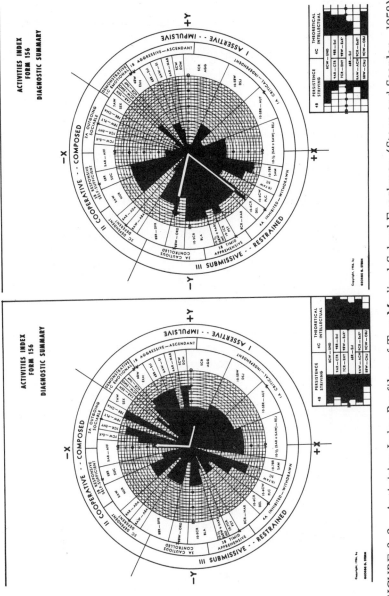

FIGURE 3-2.   Activities Index Profiles of Two Medical School Freshmen (Stern and Scanlon, 1958).

at the periphery. The two profiles shown here were both
obtained from freshman medical students. The one on the
left suggests a distant, self-assertive individual with fantasies of personal achievement and intellectual precocity.
The faculty noted independently that this student was antago-
nistic, individualistic, and dreamlike, with a suggested
capacity for work which he never fulfilled. The profile to
the right is at the opposite extreme in suggesting withdrawal,
depressed affect, lowered self-esteem, minimal drive level,
and modest intellectual characteristics. This student was
an early withdrawal who complained of the excessive work.

Group data for either needs or press may be averaged
and also presented in profile form. Figure 3-3 provides a
contrast between the average press profile of seven liberal
arts colleges and that obtained from three business administration programs. The scores have been adjusted in these
two profiles so that the value of five on any scale corresponds to the average score in a composite sample of 32 selected colleges and technical programs; any deviation from
a perfect circle, therefore, indicates a deviation from the
norm.

It is reasonably clear from the two profiles that these
liberal arts and business administration programs differ
from other types of college programs as well as from one
another. The business administration programs appear
here as markedly higher in maintaining student dependency
needs, particularly with respect to the press for abasement,
deference, and orderliness represented in the upper left
sector of the circle (note the black arrow). The liberal
arts colleges, on the other hand, are not only deficient in
this area, but are in their turn correspondingly high in the
intellectual areas summarized in the grid at the bottom of
the figure. Other aspects of the differences between these
two types of schools, as reflected in specific items differentiating between them by 40 percentage points or more,
are listed in Table 3-3.

If test responses from groups of students are reduced
to the three orthogonal dimensions, needs and press characterizing a number of institutions may be represented

TABLE 3-3. COLLEGE CHARACTERISTICS INDEX ITEMS DIFFERENTIATING
BETWEEN LIBERAL ARTS AND BUSINESS ADMINISTRATION PROGRAMS BY
FORTY PERCENTAGE POINTS OR MORE

No.	Item	Scale	Percent Response	
			Liberal Arts	Business Adminis- tration
1.	Students are discouraged from criticizing administrative policies and teaching practices	Aba	20.2	92.0
2.	The school administration has little tolerance for student complaints and protests	Aba	14.1	56.0
9.	Students address faculty members as "professor" or "doctor"	Dfr	13.5	63.3
69.	Religious worship here stresses service to God and obedience to His laws	Dfr	18.5	64.4
22.	In many classes students have an assigned seat	Ord	12.9	99.3
142.	Professors usually take attendance in class	Ord	32.2	83.0
292.	Classes meet only at their regularly scheduled time and place	Ord	34.7	90.3
47.	The school offers many opportunities for students to understand and criticize important works in art, music, and drama	Hum	85.1	40.8
77.	A lecture by an outstanding literary critic would be well attended	Hum	90.4	34.3
107.	Many students are planning postgraduate work in the social sciences	Hum	76.2	18.8
167.	When students get together, they often talk about trends in art, music, or the theatre	Hum	75.3	17.9
197.	Humanities courses are often elected by students majoring in other areas	Hum	89.9	49.1
261.	The school has an excellent reputation for academic freedom	Obj	90.6	48.6
25.	Books dealing with psychological problems or personal values are widely read and discussed	Ref	55.2	13.8
55.	There would be a capacity audience for a lecture by an outstanding philosopher or theologian	Ref	76.2	18.1
115.	Modern art and music get considerable attention here	Ref	89.6	41.3
235.	Long, serious intellectual discussions are common among the students	Ref	84.6	21.6
295.	There is considerable interest in the analysis of value systems and the relativity of societies and ethics	Ref	86.9	38.3
30.	There is a lot of emphasis on preparing for graduate work	Und	62.4	10.4
90.	Most students have considerable interest in round tables, panel meetings, or other formal discussions	Und	74.7	34.2
180.	Many students here prefer to talk about poetry, philosophy, or mathematics, as compared with motion pictures, politics, or inventions	Und	78.6	26.5

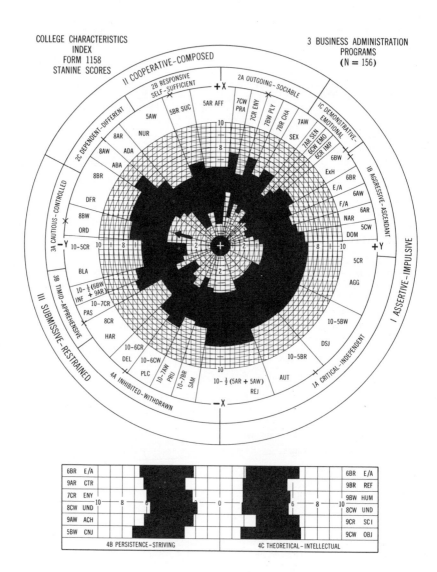

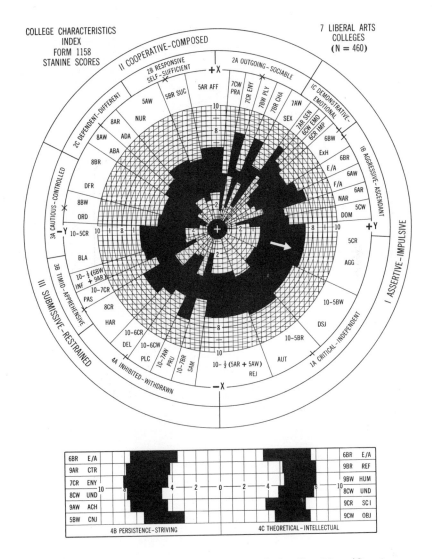

FIGURE 3-3. College Characteristics Index Profiles (Stanine Scores) Obtained from 460 Students at Seven Liberal Arts Colleges and 156 Students in Three Business Administration Programs.

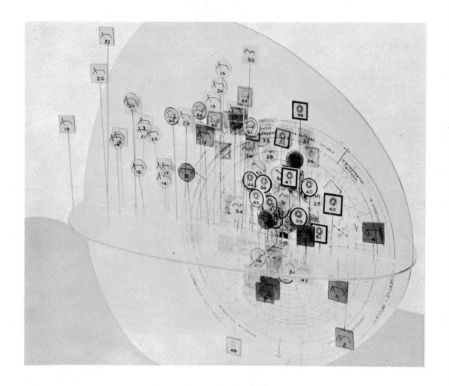

△	PRIVATE LIBERAL ARTS COLLEGES
⚘	DENOMINATIONAL COLLEGES
⌐┌┐¬	UNIVERSITY AFFILIATED COLLEGES
🎓	TEACHER - TRAINING PROGRAMS
✎	BUSINESS ADMINISTRATIVE PROGRAMS
⚛	ENGINEERING PROGRAMS
○	AI MEAN RESULTANT
□	CCI MEAN RESULTANT

FIGURE 3-4. Three-dimensional Model of Mean Activities Index and College Characteristics Index Responses from 5,348 Students at 62 Institutions.

simultaneously in a three-dimensional solid. Such a solid
is shown in Figure 3-4, based on data obtained from 5,348
students at 62 American colleges and universities; in this
solid the majority of students and colleges fall in the upper
left quadrant, representing strong trends towards dependency and conformity. The most extreme schools in this
respect are the denominational colleges. The elite liberal
arts colleges are least like the others; their scores emphasize personal independence.

Although the scoring and presentation of Index results
are seemingly complex, a machine has been designed
(Figure 3-5) to accept test response data from an IBM test
scoring machine and present the processed output in the

FIGURE 3-5. Test-processing Device for Scoring, Profiling, and
Punching Multivariate Test Data.

form of punched IBM cards and 8 1/2 x 11 profile graphs,
such as those shown in Figures 3-2 and 3-3. It is also
capable of assembling multiple-item scale responses from
other tests and transposing them to punched cards or visual
graphs either circular or rectangular in form.

Earlier Index Research

Previous research with the Indexes, based on a wide
variety of samples ranging from psychiatric patients and
industrial personnel to over 5,000 students drawn from 62
American colleges and universities, tends to support the
following conclusions:

1. Responses to needs scale items appear to be re-
sistant to faking (Schultz, 1955).

2. The social desirability of needs scale items is relatively homogeneous, none being considered important to
accept or to reject by any significant number of subjects
(unpublished data).

3. Behavioral descriptions based solely on needs profiles appear to be recognized and confirmed by peers, psychiatrists, and administrators, as well as by the subsequent
behavior of the subjects (Briggs, 1958; Chilman, 1959; Cole,
1958; Haring, Stern, and Cruickshank, 1958; Stern, 1958a;
unpublished data).

4. There are significant relationships between needs
profiles and (a) other forms of overt behavior (Gladstein,
1957; Scanlon, 1958; Stern, 1958b, 1960a, 1960b, 1962; Stern,
Stein, and Bloom, 1956; Wassertheil, 1955; see also references to item 3 above); (b) social background (an unpublished analysis of students from public and private school
backgrounds attending the same college reveals distinctive
needs profiles, regardless of the field of study elected);
and (c) career choices of both students and professionals
in various fields (Siegelman and Peck, 1960; Stern, 1954,
1960b; Stern and Scanlon, 1958; Stern, Stein, and Bloom,
1956).

5. Professionals tend generally to be higher in impulse
controls and in intellectual needs than students in the same
fields, except for teachers, who are characterized by
weaker intellectual needs than the education majors matched
with them (Stern, 1960b).

6. Student bodies tend to be characterized by needs
patterns readily recognizable as personalized versions of
the prevailing press at their institutions, although there is
greater variability among the needs of the students than in

their descriptions of their college press (Stern, 1960a, 1960b, 1962). This is not attributable to the fact that the same students are the source of both sets of data, for there is generally little relationship between the needs preferences a student records for himself and the press characteristics he attributes to the college, either at the same institution (McFee, 1961) or across institutions, as indicated in the diagonals of Table 3-4.

7. Press profiles based on miscellaneous student samples tend to be consistent with those of National Merit Scholars and Finalists, faculty, and administration at the same institutions (Pace and Stern, 1958; Thistlethwaite, 1959a, 1959b).

8. There is as much agreement in student response to subjective and impressionistic press items as there is to items more readily verifiable by reference to empirical facts (McFee, 1961).

9. Environmental descriptions based solely on press profiles appear to be recognized and confirmed by academic participants and observers (unpublished data).

10. There are significant relationships between press profiles and the types of institutions sampled (Stern, 1960b, 1962): (a) The majority of schools studied have high scores involving various aspects of constraint and dependency. The denominational schools are most extreme in their emphasis on conformity, the private liberal arts colleges least so. (b) The private liberal arts colleges are also highest in intellectual press; the image of high achievement and personal autonomy presented by these schools is sharper and further in advance of relevant student characteristics than is true of any other type of institution studied, suggesting a built-in and self-conscious strain towards academic excellence at the elite schools sampled. Variants in the orientation of this image suggest two broad dimensions: (i) arts, science or service, and (ii) appreciation versus creation. (c) The third type of school revealed by need-press analysis constitutes the remaining stronghold of the Fitzgerald tradition: fountains of knowledge where students gather to drink. A species which appeared on the decline

TABLE 3-4. MATRIX OF INTERCORRELATIONS BETWEEN ACTIVITIES INDEX
AND COLLEGE CHARACTERISTICS INDEX SCALE SCORES
(N = 1,076 students from 23 colleges)

AI Need Scale Scores	CCI Press Scale Scores														
	Aba	Ach	Ada	Aff	Agg	Cha	Cnj	Ctr	Dfr	Dom	E/A	Emo	Eny	Exh	F/A
Aba	-05	14	13	10	-16	03	13	07	01	04	09	12	12	11	02
Ach	-03	10	08	04	03	08	09	18	-07	06	03	00	16	10	13
Ada	-09	10	03	09	-12	05	10	06	-06	-09	10	01	07	08	04
Aff	11	-03	22	18	-17	-10	09	-09	20	13	04	14	-08	10	-11
Agg	11	-13	04	-12	29	08	-18	06	-08	08	-02	-11	-03	00	06
Cha	08	-09	-03	-04	12	07	-13	05	-12	04	01	02	-02	03	04
Cnj	-03	15	15	07	-19	-07	19	03	13	04	-01	02	09	08	00
Ctr	-04	06	06	06	01	11	08	12	-09	00	10	05	09	12	10
Dfr	-07	14	16	20	-27	-07	20	01	12	03	03	13	15	13	-06
Dom	05	-07	04	-03	13	03	-06	04	-03	10	02	-07	04	07	03
E/A	02	-02	02	01	05	03	-01	05	-04	01	14	04	-02	14	06
Emo	05	-05	-01	01	03	00	-01	00	-02	01	18	26	09	20	03
Eny	02	02	04	02	01	04	01	02	02	06	15	10	18	17	04
Exh	07	-06	09	01	10	01	-04	04	02	04	14	15	17	21	04
F/A	12	-11	12	-09	18	00	-09	03	09	10	-06	-08	-08	01	01
Har	-05	03	04	06	-17	-09	08	-02	09	12	-03	05	-02	-08	-06
Hum	-17	16	-05	08	-09	02	10	18	-17	00	08	09	18	05	12
Imp	-06	-02	-09	01	11	10	-04	09	-18	-05	08	06	10	07	12
Nar	09	-03	13	08	-03	-12	05	-01	15	07	-02	15	-01	05	-02
Nur	-04	14	15	20	-22	-05	15	04	06	19	06	13	08	08	03
Obj	-06	03	-04	07	-03	04	06	-01	-05	10	04	-04	-02	00	-01
Ord	06	04	19	08	-16	-09	13	-02	15	13	02	15	07	12	-07
Ply	13	-14	08	00	04	-07	-08	-17	10	10	-03	04	-15	-04	-10
Pra	03	09	13	08	-04	03	06	06	05	07	05	00	05	07	00
Ref	-02	03	-02	00	04	02	01	08	-04	05	04	01	07	06	11
Sci	-12	16	-06	-03	07	22	02	19	-16	-05	09	-05	13	06	15
Sen	-02	03	05	05	05	00	-02	-01	-01	08	01	07	05	03	05
Sex	-02	-02	04	07	-14	-11	04	-08	11	13	-01	13	-03	04	-05
Suc	-01	05	14	19	-20	-13	15	-07	17	11	00	12	-03	03	-03
Und	-13	11	-06	05	10	13	04	17	-17	-04	06	01	18	07	17

TABLE 3-4. MATRIX OF INTERCORRELATIONS BETWEEN ACTIVITIES INDEX
AND COLLEGE CHARACTERISTICS INDEX SCALE SCORES (continued)
(N = 1,076 students from 23 colleges)

AI Need Scale Scores	CCI Press Scale Scores														
	Har	Hum	Imp	Nar	Nur	Obj	Ord	Ply	Pra	Ref	Sci	Sen	Sex	Suc	Und
Aba	14	13	-01	13	22	11	12	02	05	16	12	07	-04	07	10
Ach	-05	10	08	01	03	08	02	02	06	08	15	04	04	01	15
Ada	06	15	-03	01	08	18	01	03	-01	12	13	10	-04	05	10
Aff	04	-09	00	24	22	-02	22	22	23	-10	-05	-17	16	22	-09
Agg	-21	-07	17	-11	-11	-17	-11	03	05	-07	04	-02	15	-15	-03
Cha	-04	00	10	-05	-03	-07	-10	02	-07	-05	-06	03	05	-04	-05
Cnj	08	03	-12	17	15	06	17	06	15	05	10	-05	-01	09	09
Ctr	-04	10	07	-03	05	07	00	04	06	07	14	08	05	04	11
Dfr	14	06	-09	20	22	16	20	11	14	06	05	00	-02	19	06
Dom	-15	-03	12	-01	-05	-08	-02	08	08	-06	05	-07	12	-01	-04
E/A	01	08	10	00	05	-01	-02	05	01	07	07	01	03	01	01
Emo	07	09	07	03	08	-05	-04	02	-09	07	-08	06	08	00	-02
Eny	-03	08	05	04	02	-01	02	11	10	07	09	03	02	02	02
Exh	-07	02	14	05	04	-11	01	10	05	01	02	00	11	06	-02
F/A	-18	-08	15	02	-04	-16	03	09	15	-12	04	-13	16	-05	-09
Har	16	-05	-12	06	12	09	08	00	04	00	-08	-04	-05	09	00
Hum	24	30	-02	01	08	14	-10	-12	-24	21	13	22	-15	01	21
Imp	02	13	14	-11	02	-01	-14	-07	-15	12	03	16	03	-07	09
Nar	08	-04	00	14	15	-09	16	08	11	-07	-12	-08	11	09	-05
Nur	22	14	-05	15	30	10	14	06	04	12	07	04	01	16	12
Obj	-02	03	-01	02	-01	06	-03	05	-05	01	08	-03	-02	03	01
Ord	13	-01	-10	14	17	-03	20	05	16	00	00	06	00	12	-01
Ply	-06	-12	09	06	05	-13	09	12	08	-15	-11	-15	15	03	-17
Pra	01	01	00	01	14	02	04	07	16	06	17	03	00	06	08
Ref	03	09	07	04	03	02	-03	02	-06	08	04	08	01	01	07
Sci	-08	16	11	-09	-07	12	-15	-05	-01	18	34	18	-04	-06	20
Sen	07	05	07	06	07	-02	-02	-01	-09	00	00	03	05	01	04
Sex	08	01	-01	17	15	-04	11	06	00	-04	-06	-06	11	13	-05
Suc	10	-01	-04	21	22	06	23	12	00	-01	-03	-10	09	21	02
Und	-02	16	08	-04	-01	12	-11	-04	12	16	22	17	-02	01	20

in the 1930's, this student type is apparently being saved from extinction at large state preserves (to borrow a phrase from Trow). These schools are described by their students as sources of social pleasure and togetherness, although lacking in academic strength or direction. (d) The essential details of this analysis have been supported in a subsequent analysis by Pace (1960), employing a substantially different analytic model.

Intra-institutional Need-Press Relationships

The most systematic information regarding relationships between student needs and academic press is being derived from an analysis of average scores at 43 institutions. A portion of the intercorrelation matrix employed in this analysis, representing the correlations between need and press scales, is reproduced in Table 3-5. The generally significant positive diagonal entries of this table indicate that there is a reliable tendency for students with particular needs to be found at institutions with appropriate press, although there is wide variation in the intensity of this relationship for various need-press variables.

Reading across the rows of this table indicates the kind of academic environments in which each particular student characteristic is maximized; the kinds of students to be found in any given environment are revealed down the columns. As an example, consider the needs for achievement and sex. Both the diagonal and the row entries for these two variables are approximately zero, indicating that students with strong achievement or sex needs are not unique to any particular college environment. The significant column entries, however, suggest that institutions which stress academic achievement are most likely to have student bodies with strong needs for philosophical reflectiveness and scientific research and weak needs for affiliation, dominance or play. On the other hand, students at schools which stress heterosexual activities are most likely to be play-oriented, as well as aggressive, domineering, and occupied with fantasies of unrealistic achievement.

TABLE 3-5. MATRIX OF INTERCORRELATIONS BETWEEN ACTIVITIES INDEX
AND COLLEGE CHARACTERISTICS INDEX MEANS AT 43 COLLEGES

| AI Needs Means | Aba | Ach | Ada | Aff | Agg | Cha | CCI Press Means | | | | | | | | |
							Cnj	Ctr	Dfr	Dom	E/A	Emo	Eny	Exh	F/A
Aba	-15	14	24	48	-59	-34	66	-08	11	07	17	32	25	11	-02
Ach	07	11	25	-16	24	23	-18	11	02	02	-02	-12	03	08	-09
Ada	-25	20	13	21	-13	12	31	26	-20	-09	39	18	28	30	24
Aff	49	-42	60	43	-40	-58	28	-61	71	52	-26	-10	-48	-02	-54
Agg	26	-21	-17	-60	79	52	-70	28	-20	-06	-11	-48	-29	-17	14
Cha	08	-21	-39	-37	63	39	-62	32	-38	-14	04	01	-04	-06	17
Cnj	-19	13	52	47	-59	-49	65	-34	37	25	-09	75	12	002	-28
Ctr	18	-14	-13	-48	39	32	-41	14	-04	-17	-06	-35	-11	-004	12
Dfr	-13	14	36	53	78	-40	68	-31	39	19	14	26	14	23	-11
Dom	45	-38	-01	-52	54	32	-61	-07	17	14	18	-55	-51	-05	-13
E/A	06	01	-002	-01	02	-08	10	03	-03	14	-02	-09	-07	02	-04
Emo	-30	05	-44	10	07	01	-04	28	-49	-12	-18	52	33	-01	23
Eny	-14	-05	-14	-21	16	31	-21	-06	-02	-24	11	-08	-02	15	-02
Exh	22	-20	-18	-36	50	08	-40	12	-12	-01	-27	-11	-15	-26	-12
F/A	46	-25	20	-53	55	28	-43	07	22	15	-24	-60	-45	-16	-12
Har	02	-01	33	52	-57	-48	45	-27	24	38	10	35	03	08	-21
Hum	-29	25	19	21	-10	-07	18	19	-40	-03	21	46	33	10	10
Imp	-17	01	-59	-30	47	37	-46	45	-62	-33	15	25	22	-08	25
Nar	07	04	19	29	-25	-26	37	-04	16	32	09	37	11	17	-07
Nur	-16	04	-13	62	-54	-50	53	-24	14	26	16	52	12	17	-22
Obj	-06	03	-03	05	-19	09	01	-26	12	-12	08	-14	-05	13	-01
Ord	36	-01	48	47	-58	-47	62	-37	40	26	002	13	-06	-003	-33
Ply	47	-48	09	-10	16	-04	-30	-32	35	22	-18	-31	-51	-08	-26
Pra	32	-17	61	20	-18	-12	16	-29	46	31	-01	-25	-32	16	-29
Ref	-29	30	-08	05	-06	22	07	20	-24	-01	38	23	29	23	30
Sci	-10	34	05	-39	28	46	-21	42	-19	-22	10	-31	16	-002	30
Sen	-22	16	-31	-03	11	22	-14	36	-36	-06	32	35	29	19	34
Sex	-29	-08	02	18	-23	-12	16	-01	01	23	14	31	07	02	08
Suc	-005	-10	36	54	-59	-45	57	-43	38	32	02	23	13	13	-10
Und	-23	28	-16	-33	41	53	-28	43	-39	-17	21	-01	25	17	34

TABLE 3-5. MATRIX OF INTERCORRELATIONS BETWEEN ACTIVITIES INDEX
AND COLLEGE CHARACTERISTICS INDEX MEANS AT 43 COLLEGES (continued)

AI Needs Means	CCI Press Means														
	Har	Hum	Imp	Nar	Nur	Obj	Ord	Ply	Pra	Ref	Sci	Sen	Sex	Suc	Und
Aba	65	22	-39	37	62	-36	39	-05	-02	25	-11	-06	-48	36	41
Ach	-37	-14	19	-10	-22	-18	-14	22	18	-11	07	-18	09	-09	04
Ada	21	13	03	-002	19	25	-009	03	-08	42	16	30	-08	02	31
Aff	10	-47	-38	55	52	-38	71	47	53	-46	-30	-55	15	56	-48
Agg	-75	-09	48	-47	-71	-48	-35	05	-002	-14	41	05	50	-67	-35
Cha	-35	17	37	-48	-51	-14	-41	-17	-34	08	16	31	32	-38	-20
Cnj	56	-22	-42	51	60	10	53	21	36	-15	-25	-38	-35	47	18
Ctr	-40	-005	25	-38	-48	-31	004	06	13	-06	35	15	36	-35	-22
Dfr	63	08	-47	60	71	33	51	14	22	14	-20	-11	-43	56	31
Dom	-61	-20	32	-21	-51	-62	-06	26	22	-31	25	-15	53	-42	-52
E/A	24	22	-04	12	12	-002	12	05	-15	02	-02	10	02	-12	10
Emo	30	40	02	-16	06	38	-28	-42	-61	26	-11	45	-11	-03	21
Eny	-16	16	09	-14	-31	-04	-13	07	01	10	14	12	14	-004	-06
Exh	-22	-08	11	-29	-38	-31	-08	-04	-22	-24	-06	02	17	-31	-25
F/A	-64	-35	24	-24	-54	-65	05	26	41	-39	28	-33	43	-48	-48
Har	64	02	-35	52	69	27	27	14	04	03	-46	-14	-29	43	19
Hum	59	56	-13	07	24	41	-21	-28	-65	41	-11	46	-30	04	42
Imp	-11	36	28	-61	-45	15	-55	-46	-60	24	13	52	04	-42	04
Nar	42	18	20	32	49	18	31	-01	-08	10	-12	03	-10	32	19
Nur	74	21	-36	52	77	38	34	08	-19	17	-49	04	-35	59	30
Obj	-06	14	-07	14	09	02	04	08	-03	13	20	11	04	14	04
Ord	50	-18	-42	49	61	12	54	16	39	-15	-32	-39	-34	53	14
Ply	-32	-24	01	04	-13	-45	16	23	22	-32	06	-22	39	-02	-59
Pra	-22	-38	-03	27	20	-34	46	48	71	-28	12	-40	22	23	-24
Ref	27	59	14	17	19	34	-22	-06	-44	55	19	45	-14	-08	52
Sci	-41	04	18	-37	-48	-14	-26	-10	11	10	61	16	09	-51	11
Sen	09	53	17	-09	001	31	-28	-27	-57	40	16	49	04	-14	33
Sex	26	14	-21	19	31	09	18	-11	-28	07	-24	12	02	13	03
Suc	45	01	-41	63	69	13	60	21	20	01	-20	-12	-15	55	07
Und	-26	35	35	-30	-43	01	-46	-08	-22	33	44	36	10	-46	23

Perhaps these are the qualities necessary for survival in the more extreme examples of the adolescent rating-dating complex.

Subcultural Differences Within a Complex Institution

The relationships suggested by Table 3-5 assume a degree of institutional homogeneity which is actually realized to any considerable degree only in the elite private liberal arts colleges. Although the average scale values at other institutions provide an entirely adequate basis for conceptualizing dominant need-press trends, the variability of response is great enough to suggest the likelihood of subcultural variation, particularly in the larger and more complex university-affiliated colleges.

The remaining tables are based on data from one such institution, a large eastern university with a graduating class of approximately 1,000 students. The general characteristics of this school are essentially like those just described for schools stressing heterosexual activities--the most pronounced aspects of the press as seen by the senior class involve various forms of impulse expression reflected in high scores on scales for sex, play, thrill-seeking (risk-taking), dominance, and aggression. At the same time the intellectual press is regarded as low and the faculty are denigrated.

Although there are consistent differences between men and women, as shown in Tables 3-6 and 3-7, they are both agreed in this general characterization of a low intellectual, high impulse-expression school. The major sex differences in press perception stem from the fact that the men find the school generally less stimulating than do the women, particularly in opportunities for impulse-expression. This is apparently a school with facilities oriented towards women. Sex differences in needs scores, reported in Table 3-7, are extensive; the most consistent differences are to be found in the typically higher scores for women on scales associated with dependency needs.

TABLE 3-6. COLLEGE CHARACTERISTICS INDEX STANINE MEANS
FOR SENIOR MEN AND WOMEN AT THE SAME INSTITUTION
(N = 573 men and 463 women)

Dimension	Need Scales	Men		Women		$t^{a,b}$	Total	
		$\overline{X}$	σ	$\overline{X}$	σ		$\overline{X}$	σ
Intellectual Needs	Achievement	3.35	2.64	3.41	2.45	.38	3.38	2.55
	Conjunctivity-Disjunctivity	4.21	2.45	4.10	2.32	.73	4.16	2.40
	Counteraction-Infavoidance	4.12	1.85	3.79	1.78	+2.75**	3.96	1.84
	Ego Achievement	5.82	2.05	6.23	1.85	-3.42**	6.00	1.99
	Energy-Passivity	4.10	2.00	4.01	2.18	.64	4.07	2.17
	Humanism	4.84	2.13	5.19	2.02	-2.69**	4.99	2.11
	Objectivity	3.95	2.32	3.93	2.13	.14	3.94	2.24
	Reflectiveness	5.17	2.19	5.43	2.18	1.86	5.29	2.18
	Scientism	4.63	2.41	4.12	2.25	+3.40**	4.40	2.37
	Understanding	4.22	2.25	4.01	2.22	1.50	4.12	2.26
Dependency Needs	Abasement	7.03	2.12	7.37	1.93	-2.62**	7.17	2.06
	Adaptiveness	6.05	1.67	5.76	1.74	+2.64**	5.92	1.71
	Affiliation-Rejection	4.59	1.92	4.63	1.83	.33	4.60	1.89
	Blameavoidance-Aggression	3.75	2.12	3.77	2.14	.14	3.77	2.14
	Conjunctivity-Disjunctivity	4.21	2.45	4.10	2.32	.73	4.16	2.40
	Deference	5.50	1.60	5.50	1.54	--	5.50	1.57
	Nurturance-Rejection	5.25	2.10	5.91	1.82	-5.08**	5.55	2.02
	Order	4.15	1.64	4.31	1.56	1.57	4.21	1.63
	Succorance-Autonomy	4.58	1.66	4.71	1.52	1.30	4.64	1.59

[a] Significantly larger values for senior men are indicated by a plus (+) sign, lower by a minus (-).
[b] $p < .05$ (*), $< .01$ (**).

TABLE 3-6. COLLEGE CHARACTERISTICS INDEX STANINE MEANS
FOR SENIOR MEN AND WOMEN AT THE SAME INSTITUTION (continued)
(N = 573 men and 463 women)

Dimension	Need Scales	Men X̄	Men σ	Women X̄	Women σ	$t^{a,b}$	Total X̄	Total σ
Impulse Expression	Aggression-Blameavoidance	6.25	2.12	6.23	2.14	.14	6.23	2.14
	Change-Sameness	5.46	1.56	5.56	1.51	1.00	5.50	1.53
	Dominance	6.19	1.88	6.67	1.85	-4.00**	6.41	1.87
	Ego Achievement	5.82	2.05	6.23	1.86	-3.42**	6.00	1.99
	Emotionality-Placidity	4.33	1.88	4.91	1.84	-4.83**	4.59	1.88
	Energy-Passivity	4.10	2.19	4.01	2.18	.64	4.07	2.17
	Exhibitionism-Infavoidance	5.34	2.11	5.52	1.99	1.38	5.42	2.06
	Fantasied Achievement	4.99	1.56	4.69	1.44	+3.00**	4.86	1.50
	Impulsion-Deliberation	6.05	1.72	6.43	1.56	-3.80**	6.21	1.68
	Narcissism	5.26	1.96	5.90	1.95	-5.33**	5.55	1.99
	Play	6.86	1.75	7.16	1.46	-3.00**	7.00	1.61
	Pragmatism	6.06	1.57	6.07	1.61	.10	6.07	1.56
	Risk-Harmavoidance	6.49	1.42	6.34	1.39	1.67	6.42	1.41
	Sentience	4.87	1.82	5.46	1.98	-4.92**	5.14	1.93
	Sex-Prudishness	7.51	1.75	7.19	1.39	+3.20**	7.05	1.60

[a] Significantly larger values for senior men are indicated by a plus (+) sign, lower by a minus (-).

[b] $p < .05$ (*), $< .01$ (**).

TABLE 3-7.   ACTIVITIES INDEX STANINE MEANS FOR
SENIOR MEN AND WOMEN AT THE SAME INSTITUTION
(N = 573 men and 463 women)

Dimension	Need Scales	Men		Women		$t^{a,b}$	Total	
		$\bar{X}$	σ	$\bar{X}$	σ		$\bar{X}$	σ
Intellectual Needs	Achievement	5.44	2.10	4.96	2.26	+3.43**	5.21	2.21
	Conjunctivity-Disjunctivity	4.80	2.30	4.97	2.28	1.13	4.87	2.30
	Counteraction-Infavoidance	5.41	2.08	5.16	2.40	1.79	5.28	2.28
	Ego Achievement	5.44	2.86	5.06	2.68	+2.11*	5.26	2.81
	Energy-Passivity	5.64	1.61	5.43	2.64	1.24	5.34	1.61
	Humanism	4.74	2.61	5.62	2.96	-5.18**	5.13	2.85
	Objectivity	5.00	1.20	4.94	1.42	.75	4.97	1.37
	Reflectiveness	4.95	2.27	5.30	2.03	-2.50*	5.09	2.22
	Scientism	5.32	3.20	4.38	3.42	+4.70**	4.89	3.40
	Understanding	4.94	2.22	5.03	2.27	.64	4.97	2.28
Dependency Needs	Abasement	4.78	1.85	4.93	1.82	1.36	4.84	1.84
	Adaptiveness	4.99	2.25	5.08	2.37	.60	5.02	2.34
	Affiliation-Rejection	5.27	2.57	5.81	2.33	-3.60**	5.50	2.52
	Blameavoidance-Aggression	4.00	2.39	5.33	2.24	-8.87***	4.60	2.46
	Conjunctivity-Disjunctivity	4.80	2.30	4.97	2.28	1.13	4.87	2.30
	Deference	4.60	2.02	5.28	1.93	-5.23**	4.89	2.05
	Nurturance-Rejection	4.52	2.46	5.66	2.06	-8.14**	5.02	2.42
	Order	4.91	3.13	5.38	2.84	-2.35*	5.12	3.04
	Succorance-Autonomy	4.77	2.03	5.57	1.97	-5.71**	5.12	2.08

[a] Significantly larger values for senior men are indicated by a plus (+) sign, lower by a minus (-).
[b] $p < .05$ (*), $< .01$ (**).

TABLE 3-7. ACTIVITIES INDEX STANINE MEANS FOR
SENIOR MEN AND WOMEN AT THE SAME INSTITUTION (continued)
(N = 573 men and 463 women)

Dimension	Need Scales	Men X̄	Men σ	Women X̄	Women σ	$t^{a,b}$	Total X̄	Total σ
Impulse Expression	Aggression-Blameavoidance	6.00	2.39	4.67	2.24	+8.87**	5.40	2.46
	Change-Sameness	5.40	2.21	5.57	2.14	1.21	5.46	2.21
	Dominance	5.98	2.09	5.10	2.27	+6.29**	5.58	2.29
	Ego Achievement	5.44	2.86	5.06	2.68	+2.11*	5.26	2.81
	Emotionality-Placidity	4.54	1.82	6.14	1.98	-13.33**	5.25	2.10
	Energy-Passivity	5.64	1.61	5.43	2.64	1.24	5.34	1.61
	Exhibitionism-Infavoidance	5.42	2.63	5.27	1.50	1.50	5.54	2.66
	Fantasied Achievement	6.30	2.36	4.42	2.08	+13.43**	5.45	2.46
	Impulsion-Deliberation	5.00	1.85	5.52	1.95	-4.33**	5.22	1.95
	Narcissism	4.97	2.35	5.64	2.35	-4.79**	5.26	2.40
	Play	5.51	2.49	5.38	2.24	.93	5.45	2.40
	Pragmatism	5.47	2.35	5.04	2.37	+3.07**	5.26	2.42
	Risk-Harmavoidance	5.80	2.38	4.97	2.76	+4.88**	5.43	2.62
	Sentience	4.74	1.77	5.63	1.74	-8.09**	5.13	1.82
	Sex-Prudishness	4.52	2.56	5.82	2.44	-8.12**	5.09	2.67

[a] Significantly larger values for senior men are indicated by a plus (+) sign, lower by a minus (-).

[b] $p < .05$ (*), $< .01$ (**).

Tables 3-8 and 3-9 summarize differences in the images held by various majors at this school. Reference to Table 3-9 suggests that three of the 16 groups of seniors identified here have distinctly different impressions of the institution. Business administration majors are even more extreme than the rest of the class in devaluing the school's intellectual climate, whereas education and forestry majors both find the school challenging, although for different reasons. A very similar situation has been encountered at a large southern university where education and engineering majors found the school to be high in achievement orientation, whereas majors in liberal arts described it as extremely low in this regard.

The situation is reversed with respect to impulse expression. As shown in Table 3-9, the education students find this school to be even more emotionally stimulating than does the class as a whole, in marked contrast to the restraints experienced by both the engineers and the foresters.

The differences between majors are apparently not a function of intelligence, since these groups are fairly similar in scores on the College Board Scholastic Aptitude Test, with the single exception of the engineering students, who are almost a standard deviation higher than the rest of the class in math aptitude (Table 3-10). In part the differences appear to be related to supporting needs characteristics of these students, as shown in Tables 3-11 and 3-12, but sex differences are also a factor here--the education students being largely female, the engineering and forestry students male. Analyses now in progress are expected to clarify the determinants of these relationships, and to investigate the educational significance of need-press congruence and dissonance for other campus subgroups.

Conclusions

This paper has described a technique for measuring concomitant aspects of personal needs and situational press. The primary significance of this approach lies in the fact

TABLE 3-8. COLLEGE CHARACTERISTICS INDEX STANINE MEANS--
TOTAL SENIOR CLASS OF UNIVERSITY-AFFILIATED COLLEGE
(N = 1,036)

Major	Aba	Ach	Ada	Aff	Agg	Cha	Cnj	Ctr	Dfr	Dom
Liberal Arts:										
Classics and Humanities	7.35	3.19	5.59	4.28	6.28	5.42	4.30	3.90	5.76	6.29
Social Sciences	7.78	-2.39	-5.19	4.32	6.54	5.59	4.24	3.39	5.68	6.07
Natural Sciences	7.18	3.71	5.59	4.82	6.37	5.37	4.38	3.59	5.40	6.14
Hist., Econ., and Govt.	7.27	3.32	5.90	4.45	6.15	5.16	4.29	3.63	5.75	6.36
Biol. Sciences	7.84	3.07	6.16	3.81	6.48	5.34	4.34	3.81	5.90	6.49
Miscellaneous	7.50	3.10	5.73	4.29	6.52	5.27	3.69	3.66	5.64	6.41
Business Administration	7.43	-2.67	5.96	4.08	6.50	5.26	3.88	3.58	+5.93	6.36
Fine Arts	7.27	3.53	6.34	4.99	6.02	5.73	4.08	4.28	5.10	6.39
Education	7.27	3.74	5.99	4.92	6.13	+5.83	4.41	4.27	5.33	6.80
Speech and Dramatic Arts	8.25	-2.45	6.03	4.30	6.65	5.43	3.82	3.35	5.74	7.43
Home Economics	7.52	3.85	5.85	4.80	6.07	5.21	4.08	4.02	5.61	7.05
Architecture	7.42	3.23	+6.94	4.23	6.86	5.16	3.55	4.15	4.88	7.01
Engineering	6.84	3.42	5.93	4.43	5.86	5.65	3.32	4.11	5.84	-5.79
Forestry	-5.69	3.97	6.10	+5.53	5.77	5.65	4.12	+4.81	-4.90	-5.51
Journalism	-5.57	3.95	5.68	4.53	+7.22	5.46	3.66	3.66	5.31	7.00
Nursing	6.54	4.56	6.34	4.64	5.51	5.72	5.04	4.38	4.87	6.54
TOTAL	7.17	3.38	5.92	4.60	6.23	5.50	4.16	3.96	5.50	6.41

Plus (+) and minus (-) signs indicate means differing between groups of majors enough to be estimated
as statistically significant in the region of the .01 level or beyond.

TABLE 3-8.　COLLEGE CHARACTERISTICS INDEX STANINE MEANS--
TOTAL SENIOR CLASS OF UNIVERSITY-AFFILIATED COLLEGE (continued)
(N = 1,036)

Major	E/A	Emo	Eny	Exh	F/A	Har	Hum	Imp	Nar	Nur
Liberal Arts:										
Classics and Humanities	6.06	4.64	3.97	5.73	4.84	3.51	4.98	6.18	5.87	5.43
Social Sciences	5.92	4.38	3.58	5.41	4.75	3.44	5.11	6.60	5.50	5.42
Natural Sciences	5.83	4.41	3.93	5.30	4.61	3.49	4.78	5.92	4.96	5.35
Hist., Econ., and Govt.	5.95	4.31	4.18	5.41	4.90	3.45	5.20	6.24	5.58	5.32
Biol. Sciences	6.09	4.38	3.55	5.61	4.56	3.51	4.67	5.62	5.07	5.28
Miscellaneous	5.81	4.44	3.57	5.39	4.91	3.56	4.88	5.80	5.57	5.38
Business Administration	5.76	4.07	-3.41	4.99	4.48	3.31	-4.41	6.25	5.24	4.99
Fine Arts	6.10	4.75	4.48	5.53	5.17	3.72	5.07	6.16	5.80	5.80
Education	+6.63	+5.18	4.38	+5.91	4.95	3.72	5.51	+6.64	+6.09	+6.26
Speech and Dramatic Arts	6.15	4.66	3.64	5.21	5.28	3.27	4.66	6.49	6.05	4.95
Home Economics	6.64	5.08	4.51	5.63	4.88	3.59	5.85	6.84	5.95	6.16
Architecture	5.23	4.50	4.35	5.20	5.07	3.76	5.24	6.30	4.83	5.16
Engineering	5.53	4.23	4.14	5.02	4.82	3.61	4.93	-5.49	5.12	5.19
Forestry	5.33	4.22	4.36	-4.63	4.92	3.65	-4.10	-5.60	-4.77	5.16
Journalism	5.69	4.57	3.43	5.45	4.46	3.58	4.17	6.45	4.91	5.43
Nursing	6.05	5.29	5.18	5.45	5.32	4.25	5.49	6.64	6.34	6.47
TOTAL	6.00	4.59	4.07	5.42	4.86	3.58	4.99	6.21	5.55	5.55

Plus (+) and minus (-) signs indicate means differing between groups of majors enough to be estimated
as statistically significant in the region of the .01 level or beyond.

TABLE 3-8. COLLEGE CHARACTERISTICS INDEX STANINE MEANS--
TOTAL SENIOR CLASS OF UNIVERSTY-AFFILIATED COLLEGE (continued)
(N = 1,036)

Major	Obj	Ord	Ply	Pra	Ref	Sci	Sen	Sex	Suc	Und
Liberal Arts:										
Classics and Humanities	3.72	3.89	6.94	5.65	5.19	4.07	5.20	7.13	4.48	4.15
Social Sciences	3.83	4.51	7.27	-5.54	5.26	4.07	4.99	+7.60	4.85	3.86
Natural Sciences	3.94	3.77	7.09	6.00	4.85	4.34	5.02	7.10	4.94	4.07
Hist., Econ., and Govt.	3.74	4.04	7.10	6.05	4.98	4.19	-4.66	7.15	4.50	4.24
Biol. Sciences	3.93	4.73	6.98	6.21	5.65	4.33	4.79	7.06	3.99	3.78
Miscellaneous	3.31	4.08	6.86	6.26	5.15	4.11	-4.67	7.05	4.15	3.81
Business Administration	3.53	4.09	7.17	6.25	4.85	3.76	-4.53	7.32	4.58	-3.39
Fine Arts	4.14	4.36	7.13	6.13	5.52	4.17	5.62	7.00	4.77	4.29
Education	+4.26	4.54	7.34	+6.31	+5.89	4.75	+5.66	7.36	4.67	4.44
Speech and Dramatic Arts	2.88	4.24	7.60	6.53	4.64	3.66	4.77	7.59	4.57	3.64
Home Economics	3.97	4.84	6.68	6.38	5.85	4.81	+5.87	7.05	4.91	4.56
Architecture	3.40	3.95	6.74	6.34	5.00	4.42	5.29	6.91	4.56	3.57
Engineering	4.28	-3.66	-6.35	5.84	5.23	4.78	4.98	-6.62	4.86	4.27
Forestry	+4.60	4.22	-6.08	5.60	4.77	+5.62	4.93	-5.74	4.84	4.47
Journalism	3.93	3.47	7.25	6.37	4.97	-2.89	5.46	7.15	4.75	3.57
Nursing	4.63	4.83	6.79	6.12	6.07	4.84	5.76	6.33	4.47	4.68
TOTAL	3.94	4.21	7.00	6.07	5.29	4.40	5.14	7.05	4.64	4.12

Plus (+) and minus (-) signs indicate means differing between groups of majors enough to be estimated
as statistically significant in the region of the .01 level or beyond.

TABLE 3-9. SUMMARY OF COLLEGE CHARACTERISTICS INDEX SCALES
CONTRIBUTING TO DIFFERENTIATION BETWEEN SENIORS
IN 16 DIFFERENT MAJORS AT THE SAME INSTITUTION

Major	N	Intellectual Needs	Dependency Needs	Impulse Expression
Liberal Arts:				
Classics and Humanities	77			
Social Sciences	65	Ach-	Ada-	Pra-, Sex-
Natural Sciences	42			
Hist., Econ., and Govt.	110			Sen-
Biological Sciences	32			
Miscellaneous	66			Sen-
Business Administration	88	Ach-, Eny-, Hum-, Und-	Dfr+	Sen-
Fine Arts	71			
Education	211	E/A+, Obj+, Ref+	Nur+	Cha+, E/A+, Emo+, Exh+, Imp+, Nar+, Pra+, Sen+
Speech and Dramatic Arts	25	Ach-		
Home Economics	34			Sen+
Architecture	28		Ada+	
Engineering	64		Ord-	Dom-, Imp-, Ply-, Sex-
Forestry	84	Ctr+, Hum-, Obj+, Sci+	Aba-, Aff+, Dfr-	Dom-, Exh-, Imp-, Nar-, Ply-, Sex-
Journalism	24	Sci-	Aba-, Bla-	Agg+
Nursing	15			

Plus (+) signs following scale name indicate means significantly high
at .01 level or beyond, minus (-) signs indicate significantly low means.

TABLE 3-10. SCHOOL OR COLLEGE COMPARISON ON CEEB--1959

Upper Limit of Raw Score Intervals	1957 Base Year %iles		1958 All School %iles		1959 All School %iles		Comparisons of Distributions by Colleges, 1959 (Cumulative Percentages Reported) Business Admin.		Engi- neering		Fine Arts		Home Econ.		Liberal Arts		Nursing		Speech and Dr. Arts	
	V	M	V	M	V	M	V	M	V	M	V	M	V	M	V	M	V	M	V	M
799																				
779						99+														
759						99+														
739		99+		99+	99+	99				99+		99+				99+				
719	99+	99	99+	99	99+	98		99+	99+	99+		99+			99+	99+			99+	99+
699	99	98	99	99	99	97		99+	99+	97	99+	99+		99+	99+	99		99+	99+	98
679	98	97	98	99	98	95	99+	99+	99+	95	99+	99	99+	97	99	97	99+	98	99+	98
659	96	96	98	98	96	93	99+	99+	98	94	98	98	99	95	99	95	95	98	96	97
639	96	94	96	96	94	90	99	99	97	87	97	97	94	87	95	93	91	96	93	94
619	94	91	94	94	90	84	99	98	95	78	95	95	92	86	92	90	89	94	88	93
599	90	86	92	91	85	80	96	96	93	72	93	91	92	83	88	85	80	89	80	90
579	86	82	89	87	81	75	93	95	85	56	90	89	91	78	84	81	78	87	75	82
559	81	77	84	81	74	68	90	92	82	46	87	86	89	78	79	76	72	77	69	76
539	74	70	78	74	67	62	85	85	78	37	79	82	80	73	71	69	65	68	64	72
519	67	62	72	67	60	54	79	79	72	29	70	74	75	68	64	64	59	64	57	60
499	59	53	66	58	52	45	72	76	67	18	61	67	70	56	57	56	52	55	46	46
479	52	45	58	49	44	37	66	69	59	11	53	57	59	43	49	46	48	49	38	41
459	44	37	50	40	36	30	55	61	47	5	47	48	49	30	41	39	37	43	31	34
439	35	28	41	31	27	22	44	53	39	4	41	40	37	24	33	31	26	36	23	21
419	27	20	32	23	19	15	33	42	28	3	32	33	30	17	25	22	20	30	19	21
399	21	15	25	17	13	10	24	33	20	2	21	26	21	13	17	15	13	17	12	8
379	15	11	17	12	8	6	18	23	14	1	17	18	10	8	12	10	7	9	12	6
359	10	7	12	8	4	4	9	16	9		9	11	2	6	7	5	2	4	5	6
339	6	5	8	5	2	2	5	12	5		7	10		6	4	4		2	4	1
319	3	3	5	3	1	1	1	8	3		4	4		3	2	2			1	
299	2	1	2	1	1-	1-		4	2		1	4			1-	1-				
279	1	1	1	1		1-		3			1	1			1-	1-				
259	1-	1-	1-	1-		1-		1-			1-	1-			1-	1-				
Means	489	505	495	514	499	518	477	522	492	601	489	485	476	481	506	514	520	509	512	486
Standard Deviations	90	90	88	86	124	127	76	87	85	71	86	89	82	92	126	130	86	89	88	81
Number in Classes	1995		1922		2285		251		186		270		63		1367		47		101	

TABLE 3-11.   STERN ACTIVITIES INDEX STANINE MEANS--
TOTAL SENIOR CLASS OF UNIVERSITY-AFFILIATED COLLEGE
(N = 1,036)

Major	Aba	Ach	Ada	Aff	Agg	Cha	Cnj	Ctr	Dfr	Dom
Liberal Arts:										
Classics and Humanities	4.88	5.01	4.85	5.04	5.05	5.74	4.45	5.00	5.01	5.19
Social Sciences	4.64	4.72	4.84	5.80	5.40	5.39	4.52	4.72	4.51	5.59
Natural Sciences	4.58	5.70	4.95	-4.29	4.76	-4.38	5.25	6.00	4.66	-4.68
Hist., Econ., and Govt.	4.75	5.55	4.86	5.64	+6.41	5.46	4.61	5.52	4.29	+6.43
Biological Sciences	5.00	5.28	5.00	5.33	5.75	4.85	5.31	5.28	4.63	6.08
Miscellaneous	4.59	5.08	4.88	5.75	5.99	5.89	4.71	5.14	4.55	5.80
Business Administration	4.50	5.08	4.54	6.00	5.44	5.32	4.51	5.35	4.78	5.98
Fine Arts	4.86	+5.77	5.43	5.20	5.09	5.99	4.72	5.60	5.11	5.05
Forestry	5.16	5.12	5.36	-4.39	+5.98	5.67	4.92	5.40	4.58	5.70
Architecture	4.74	5.94	5.32	5.35	6.21	5.90	4.68	5.37	5.12	5.82
Education	5.18	4.94	5.22	+6.01	-4.83	5.32	+5.36	5.28	+5.47	5.38
Engineering	4.61	5.45	4.72	5.14	5.81	5.23	5.05	5.32	4.84	5.66
Journalism	4.62	5.97	5.45	5.56	5.13	5.71	4.92	5.54	4.54	5.50
Speech and Dramatic Arts	4.25	5.28	4.94	5.40	5.43	5.95	4.69	5.32	4.53	5.48
Nursing	5.52	5.39	5.80	6.14	-3.87	4.91	5.75	5.73	+6.40	4.67
Home Economics	4.77	4.60	4.75	+6.35	-4.33	5.57	4.53	4.72	5.40	5.11
TOTAL	4.84	5.21	5.02	5.50	5.40	4.63	4.87	5.28	4.89	5.58

Plus (+) and minus (-) signs indicate means differing between groups of majors enough to be estimated as statistically significant in the region of the .01 level or beyond.

TABLE 3-11. STERN ACTIVITIES INDEX STANINE MEANS--
TOTAL SENIOR CLASS OF UNIVERSITY-AFFILIATED COLLEGE (continued)
(N = 1,036)

Major	E/A	Emo	Eny	Exh	F/A	Har	Hum	Imp	Nar	Nur
Liberal Arts:										
Classics and Humanities	5.44	+5.59	-4.54	5.36	5.39	5.09	4.87	+5.74	5.53	5.13
Social Sciences	5.30	+5.67	5.09	5.32	-4.81	4.77	5.30	5.29	4.89	4.98
Natural Sciences	4.43	-4.42	5.77	4.50	4.85	4.90	4.48	4.54	4.73	4.40
Hist., Econ., and Govt.	+6.10	5.13	5.54	6.19	+6.65	4.12	5.25	5.30	5.24	4.69
Biological Sciences	5.50	4.88	5.38	5.51	+6.44	3.97	5.32	4.50	5.55	5.19
Miscellaneous	5.62	4.94	5.09	5.70	5.78	4.20	5.38	5.41	5.08	4.86
Business Administration	5.32	-4.57	5.16	5.56	+6.12	-3.27	4.38	5.03	4.82	4.40
Fine Arts	-4.35	+5.59	5.58	5.59	-4.94	4.61	5.46	5.35	5.50	5.10
Forestry	5.14	-4.06	5.82	4.89	5.65	-3.89	4.44	4.70	-4.54	-4.18
Architecture	5.44	4.82	5.63	5.47	5.60	3.90	4.95	5.55	4.76	4.43
Education	5.22	+6.00	5.42	5.73	-4.71	+5.14	+5.88	5.34	5.65	+5.88
Engineering	4.86	-4.18	5.39	4.94	+6.40	4.65	-4.04	4.77	4.97	4.25
Journalism	6.06	5.28	5.59	5.55	4.59	5.47	5.93	5.38	4.87	5.21
Speech and Dramatic Arts	5.51	6.14	5.02	+7.78	6.34	5.19	5.18	+6.35	+6.64	5.42
Nursing	4.60	5.82	5.81	4.37	-4.17	5.46	5.14	4.76	5.52	+7.08
Home Economics	4.81	5.98	4.65	5.69	-4.19	+5.62	5.05	5.63	+6.39	5.66
TOTAL	5.26	5.25	5.34	5.54	5.45	4.57	5.13	5.22	5.26	5.02

Plus (+) and minus (-) signs indicate means differing between groups of majors enough to be estimated as statistically significant in the region of the .01 level or beyond.

TABLE 3-11. STERN ACTIVITIES INDEX STANINE MEANS--
TOTAL SENIOR CLASS OF UNIVERSITY-AFFILIATED COLLEGE (continued)
(N = 1,036)

Major	Obj	Ord	Ply	Pra	Ref	Sci	Sen	Sex	Suc	Und
Liberal Arts:										
Classics and Humanities	4.62	5.14	5.51	4.92	5.33	4.74	5.39	4.94	5.19	5.26
Social Sciences	5.32	4.65	5.98	4.76	5.24	4.53	5.40	5.28	5.28	4.86
Natural Sciences	5.50	5.30	4.92	5.17	5.55	+6.42	4.77	4.81	4.95	+5.99
Hist., Econ., and Govt.	4.73	5.07	5.79	5.10	4.71	4.55	5.01	4.74	4.93	4.87
Biological Sciences	5.15	5.06	5.13	6.14	5.75	+6.73	5.27	4.94	5.25	5.85
Miscellaneous	4.94	4.47	5.79	4.96	4.97	4.75	4.54	4.43	4.50	5.19
Business Administration	5.34	5.12	+6.19	5.64	-4.05	4.37	4.61	4.92	5.08	-4.19
Fine Arts	5.10	4.88	4.98	5.12	+5.82	4.70	5.15	4.88	4.93	4.77
Forestry	5.27	4.69	-4.81	5.75	4.58	+5.77	4.59	4.32	-4.25	4.73
Architecture	5.14	4.84	5.62	5.62	5.37	5.01	5.29	4.42	4.57	4.95
Education	4.92	+5.60	5.25	5.13	5.54	4.67	+5.54	+6.04	-4.12	5.04
Engineering	4.83	5.18	5.35	+6.18	4.69	+6.52	4.78	4.42	5.02	5.40
Journalism	5.20	5.15	4.55	4.44	5.12	-3.34	5.40	5.35	4.37	5.08
Speech and Dramatic Arts	-3.96	5.05	5.80	4.83	4.68	3.48	+6.08	5.59	4.92	-3.79
Nursing	4.83	5.75	4.58	5.22	5.69	4.46	5.28	5.51	5.94	5.39
Home Economics	4.44	5.60	6.24	5.46	5.03	3.95	5.63	+6.18	5.46	-3.74
TOTAL	4.97	5.12	5.45	5.26	5.09	4.89	5.13	5.09	5.12	4.97

Plus (+) and minus (-) signs indicate means differing between groups of majors enough to be estimated as statistically significant in the region of the .01 level or beyond.

TABLE 3-12. SUMMARY OF ACTIVITIES INDEX SCALES
CONTRIBUTING TO DIFFERENTIATION BETWEEN SENIORS
IN 16 DIFFERENT MAJORS AT THE SAME INSTITUTION

Major	N	Intellectual Needs	Dependency Needs	Impulse Expression
Liberal Arts:				
Classics and Humanities	77	Eny-		Emo+, Eny-, Imp+, Risk+
Social Sciences	65			Emo+, F/A-
Natural Sciences	42	Sci+, Und+	Aff-	Cha-, Dom-, Emo-
Hist., Econ., and Govt.	110	E/A+	Bla-	Agg+, Dom+, E/A+, F/A+
Biological Sciences	32	Sci+		F/A+
Miscellaneous	66			
Business Administration	88	Ref-, Und-		Emo-, F/A+, Ply+, Risk+
Fine Arts	71	Ach+, E/A-, Ref+		E/A-, Emo+, F/A-
Education	211	Cnj+, Hum+	Aff+, Bla+, Cnj+, Dfr+, Nur+, Suc+	Emo+, F/A-, Risk-, Sex+
Speech and Dramatic Arts	25	Und-		Exh+, Imp+, Nar+
Home Economics	34	Und-	Aff+, Bla+	Agg-, F/A-, Nar+, Risk-, Sex+
Architecture	28			
Engineering	64	Hum-, Sci+		Emo-, F/A+, Pra+
Forestry	84	Sci+	Aff-, Bla-, Nur-, Suc-	Agg+, Emo-, Nar-, Ply-
Journalism	24	Sci-		
Nursing	15		Bla+, Dfr+, Nur+	Agg-, F/A-

Plus (+) signs following scale name indicate means significantly high
at .01 level or beyond, minus (-) signs indicate significantly low means.

that it provides a basic taxonomy for classifying both persons and situations in comparable terms. Research to date,
largely in college settings, tends to support its validity
and utility. The ultimate value of these techniques is expected to lie not only in the description of learning environments, however, but also in a more general contribution
to research and theory on the relationships between psychological aspects of organizational structures and the personality characteristics of the group members.

4 | John Ross
University of Western Australia

Factor Analysis and Levels of Measurement in Psychology

It is to psychoanalysis and factor analysis, two disciplines as distant from one another as any in psychology, that we owe our conception that human behavior may be investigated on different levels. Psychoanalysis has taught us that it may be possible to penetrate beneath the surface of behavior into recesses where there are forces that show themselves only indirectly. We have come to believe that by using the couch and other stimuli to free mental play, we can investigate people in depth--that is, on another level than is normally possible. Factor analysis has shown us that by mathematical analysis of covariation it is possible to discover factors which underlie the surface level of our measures, and thus, by a number magic dimly understood by most of us, in some sense to follow Freud in his descent to the depths of personality. But both the psychoanalytic and the factor analytic pedagogues, not having taught their lessons well, have left us with a haze of misconceptions and ill-considered equations, as well as the shining prospect of distant paths converging upon a common truth. Cattell (1957) has recently unearthed factors interpreted in terms of the Freudian Ego, Id, and Super-Ego, which would seem

This paper was read while the author was affiliated with Educational Testing Service.

to indicate that the point of convergence has been nearly reached if it is not, in fact, upon us.

The purpose of this paper is to examine the concept of levels as we find it in personality theory and in factor analysis, to show that the deep-level variables of personality theorists and the factors of factor analysts by no means necessarily correspond, and to try to show, for a specific personality test, how we might use factor analysis to decide whether or not it gets at deep-seated or superficial variables of personality. The test to be discussed is the Myers-Briggs Type Indicator, which is intended to make assessments in terms of variables based upon Jung's system of psychological types.

Levels of Analysis in Psychology

The Psychoanalytic Concept of Levels

Let us first see what is meant by the psychoanalytic concept of levels. Freud's central concept is the wish (cf. Holt, 1915), and in his conception of mind the wish may or may not be expressed directly in behavior. It may vary in another respect in being either conscious or unconscious. (Whether this is a difference in the state of the wish, or whether Freud means that the wish is unrecognized, or that both are true, is unclear.) Expression is not such an all-or-none matter as is implied above. Wishes may be expressed directly in behavior or indirectly through symbols, in fantasy, in disguise, or in conjunction with another wish. In the latter case, behavior literally has a double meaning, so Freud would say, and he actually discusses wit, especially double-entendres, in these terms. Broadly, Freud would say we go deeply into behavior when we discover the wishes it expresses, more deeply when we discover the unconscious wishes, and most deeply of all when we probe for the unconscious wishes most circuitously expressed.

With the elaboration of concepts of character structure and the defense mechanisms of the ego, depth analysis came to have a second meaning. To understand the individual on a deep level came to mean to understand the control mechanisms that he uses to govern the expression of his wishes, and, so we have begun to think more recently, the whole of his perceptual and cognitive functioning (cf. Rapaport, 1959).

Later modifications of the Freudian position have substituted motive for wish and added new motives, but the idea of expression is still fundamental, and on it is based the idea of a deeper, covert level beneath the overt behavior we observe.

The Factor Analytic Concept of Levels

Let us next ask what factor analysts mean by the concept of levels. Factors are usually held to be underlying variables, but due to an ambiguity in the term "underlying" and in the whole family of terms of which it is a member, this can mean different things to different people. The ambiguity goes as follows: Given a patterned configuration of any kind, say a graphic design or a social structure, we may examine the details and then become aware of something underlying them. What we become aware of may be the pattern itself or the forces, whatever they were--artistic tradition in the one case, let us say, and economic processes in the other--which produced the pattern. Both may equally be said to underlie the relationships among details, but they are quite distinct. In behavior itself the two possibilities are open, and some factor analysts take one option in interpreting factors, while some prefer the other. Burt (1941) and Cattell (1957) seem to mean by a factor a salient dimension within the pattern. Thurstone (1947), however, seemed to mean some underlying causal component for which a real (neurological) counterpart might eventually be found.

Clearly, factors in the first sense may not be the variables at a deeper level which psychoanalysts have taught us to look for. (Although Toulmin (1948-49) believes that they are really dealing with patterns in behavior and erroneously postulate covert forces.) While both can be said to underlie behavior, they belong to different universes of discourse, and to confuse the two would be what Ryle (1950) calls a category mistake.

If factors may be underlying causes, however, it is certainly more reasonable to ask if they may not correspond to the deeper level variables of depth psychology. Some factor analysts would argue more forcefully still and say that if the variables proposed by depth psychologists are genuine they should emerge as factors. It is this argument that we consider next.

Personality Models and Factor Models

Elaborate though it is, Freud's system is still only an energy model of personality, which is to say that it is an elaborate system of forces and counter-forces where force as such prevails. (Thus Freud's problems with the source of the Ego's power.) The real innovation of ego-psychology was to modify Freud's conception, so that some elements in the model, because they held an executive, controlling function, could have an effect disproportionate to the force they could exert. It is probably no accident that this revolution in psychoanalytic theory has corresponded in time with a technological revolution in which concern has shifted from the production of energy to mechanisms for its control.

The factor analytic model is expressed in the fundamental factor equation

$$X_{ia} = \sum_g a_{ig} W_{ga} \quad ,$$

that is, that the score (X_{ia}) of an individual (i) on an observed variable (a) is the weighted sum of his scores on a set of factor variables (a_{ig}), each having a weight (W_{ga}) which depends on the variable (a) and the factor (g) only and not on the individual.

The factor model, then, assumes that the magnitude of a behavioral effect (ability to solve problems, compulsivity, etc.) may be considered as the sum of separate effects each produced by a separate agent. The analytic technique is one which endeavors to find out (i) how many agents there are, (ii) how much each contributes to each behavioral effect considered in the analysis, and (iii) the identity of the agent. Factor analysts call these items of information (i) the number of factors, (ii) the factor loadings, and (iii) the interpretation of the factors, respectively. Sometimes one takes a fourth step (iv) of finding the scores of individuals on the factors, since they may be estimated from the behavioral test scores.

Let us now consider how well the assumptions demanded by factor analysis are met by reality as Freud imagined it. It is clear at once that the fit between the world of psychoanalysis and the constraints of factor analysis is not good, because the wish of psychoanalysis is not supposed to produce any constant effect along a behavioral dimension and because the effects that wishes do produce are not supposed to be invariably additive. The point may be most easily demonstrated by an example.

Psychoanalysts argue that there is a phenomenon of reaction formation in which a wish leads to its behavioral opposite; e.g., a wish to be hostile leads to overconcern for the welfare of others. Let us simplify things a little and assume that anxiety level determines whether reaction formation occurs or not, and then inquire into the probable results of a factor analytic study of a set of tests depending upon anxiety, hostile wishes (covert hostility), and hostility directly expressed in behavior (overt hostility). We may consider three cases, increasing somewhat in complexity:

Case 1. Assume that we have covert hostility (Hc) and anxiety (A) and assume that if anxiety is above a given level K, overt hostility (Ho) is inversely related to covert hostility (cf. Wallach, Green, Lipsitt, and Minehart, 1962). Formally,

$$Ho = Hc \quad \text{for} \quad A \leq K$$

$$Ho = -Hc \quad \text{for} \quad A > K \ . \tag{1}$$

Assume further that we have a set of measures (M_g) which are all linear functions of anxiety, covert hostility, and overt hostility. Formally we have a set (M_g) where

$$M_{gi} = a_g A_i + b_g Hc_i + c_g Ho_i \quad . \tag{2}$$

By conditions **(1)**, we can say

$$M_{gi} = a_g A_i + (b_g + c_g)Hc_i \quad \text{for} \quad A_i \le K$$

$$M_{gi} = a_g A_i + (b_g - c_g)Hc_i \quad \text{for} \quad A_i > K \ .$$

(3)

Consider now a matrix of scores M for n tests and N individuals. Any given score can be expressed as $a_g A_i + \alpha_g Hc_i$
or as $a_g A_i + \beta_g Hc_i$, depending upon A_i . If we arrange
the scores as follows:

$$
\begin{Vmatrix}
a_1 A_a & + \alpha_1 Hc_a & a_2 A_a & + \alpha_2 Hc_a & \cdots \\
a_1 A_b & + \alpha_1 Hc_b & a_2 A_b & + \alpha_2 Hc_b & \cdots \\
\vdots & & \vdots & & \vdots \\
a_1 A_m & + \alpha_1 Hc_m & a_2 A_m & + \alpha_2 Hc_m & \cdots \\
a_1 A_{m+1} & + \beta_1 Hc_{m+1} & a_2 A_{m+1} & + \beta_2 Hc_{m+1} & \cdots \\
\vdots & & \vdots & & \vdots \\
a_1 A_N & + \beta_1 Hc_N & a_2 A_N & + \beta_2 Hc_N & \cdots
\end{Vmatrix} ,
$$

separating the A values above K from those less than or
equal to K, it becomes clear that the rank of the score
matrix M is 3, since it can be expressed as the product of
two matrices S and F where

$$
S = \begin{Vmatrix}
A_a & Hc_a & 0 \\
\vdots & \vdots & \vdots \\
A_m & Hc_m & 0 \\
A_{m+1} & 0 & Hc_{m+1} \\
\vdots & \vdots & \vdots \\
A_N & 0 & Hc_N
\end{Vmatrix}
\quad \text{and} \quad
F = \begin{Vmatrix}
a_1 & a_2 & \cdots & a_n \\
\alpha_1 & \alpha_2 & \cdots & \alpha_n \\
\beta_1 & \beta_2 & \cdots & \beta_n
\end{Vmatrix}
$$

and neither matrix reduces in rank. Thus, rather than just hostility and anxiety, we would find three factors.

Case 2. Assume now that anxiety and covert hostility are linked in such a way that

$$Ho = CHc \quad ,$$

where C takes on r values as A passes through r different ranges. Clearly, here the rank of the score matrix will be r, n, or N, whichever is smaller. That is to say we would have, generally, r factors instead of just two.

Case 3. If C is a continuous function of A, the rank will be n or N, whichever is smaller, which is to say that the factor pattern would show no simplification at all. We have here a case where a model with two underlying variables generates a complex factor structure because of what we might call a control parameter which determines the weighting of variables in an arithmetic formula.

Factor analysis fails to reveal the variables that are there because the method of analysis makes assumptions about the way the variables are expressed in behavior which are not true in this case.

It may be noted that Saunders (1956) has described an approach to handling the case where the regression coefficient of one variable on another is a simple function of the value of a third variable. Saunders calls such a third variable a moderator variable.

The Non-neutrality of Factor Analysis

The point which is brought out by the example is that factor analysis is not neutral with respect to theoretical models. It will reveal as many variables as the model claims only when the assumptions of the model about the way the variables act are congruent with those implicit in factor analysis. There is, therefore, a class of models, the Freudian among them, which, if true, would not be shown to be true in any simple way by linear factor analysis.

The Example of the Myers-Briggs Type Indicator

The point just made may be drawn out in detail by considering the case of the Myers-Briggs Type Indicator, which rests on a theory having some features in common with the ego-psychology mentioned previously.

The similarity exists because the test sets out to measure four interlocking variables which are conceived not as personality traits, but as deep-seated individual differences exercising a wide, but somewhat loose control over the domains of cognitive function, interests, values, and personality development.

Since the Myers-Briggs test represents a considerable effort to make assessments in terms largely consistent with Jung's thinking about individual differences and is of interest in its own right, it will be described in some detail. It is made up of forced-choice questions which, for the most part, call for a behavior report. In most cases the subject is offered the choice of two alternatives. Some of the questions are not behavior reports but ask the subject to indicate a preference (e.g., between pairs of words) or to make a value judgment (e.g., "Do you think it is a worse fault (A) to show too much warmth? (B) not to have warmth enough?"). While no formal study has yet been made of the social desirability of the alternatives, pains were taken to try to find alternatives that would be about equal in terms of social desirability.

For the purposes of the basic scoring, the items fall into four non-overlapping groups, each group providing the basis for one scale or index. The scales, then, are strictly independent in terms of the raw test responses from which they are computed, a point to be borne in mind in evaluating data on the correlations between the scales.

As was mentioned earlier, the four scales do not simply stand side by side, but comprise the elements of an interlocking system. Their aim, furthermore, is not so much to measure as to classify. The exposition is probably easiest if we begin with the judgment-perception or J-P scale. The idea underlying this scale is that a great part of cognitive activity can be regarded as consisting of one of two things, either coming to conclusions about something, or gathering information. We may describe people engaged in coming to conclusions as possessing a judging attitude, and people who are engaged in becoming aware of something as possessing a perceptive attitude. While individuals alternate between the two, the notion is that one attitude is more characteristic of most people than the other, so that most people may be classed in terms of the attitude which is more characteristic.

The next two scales interlock with the J-P scale. Two distinct and contrasting ways of perceiving are considered to operate--the process of sensing, which is a direct form of perception, and the process of intuition, which is indirect, wholistic, and typically enriched by information which the perceiver adds to what is given in the stimulus. We might draw the distinction in terms of more or less stimulus-bound perception. The sensing-intuition or S-N scale is designed to distinguish between those people who prefer and usually engage in sensing perception and those who engage in intuitive perception.

A most important point in understanding the test, and the theory it is built on, is that the behavioral distinction is regarded as derivative, rather than basic. The basic difference in individuals is with respect to a decision, early in the course of development, to cultivate one form of perception or the other. While all individuals engage in both forms of behavior, they are all considered to have developed greater reliance upon one process than the other, to have developed greater skill with one process than the other, and so to feel more comfortable in one mode of perception than the other.

Just as there are two methods of perceiving, there are also considered to be two bases for the activity of making judgments. One basis is thinking, which is described as "a logical process, aimed at an impersonal finding." The other is feeling, which, in contrast, is subjective and personal, rather than objective and impersonal. Once

again the normal individual is considered to exercise both
forms of judgment, but here also there is thought to be an
early bifurcation in the course of development, with some
individuals preferring and developing thinking as a basis for
judgment, others developing feeling. As with the S-N scale,
the thinking-feeling or T-F scale is not meant to determine
which form of behavior is more typical, but which of the
two courses of development an individual has taken.

It will be obvious that there is a close similarity between the variables so far described and elements of Jung's
typology. There are obvious differences, too. Jung does
not refer to the J-P distinction directly, although he does
refer to the function of feeling as "a kind of judging" (Jung,
1959). More importantly, the functions of sensation, intuition, thinking, and feeling are not so tightly organized by
Jung as in the Myers-Briggs scheme. I do not wish to examine the similarities and differences in detail, but I do want
to point out that the Myers-Briggs scheme is not to be taken
as identical to the Jungian.

We may perhaps best summarize the relationships so
far by saying that people differ with respect to the aims
(judgment and perception), with respect to preferred basis
for judgment (thinking and feeling), and with respect to preferred techniques for perception (sensation and intuition).
The last element of the system, continuing in this vein, has
to do with the objects toward which interest is directed.
The extravert's interest is in the external world of people
and objects, the introvert's in the interior world of concepts
and ideas. The extraversion-introversion or E-I scale
attempts to classify subjects with respect to the object of
their interest. Again, while recognizing that people display
both interests, it is contended that people differ fundamen-
tally in terms of which object of interest they prefer and
are, in this sense, either extraverts or introverts.

The outline given is sketchy and has deliberately blurred
over some details in order to bring out sharply the structure
of the theory. To summarize: the J-P scale deals with a
distinction of aim or attitude, the T-F with a difference in
the basis of judgment, the S-N with a difference in the tech-

nique of perception. Finally, the E-I scale deals with a difference in the direction of interest. Each scale is intended to classify people with respect to a different turn taken in the course of development.

The test as a whole, the four scales in combination, attempts to assign subjects to one of 16 type categories. The subject can be E or I, S or N, T or F, and J or P. The testing premise, as I have tried to indicate in the exposition, is that the subject's type will not absolutely determine his behavior, but will facilitate some aims, some interests, and some processes, and make others more difficult and less likely. The relationship between type and behavior is thus one in which the type structures the behavior, giving it a prevailing character without in any way binding it. The method of the test is to try to infer a subject's type from his reports of his characteristic behavior and from a record of his preferences and value judgments.

The question now is what should one expect a factor analysis to show if the model behind the test were true. One feels that the answer might be to look for coincidence between the Myers-Briggs scales and the second-order factors that emerge from large-scale explorations of trait interrelationships. Factors, after all, are supposed to be on a deeper level than traits, at least in reflecting more truly the workings of the mind. Second-order factors can be considered to reflect even more deep-seated processes, whose operations are not apparent in an immediate analysis of the data, but which emerge in the interrelationship of the variables reflecting the first level of mental operations. On closer examination, however, it is clear that one would be misled in equating the Myers-Briggs scales with factors at any level. The model on which the Myers-Briggs test is built proposes not that a set of type variables enters into the determination of a subject's standing on a behavioral variable, but that they govern what source variables enter into the determination of behavior. One has, to put it in mathematical and logical terms, a distinction between Boolean and arithmetical functions. It is not the claim that

the Myers-Briggs variables enter into the mathematical
functions by which behavior is predicted. They rather are
claimed to make a difference in specifying the equations
which are appropriate to predict behavior. Legitimate
statements in terms of the model take the form: If it is true
that the subject is E and not I, S and not N, etc., then his
competence in abstract thinking (A) will be given by the
equation

$$A = f_{ES..} (V_1, V_2, \ldots) \quad .$$

The type variables enter, not into the arithmetic, but into
the conditions determining which piece of arithmetic is appropriate.

If this analysis is correct, it follows that finding the
Myers-Briggs scales to coincide with factors would not
support its case, but would rather support some opposed
model.

The question then is how does one decide if this test is
measuring structural variables which exercise control over
the variables determining behavior. The most appropriate
method would seem to be first to classify subjects into types
on the basis of their Myers-Briggs scores, and then to
examine the structure between other variables, by factor
analysis or any other available technique, in order to see if
there is a genuine difference in the process of determining
behavior. However, there are at least three difficulties in
the way of such a program: (1) It is difficult to find large
numbers of subjects in some categories because the frequency of some types is small. (2) The analysis will be
complicated by the problem of curtailed variance on some
variables related to the Myers-Briggs scales unless pains
are taken to avoid or correct for curtailment. (3) We do not
possess well worked-out methods for comparing and assessing differences between structures. Though there are difficulties, they do not seem insoluble, and it does seem that
in this case, and in other cases where we set out to measure
structures which lie at a level below the surface of behavior,
it is necessary to devise a method for assessing our test

devices which has adequate regard for our psychological model and the major competitors to it.

Conclusions

The conclusions we draw are clearly that we should look carefully both at our personality models and at the assumptions of factor analytic methods and be sure that the two are in harmony before we use the one to test the veridicality of the other. If we do, we will find a mismatch in many cases and an indication that some other technique is called for, or, that if factor analysis may be used, it has to be used in conjunction with other techniques and interpreted in a way appropriate to the model.

John Ross

University of Western Australia
and

Samuel Messick

Educational Testing Service

5

Commentary:
Trait Inferences and
the Psychometrics
of Inventory Scales

Theories of personality and instruments to measure personality were developed as matters of practical necessity. If Freud and Woodworth had been aware of all the difficulties that we recognize today, neither psychoanalysis nor personality inventories might have been with us. Woodworth's hope that people would or could answer relevant questions truthfully now seems very naive. Just as we have begun to examine our personality theories systematically, determining what is central, what peripheral, and what nets of propositions may be formed, so we are also beginning to systematize our measurement techniques, learning how to make inferences from the responses we observe to the variables responsible for them. What we are learning with inventories is to build in appropriate controls for distracting influences and, more basically, to model relationships among items in the inventory according to the theoretical structure about which inferences are to be made (cf. Loevinger, 1957). We are learning how to do properly what has been done improperly for a long time.

Comrey's paper (Chapter 2) proposes a technique to build better inventories for people who want to make inferences about factors. His point is that item unreliability is so great that we cannot build solid factor scales by factor

83

analyzing items; more importantly, we can seldom be sure
if factors from one study are the same as those from another if both begin with item intercorrelations. Comrey
says we should prefabricate by constructing reliable item-
homogeneous building blocks. The particular standards
adopted for homogeneity are crucial, however, since a
requirement of high inter-item correlations or a Guttman-
type of reproducibility would likely lead to highly specialized and perhaps artificial dimensions (Cattell, 1957);
whereas a requirement of substantial Kuder-Richardson
reliability could be achieved through the cumulative effect
of a common factor running through items with quite modest
intercorrelations (Cronbach, 1951).

Granted that factored homogeneous item scales have
many desirable psychometric properties, Comrey's
strategy is nevertheless faced with two difficulties: (1)
We do not know how factor structure stabilizes as the reliability of the entering variables increases. The function
relating instability of the one--however defined--to unreliability of the other is probably non-linear, and may well be
fairly flat over a wide region, increasing rapidly after
that. Without knowing a little about the function, we cannot
be sure that the increase in reliability from item to scale
pays worthwhile dividends in factor stability, although such
may well be the case. (2) The second point is that no set
of items is absolutely homogeneous in terms of the stimulus variables they present or the processes they engage.
A scale may well be factorially pure in the context within
which it was established; yet in another context the items
may be pulled apart. If the items have been glued together
as a scale, an analysis which might otherwise bring out a
lack of homogeneity would not do so. Ensuring that the
scales hold together on "logical" grounds helps to some extent, but care should be exercised that some presumably
"content" homogeneity is not due to response sets or stylistic consistencies. This joint statistical and logical criterion should also be applied gingerly, however, since the
logical requirements rarely reflect an explicit psycholog-

ical theory and may unwittingly rule out important areas of
personality functioning not presently permitted by our
"logical" constraints. It is less likely, of course, that a
scale which is factorially pure in a broad context and looks
homogeneous on other grounds would fall apart, but both
criteria together by no means guarantee homogeneity in
any fundamental sense.

Specifying the guarantees that would be sufficient is by
no means easy. The question brings us to some deep concerns about factor analysis and, indeed, face to face with
the whole question of developing normative statements
about personality from the study of individual differences.
Factor analysts usually rely on two assumptions: (1) that
any task (answering a question, solving a problem, making
a decision) calls upon the same processes in all individuals;
and (2) that the processes (abilities, personality traits)
correspond to task demands or behavioral characteristics
(cf. number ability, rhathymia-restraint). Given the first
assumption, the factor equation gains empirical force and
implies a strategy for analyzing out factors; given the
second, factor interpretation becomes the straightforward
business it is usually considered to be. But what if it were
otherwise? Suppose we were all born with neuronal black-
boxes that could be hooked together in idiosyncratic ways,
and each had a wide choice in how we coupled them to behavior. The rank of the hypothetical matrix of scores on
all personality variables would not tend to some finite k,
the number of black boxes, or k', the number of fundamental personality factors. And, worse still, our factor
interpretations would become as erroneous as the hypos-
tatization of faculties.

If a program like Comrey's is to be followed, at least
three things seem to be necessary: (1) to learn more about
the relationship between the stability of factor structures
and the reliability of the variables; (2) to keep checking
that the scale packages are really pure; and (3) to test
the packages with the most diverse samples that can be
found. If individuals really do differ in the calamitous way

we have suggested, factor studies in groups of different
cultures should give grossly different structures, and, to
the extent they do not, we may be more confident that the
study of individual differences will lead to normative statements and that pure factor packages are genuinely pure.

Stern's approach (Chapter 3) is also partly factor
analytic, but his major concern is with interaction. Since
his model is explicitly interactional, his measures must
be tailored to fit; so he uses two inventories, one to get at
the needs of the individual and the other to get at the
press of the situation. The idea that the value of a personality trait depends on the situation has been slow in re-
gaining explicit recognition in psychology and particularly
in measurement. Both personality and ability theorists
have tended to be absolutists. Worse still, they have frequently combined utilitarian standards with their absolut-
ism, basing their approach on the belief that to be "high"
on an ability (and even on many traits) always pays off.
The fog is clearing. Research in cognitive styles recog-
nizes the relativity of their value (cf. Klein, 1958; Witkin,
1959), and Stern's work very clearly bases its approach on
the idea that what pays off is need-press match.

Whether the area of interaction between individual and
situation is the appropriate place to look for variables is
another matter. Stern certainly thinks so, and he happily
uses the same names for needs and press. The individual,
for example, needs achievement and the situation demands
it. Quite possibly, however, we need one language to talk
about individuals--their needs, motives, skills and the
like--another to talk about situations, and still a third
to talk about the interaction of the two. But, given the
Murray (1938) approach and vocabulary, Stern's work is
an illustration of how two or more inventories may be constructed and employed to evaluate interactions and functional relations between variables operating in different
domains. Appropriate measurement of variables within
each domain must first be demonstrated, however, before
their interactions can be properly appraised.

Stern has attempted to evaluate relations between his need measures by factoring scores on the Activities Index. Similar analyses will presumably be undertaken for the measures of environmental press from the College Charac- teristics Index, followed by a comparison of the obtained structures. His finding of three basic dimensions under- lying the various need scales and of the compelling circular array of scale vectors in the plane of the first two factors is particularly interesting in that it would seem to require somewhat more than the usual type of factor interpretation. Not only should the basic dimensions be characterized, but the fairly restrictive structural relations successively occurring between scales in the obtained circular pattern should also be validated to appraise the extent to which the structural relations between the scales parallel structural relations between other non-test manifestations of the needs being measured (Loevinger, 1957). To the extent that such structural validity is obtained and the reported rela- tionships are not due to restrictions of the test format or the measurement model, then a psychological theory which encompasses the results would deal not only with the number and nature of basic need variables but also with the struc- ture of need systems.

Ross (Chapter 4) also favors a factor analytic approach but for a very different purpose. He suggests its use not to develop item homogeneous dimensions or to appraise relations between scales, but to provide a basis for infer- ence about the nature of certain variables--as a way of deciding whether particular scales (in his case the Myers- Briggs Type Indicator) reflect correlated traits or type clusters. He argues that the factor model assumes that scores on a measure are a linear function of scores on a set of relevant factors or source variables; whereas the type conception underlying the Myers-Briggs inventory implies that the type variables do not determine standing on behavioral variables but instead govern the selection of which particular source variables determine behavior. If it is found by factor analysis that the type scales correspond to factors, then this particular type conception is not supported. The inference seems to follow in only one direction, however, since a failure to find a factorial basis for the type scales does not necessarily support the type model--some other violation of the factor model might lead to similar negative results.

Although all three of the papers discussed utilize factor analysis to some extent, the respective purposes of its application are somewhat different. Comrey sought a factorial basis for personality scales to support inferences from scale scores to underlying trait dimensions; Stern attempted to explicate relations between scales and to identify basic dimensions of need structure; and Ross used factor analysis as a basis for inferring the nature of the underlying variables, arguing that if the factor model adequately describes obtained relationships in terms of correlated traits, then some other incompatible model does not apply. The present discussion has attempted to emphasize that such inferences about the nature of underlying variables and about the structure of the domain depend partly upon the measurement model employed, and to show the necessity for validating at some point the structural relationships between items or scales permitted or imposed by the model against structural relations observed between other manifestations of the traits (Loevinger, 1957).

PART II

Response Styles in

Personality Measurement

6 | Allen L. Edwards
University of Washington

The Social Desirability Hypothesis: Theoretical Implications for Personality Measurement

Several years ago I reported in a monograph (Edwards, 1957a) the results of research bearing on the social desirability variable in personality assessment. I interpreted the results as supporting the hypothesis that scores on many personality scales of the true-false type could be largely accounted for by individual differences in the tendency to give socially desirable responses to items in the scales. Part of the evidence bearing upon this hypothesis consisted of the correlations obtained between Minnesota Multiphasic Personality Inventory (MMPI) scales and scores on another scale which I called the Social Desirability (SD) scale.

It will be clear to anyone who reads the monograph that I in no way restricted the social desirability hypothesis to the MMPI scales, nor was the evidence confined only to the correlations between the MMPI scales and the SD scale. It is my interpretation--that scores on the SD scale measure the tendency to give socially desirable responses and that

Presidential address delivered to the Division of Evaluation and Measurement, American Psychological Association, September 1960, under the title "Social Desirability or Acquiescence in the MMPI? A Case Study with the SD Scale." Permission to reproduce this text, which will appear in the Journal of Abnormal and Social Psychology in a somewhat different form, has been granted through the courtesy of Daniel Katz, Editor, and the American Psychological Association.

91

the correlations of the SD scale with the MMPI scales support the social desirability hypothesis--which has been
questioned; therefore this paper is primarily concerned with
the MMPI and SD scales.

Some critics have suggested that the SD scale is a measure not of the tendency to give socially desirable responses
but of the tendency to acquiesce, to give True responses to
the items in the scale. It has also been suggested that many
of the MMPI scales reflect the tendency to acquiesce and that
the correlations between the SD scale and the MMPI scales
reflect individual differences in the tendency of subjects to
give acquiescent responses to scale items.

The question before us, then, is a controversial one.
I propose to review briefly the history of the controversy by
stating first the argument for the social desirability hypothesis and then the argument for the acquiescence hypothesis.
I shall then present some new evidence which bears upon
these alternative hypotheses.

The Social Desirability Hypothesis

Relationship Between Probability of Item Endorsement and Social Desirability Scale Value

My first research (Edwards, 1953a) on social desirability dealt with the relationship between the social desirability scale value of a personality statement and the probability of its endorsement. This study is particularly relevant to the points I shall develop later about the acquiescence
and social desirability hypotheses, and I shall therefore
describe both its procedures and its results.

Psychological scaling methods have long been used to obtain scale values for statements of opinion. For example,
if we have a set of statements of opinion relating to capital
punishment, we can have judges rate how favorable or unfavorable to capital punishment they believe each statement
to be. Psychological scaling methods can then be applied to
the distributions of ratings to obtain a scale value for each
statement. The statements can then be ordered on a con-

tinuum ranging from highly unfavorable to highly favorable opinions.

The same methods, I believed, could be applied to obtain social desirability scale values for personality statements. I therefore asked judges to rate the degree of social undesirability or social desirability of the behavior, trait, or characteristic represented by each personality statement in a set of 140. I then used the method of successive intervals to obtain for each statement a social desirability scale value which orders it on a continuum ranging from highly undesirable, through neutral, to highly desirable. I call this the social desirability continuum.

The statements were then printed in the form of a personality inventory and administered to a new group of subjects under standard instructions to describe themselves. For this group the proportion endorsing or answering True to each statement was found. This proportion I refer to as the probability of item endorsement. If we now plot the probability of item endorsement against the social desirability scale value, we can see whether there is any relationship between the two variables.

The relationship that I found is shown in Figure 6-1. The X or horizontal axis is the social desirability continuum, with the left end representing statements with socially undesirable scale values and the right end statements with socially desirable scale values. The Y or vertical axis is the probability of item endorsement. It is evident that the probability of item endorsement, or of a True response, is a linear increasing function of the social desirability scale value. The more socially desirable a statement is, the greater is the probability of item endorsement. The product-moment correlation between the two variables is .87.

I first presented the results shown in Figure 6-1 at a meeting of the Western Psychological Association in 1952. The research has since been replicated many times (Edwards, 1955, 1957b, 1959; Hanley, 1956; Kenny, 1956; J. B. Taylor, 1959; Wiggins and Rumrill, 1959; Cowen and Tongas, 1959; Hillmer, 1958; Wright, 1957). These replications have involved variations in the scaling method used

to obtain the social desirability scale values, variations in
the technique used to obtain the descriptions of subjects,
variations in the set of personality items, and a range of
different groups of subjects. In each instance the results

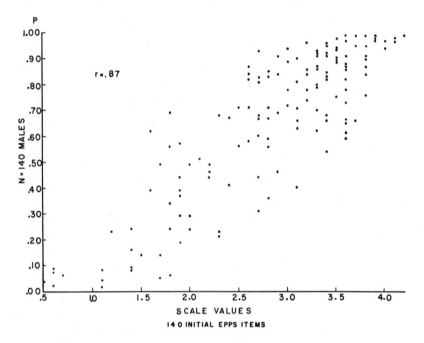

FIGURE 6-1. The Relationship Between Probability of Item Endorsement and Social Desirability Scale Value. (Reproduced from Edwards, 1953a.)

have been consistent with those I originally reported. Therefore I believe that the relationship between probability of
item endorsement and social desirability scale value is a
general phenomenon rather than an isolated result obtained
under rather restricted conditions.

The SD Scale

    Consider now one way in which we might key a given
set of personality statements. Suppose, for example, that

if a statement has a socially desirable scale value we key
the True response, whereas if the statement has a socially
undesirable scale value we key the False response. The
resulting scale would be of a kind that I have called a social
desirability or SD scale, one in which all of the items are
keyed for socially desirable responses. A socially desirable response is defined as a True response to an item with
a socially desirable scale value or a False response to an
item with a socially undesirable scale value. The score on
an SD scale is the number of socially desirable responses.

The first SD scale I constructed (Edwards, 1953b) consisted of 79 items from the MMPI. These 79 items were
subsequently analyzed and reduced to the 39 which best differentiated between a high and a low scoring group (Edwards,
1957a). There is evidence (Edwards, 1957a) to show that
the results obtained with the 79-item and the 39-item SD
scale are comparable, and the distinction between these
two SD scales need not concern us. However, with but few
exceptions, the research I shall be reporting upon was done
with the 39-item SD scale.

I have pointed out that all of the items in the SD scale
are keyed for socially desirable responses. The simplest
statement of what the SD scale is measuring is that it measures the tendency of subjects to give socially desirable responses in self-description under the standard instructions
ordinarily used with personality inventories. To determine
the degree to which other personality scales might also be
measuring this same tendency, I correlated scores on the
79-item SD scale with a number of other personality scales
(Edwards, 1953b). In general, the correlations I obtained
with other personality scales of the true-false type were
of substantial magnitude. Furthermore, the signs of the
correlations were in the direction predicted by the social
desirability hypothesis. For example, if a high score on a
given scale indicated a socially undesirable trait, that is,
if it was necessary to make a large number of socially undesirable responses to obtain a high score, then the correlation of this scale with the SD scale was negative. On the

other hand, if it was necessary to make a large number of socially desirable responses to obtain a high score on a given scale, then the correlation of this scale with the SD scale was positive. These results indicated to me that if the SD scale was measuring the tendency to give socially desirable responses, as I believed it was, then the scores on the other scales I had investigated were, to a remarkable degree, reflecting the same tendency.

Correlations subsequently obtained by Fordyce (1956) between the 79-item SD scale and the clinical and validity scales of the MMPI and by Edwards, Heathers, and Fordyce (1960) between the 39-item SD scale and 11 "new" MMPI scales, described by Hathaway and Briggs (1957), are also consistent with the social desirability hypothesis.

The Acquiescence Hypothesis

Two articles by Cronbach (1946, 1950) on response sets have aroused much interest in the particular response set which Cronbach called, as had Lentz (1938) before him, acquiescence. Acquiescence, according to Cronbach, refers to the tendency of a subject to agree with or respond True to a test item when he is in doubt about the appropriate or correct response. Items in personality inventories are likely to produce such doubt, since subjects must interpret the content of the item along with the meaning of such terms as few, seldom, frequently, occasionally, sometimes, and often (Allport, 1937; Benton, 1935; Watson, 1959). If a personality item does evoke doubt, about the appropriate response, it is also likely to evoke acquiescent tendencies. If a personality scale has a majority of items which are keyed False, and if these items arouse doubt about the appropriate response, then a highly acquiescent subject is apt to respond True to these keyed False items, thus obtaining a lower score than he would if acquiescence were not involved. Thus, instead of measuring the trait we think the scale is measuring, the scores may be reflecting the acquiescent tendencies of the subjects.

Acquiescence and the SD Scale

The argument for the acquiescence hypothesis, as I have presented it, can be applied to the 39-item SD scale in which 30 of the 39 keyed socially desirable responses are False. If the argument is valid, the more acquiescent subjects should obtain low scores, the less acquiescent, high scores. Therefore we must ask whether a high score on the SD scale measures the tendency to give socially desirable responses or the tendency to be nonacquiescent. I was quite aware of this possible double interpretation of scores on the SD scale, and my reasons for rejecting the acquiescence interpretation in favor of the social desirability interpretation are, I believe, clearly stated in my monograph.

Let us look once again at Figure 6-1. Suppose we take only items from the socially desirable end of the continuum and key all of these items for the True response. Then a high score on this SD scale may be a measure either of a strong tendency to give socially desirable responses or of a strong tendency to be acquiescent--or it may, of course, reflect both tendencies. If the original 39-item SD scale is primarily a measure of acquiescence and if this is also the case with the all-True SD scale, then scores on the two scales should correlate negatively, since the acquiescent subject will obtain a high score on the all-True SD scale and a low score on the 39-item SD scale, in which 30 of the 39 items are keyed False. But the correlation should be positive if both the original 39-item SD scale and the all-True SD scale are primarily measures of the tendency to give socially desirable responses. The correlation proved to be positive (.70) and therefore consistent with the social desirability hypothesis. The all-True SD scale and another SD scale in which the True-False keying was balanced were also correlated with two MMPi scales, the D or Depression scale in which a majority (67 percent) of the items are keyed False and the Sc or Schizophrenia scale in which a majority (78 percent) of the items are keyed True. These correlations were consistent with the social desirability hypothesis but not with the acquiescence hypothesis. On the basis of these and other findings I rejected the acquiescence interpretation of the SD scale in favor of the social desirability interpretation.

At the time my monograph was in press, Fricke (1956) published an article presenting results which he interpreted as supporting the idea that the imbalance in the True-False keying of the various clinical and validity scales of the MMPI made them most susceptible to the acquiescence response set. Fricke has since indicated in correspondence that he believes this is also the case with the SD scale. Wiggins (1959) has also taken the position that the imbalance in the keying of the 39-item SD scale results in its being a measure of acquiescence. Thus Wiggins believes the various reported correlations between the SD scale and the MMPI scales to be evidence of the influence of acquiescence rather than of social desirability in the MMPI. In support of this belief he cites a negative correlation he obtained between a "response bias" scale developed by Fricke (1957) and the SD scale. Jackson and Messick (1958), in their review of response sets, also state that the correlations between the SD scale and the MMPI scales may reflect acquiescence, since the SD scale contains a disproportionate number of items keyed False.

I have already cited certain evidence to indicate why I do not agree with the acquiescence interpretation given the SD scale by Fricke, Wiggins, and Jackson and Messick. Nor do I share their apparent conviction that the imbalance in the True-False keying of the MMPI scales makes these scales susceptible to acquiescent tendencies. And, as I shall show later, the correlation between the SD scale and Fricke's response bias scale is of the same sign and of just about the same magnitude as would be predicted by the social desirability hypothesis. What is at issue, then, is quite clear. It is this: Can the correlations between the SD scale and the MMPI scales be more adequately accounted for by the acquiescence hypothesis or by the social desirability hypothesis?

New Evidence Bearing upon the Two Hypotheses

The Acquiescence Hypothesis

Before presenting some new evidence bearing upon
these two hypotheses, and so that there may be no misunder-
standing, let me summarize the argument for the acquiescence hypothesis as it has been stated by Fricke, Wiggins,
and Jackson and Messick. If a majority of the items in both
an MMPI scale and the SD scale are keyed False, then on
both scales the more acquiescent subjects should obtain low
scores, the less acquiescent, high scores. If both scales
are measuring acquiescence, the correlation between the
SD scale and this MMPI scale should be positive. On the
other hand, if a majority of the items in an MMPI scale are
keyed True, and if the acquiescence hypothesis is correct,
then this scale and the SD scale should correlate negatively.

Let us accept, for the moment, the statement of Fricke,
Wiggins, and Jackson and Messick that it is possible to
evaluate the role of acquiescence in a scale by considering
the percentage of items keyed True (or False) and using
this percentage as an index of the acquiescence set. I have
obtained this index--the percentage of items keyed False--
for each of 43 MMPI scales.[1] Figure 6-2 shows the SD
correlations[2] plotted against the proportion of keyed False
items in each of the 43 MMPI scales.

---

[1] The abbreviated code names for the 43 MMPI scales, as given by
Dahlstrom and Welsh (1960), are as follows: L, F, K, Hs, D,
D-S, D-O, Hy, Hy-S, Hy-O, Pd, Pd-S, Pd-O, Mf-m, Pa, Pa-S,
Pa-O, Pt, Sc, Ma, Ma-S, Ma-O, Si, Dy, St, At, Ho, Pv, Do, Re,
A, R, Ad, Dn, Es, Eo, No, Nu, Pn, Cn, Ca, Ne, and B.

[2] All of the correlations are with the 39-item SD scale. The correlations between the SD scale and the total, subtle, and obvious scales
of the MMPI are from an unpublished study by Fordyce and Rozynko
reported by Edwards (1957a). The SD correlation with the B scale
is reported by Wiggins (1959). The remaining correlations are
based upon a sample originally tested by Merrill and Heathers
(1956).

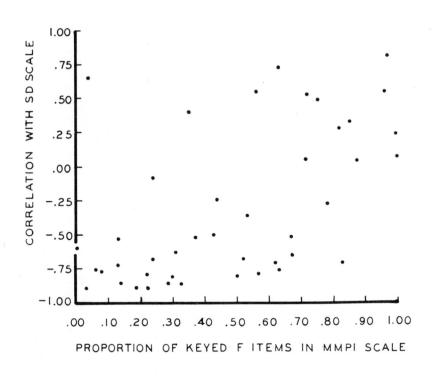

FIGURE 6-2. Correlations of 43 MMPI Scales with the SD Scale as a Function of the Proportion of Keyed False Items in the MMPI Scales.

There is clearly some tendency for the SD correlations with the 43 MMPI scales to be related to the imbalance in the True-False keying of the scales. The product-moment correlation between the two variables is .55. Thus, approximately 30 percent of the variation in the SD correlations can be accounted for by the imbalance in the True-False keying.

The Social Desirability Hypothesis

Let us now see how well the social desirability hypothesis accounts for the same SD correlations. If the distribution of social desirability scale values of the items in a personality test is known, each item in the scale may be classified by the social desirability or undesirability of the keyed response. If the scale contains a large proportion of keyed socially desirable responses, the correlation between this scale and the SD scale should be positive, according to the social desirability hypothesis. On the other hand, if it contains a large proportion of keyed socially undesirable responses, then the correlation with the SD scale should be negative. If the keying of the items is relatively balanced for socially desirable and socially undesirable responses, then the correlation with the SD scale should be low. Social desirability scale values for the MMPI items have been obtained by Heineman (1953); using these values, I have classified the items in each of the 43 MMPI scales in terms of whether the keyed response is socially desirable or undesirable.

I should point out that the social desirability of a keyed response is not necessarily a fixed characteristic of an MMPI item for all scales. For example, a given item may appear in more than one MMPI scale with the True response keyed in some scales and the False response in others. Thus, in some scales a given item may be keyed for a socially desirable response and in others for a socially undesirable response. This of course was also the case when we considered the imbalance in the True-False keying of the MMPI items.

Figure 6-3 shows the SD correlations plotted against the proportion of keyed socially desirable responses in the 43 MMPI scales.[3] We have a much closer relationship here than we had when these correlations were plotted against the proportion of keyed False items in the scales. The product-moment correlation between the two variables in Figure 6-3 is .92, and we can account for approximately 85 percent of the variance in the SD correlations with the

---

[3] Fricke's response bias scale is located in Figure 6-3 by the point with coordinates .40 and -.59 and is in accord with the trend for the other points shown in the figure.

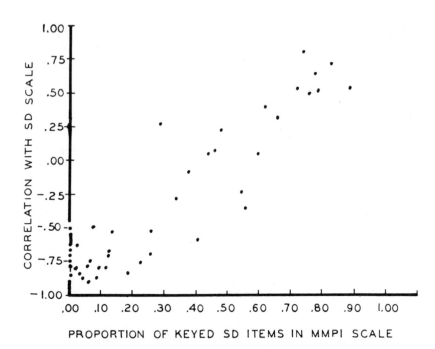

FIGURE 6-3. Correlations of 43 MMPI Scales with the SD Scale as a Function of the Proportion of Keyed Socially Desirable Responses in the MMPI Scales.

43 MMPI scales in terms of the proportion of keyed socially desirable responses in the scales.

Partial and Multiple Correlations

The proportion of keyed False items could account for only 30 percent of the variance in the SD correlations, and even this figure is spuriously high, as we shall now see. Consider the relationship shown in Figure 6-4. The X or horizontal axis gives the proportion of keyed False items in each MMPI scale and the Y or vertical axis gives the proportion of keyed socially desirable responses for the scales. Evidently there is some relationship between the imbalance in the True-False keying for a scale and the imbalance in the social desirability keying for the same scale.

In other words, those scales which tend to have a large proportion of keyed False items also tend to have a large proportion of keyed socially desirable responses. The product-moment correlation between the two sets of proportions shown in Figure 6-4 is .42.

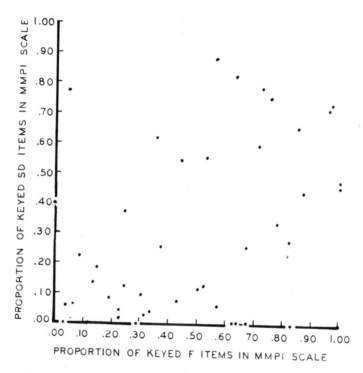

FIGURE 6-4. Relationship Between the Proportion of Items Keyed for Socially Desirable Responses in 43 MMPI Scales and the Proportion of Items Keyed for False Responses in the Scales.

What happens to the correlation of .55 between the proportion of keyed False responses in a scale and the correlations with the SD scale when we partial out the proportion of keyed socially desirable responses? As shown in Table 6-1, the partial correlation is .46. So, you see, if we hold constant or partial out the proportion of keyed

socially desirable responses, the correlation between the
proportion of keyed False responses and the SD correlations drops from .55 to .46. On the other hand, there is a
partial correlation of .91 between the proportion of keyed
socially desirable responses and the SD correlations, holding the proportion of keyed False responses constant; this
value does not differ greatly from the original zero-order
correlation of .92. It thus appears that the variation in the
correlations of the MMPI scales with the SD scale can be
more adequately accounted for by the fact that the MMPI
scales vary in the degree to which they are keyed for socially desirable responses than by the fact that these same
scales also vary in the degree to which they are keyed for
False responses.

TABLE 6-1. CORRELATION BETWEEN
SD SCALE CORRELATIONS OF MMPI SCALES
AND ITEM PROPERTIES OF THE MMPI SCALES

Correlation	Proportion Keyed F	Proportion Keyed SD
Zero-order	.55	.92
Partial	.46	.91
Multiple	.94	

We can examine the same point in a slightly different
way by looking at the multiple correlation between the SD
correlations and the proportion of keyed socially desirable
responses and the proportion of keyed False responses.
The zero-order correlation between the SD correlations and
the proportion of keyed socially desirable responses in the
MMPI scales is .92. The gain in efficiency by taking into
account also the proportion of keyed False responses in the
MMPI scales is very slight. The multiple correlation, for
example, is only .94. Thus the proportion of keyed False

responses accounts for very little of the remaining variation in the SD correlations after we have considered the
proportion of keyed socially desirable responses in the
scales.

On the basis of this evidence, I think we can conclude
that the imbalance in the True-False keying of the items in
the MMPI scales is of relatively little importance compared
with the imbalance in the social desirability keying in accounting for the correlations of the MMPI scales with the SD
scale.

Concluding Remarks

In applying the acquiescence hypothesis to personality
scales, little attention has been given to the problem of
what kinds of items are likely to evoke acquiescent tendencies. For example, in a recent paper Couch and Keniston
(1960) define acquiescence as the tendency to give Agree
(or True) responses to items regardless of the item content. We have seen, however, that the probability of a
True response to a personality item is an increasing linear
function of the social desirability scale value of the item.
If acquiescence exists as a personality trait in the sense
defined by Couch and Keniston, then the probability of a
True response for an acquiescent subject must be greater
than for a nonacquiescent subject for all items, regardless
of the social desirability scale values of the items. In other
words, we would have two regression lines for probability
of item endorsement, one for acquiescent and one for nonacquiescent subjects, with that for acquiescent subjects
having the greater Y-intercept. This is an interesting possibility but one for which as yet there is no supporting evidence.

Rather than regarding acquiescence as independent of
item content, I would agree with Cronbach that response
sets operate only when items are difficult or ambiguous.
Response sets, as he points out, do not operate apart from
the items which evoke them. It is only when an item is in

some way unclear, so that the subject is in doubt about the appropriate or correct response, that response sets become important.

In an achievement test, for example, a difficult item is by definition one to which only a few subjects know the correct response. Thus a difficult item can be said to evoke doubt about the response among more subjects than will an easy item. Difficult items, in other words, provide greater opportunities for acquiescent responses to occur than do easy items. If a test consists of a series of very easy items, we may expect few of the total responses to reflect acquiescent tendencies. As the difficulty level of the items increases, we may expect an increasing number of responses to reflect acquiescent tendencies.

Suppose, for example, we divide the items in an achievement test into those that are difficult and those that are easy. Then scores based only upon the easy items are apt to be relatively free from acquiescent tendencies, and scores based only upon the difficult items may be very much influenced by acquiescent tendencies, because only difficult items provide many opportunities for acquiescent responses to occur.

I believe the situation with respect to personality tests is somewhat similar. Scores on personality tests will be influenced by acquiescent tendencies only to the degree to which the test contains items which are difficult or ambiguous and thus provide opportunities for acquiescent responses to occur. But we must consider not only the interaction between the items and acquiescent tendencies but also the interaction between the items and social desirability tendencies. There is evidence to indicate that the tendency to give socially desirable responses is so powerful, so dominant, that if it is evoked by an item, acquiescent tendencies are of little importance. Items which evoke the social desirability set are those with socially desirable or socially undesirable scale values. I would assume, therefore, that if a personality test contains mainly items with socially desirable or socially undesirable scale values, scores on the test will be little influenced by acquiescent tendencies.

With neutral items the socially desirable response is not obvious and the social desirability set cannot operate in the same way as with nonneutral items. I would assume, therefore, that responses to neutral items may be much more influenced by acquiescent tendencies than responses to nonneutral items.

If I am correct in this analysis, then it is the neutral items in a personality test which will provide opportunities for acquiescent tendencies to influence scores on the test. If the neutral items are consistently keyed for True responses, then we may expect the more acquiescent subjects to obtain higher scores on the test than nonacquiescent subjects. If the neutral items are balanced in their True-False keying, then we may expect acquiescent tendencies to have little influence on the total test scores.

If most of the items in a test have nonneutral social desirability scale values and only a few items have neutral social desirability scale values, then acquiescent tendencies should have relatively little influence upon the total test scores. An examination of many personality scales leads me to suggest that this is most often the case. Very few of these scales contain many neutral items in relation to the total number of items in the scale. Under this condition, we may expect scores on a scale to be relatively little influenced by acquiescent tendencies, regardless of whether or not there is an imbalance in the True-False keying of the items. The SD scale, in which all of the items have socially desirable or socially undesirable scale values, is, I believe, a case in point.

If most of the items in a personality scale have nonneutral social desirability scale values, then the nature of the social desirability keying of the items is important for evaluation not only of the social desirability set but also of the acquiescence set. Acquiescence, for example, has sometimes been investigated by obtaining the correlation between the separate scores on the keyed True and the keyed False items in a scale. A negative or low correlation between the scores based upon the keyed True items and the keyed False items has been interpreted as evidence of the influence of acquiescence. I wish to emphasize, however, that this is not necessarily the case. For example, the social desirability hypothesis would predict a negative correlation between the part scores if the True items are consistently keyed for socially desirable responses and the False items for socially undesirable responses, or vice versa; a low correlation if the True items are consistently keyed for socially desirable or socially undesirable responses and if there is a balance in the social desirability keying of the False items, or vice versa; and a positive correlation between the part scores if the items in both sets are consistently keyed for either socially desirable or socially undesirable responses. Thus, what may on the surface appear to be the influence of acquiescence may, upon closer examination, be the result of social desirability.

Finally, I should like to say that for the reasons given I regard the attempt to evaluate acquiescent tendencies in terms of an imbalance in the True-False keying of all of the items in a test as completely inadequate. To determine the imbalance in the True-False keying is a very easy approach, but one which overlooks the complexity of the problem.

7 | Jerry S. Wiggins
Stanford University

Definitions of Social Desirability
and Acquiescence in
Personality Inventories

Stylistic consistencies in subjects' responses to person-ality tests are mediated by the form in which the stimulus materials, or items, are presented to the subject. The test format does not <u>create</u> stylistic consistencies in sub-jects; it defines the sample of stylistic responses to be measured on any occasion. Nevertheless, there are some response measures that are so closely related to the struc-ture of a test that they appear to tell us more about the measurement method than they do about the subjects. Con-sequently, investigations of response styles may lead to the detection of stylistic consistencies which are personality traits in their own right or they may uncover sources of method variance that increase our understanding of the instruments themselves.

This paper is concerned with two stylistic measures that may have implications for both personality assessment and inventory measurement. For reasons that I hope will become clear later, these styles have been termed "hyper-communality" and "acquiescence." Psychiatric inventories, such as the MMPI, provide some occasion for the emergence

This paper will be published in revised form in the <u>Psycholog-ical Bulletin</u>. Permission to reproduce it here has been granted by Harry Helson, Editor.

109

of these styles, but their detection has generally been complicated by the prevalence of two other response measures.
These two measures have been formulated by Berg (1955)
and studied by Barnes (1956a) within the framework of the
Deviation Hypothesis. To preserve the penetrating simplic-
ity of Berg's theorizing, these tendencies will be referred
to as simply "Deviant True" and "Deviant False." Before
considering these latter tendencies, I would like to discuss
some item characteristics that have special bearing on
stylistic response scales. I shall then briefly consider a
number of special scales that have been proposed as individual difference measures of response styles. Finally, I
will attempt to relate these scales to the Deviation Hypothesis within the context of the MMPI.

Controversiality, Communality, and Social Desirability

There are three closely related but conceptually distinct aspects of personality inventory items that have relevance for the measurement of stylistic tendencies. These
are the measures of controversiality, communality, and
rated social desirability. We speak of high item controversiality when an item is endorsed by about half of a normative group and answered "false" by the other half. The
limits of this range have been generally set at between 40
and 60 percent endorsement. In one sense, item communality is the opposite of controversiality. Items that display
strong modal tendencies for one of the response options have
a high degree of communality. The normative group is
relatively uniform in its endorsement or rejection of the
item. Although the term social desirability has been applied
to several concepts, it may be most unambiguously defined
in terms of the set of operations, first described by Edwards
(1957a), whereby items are scaled by judges' ratings along
a continuum of favorability or acceptability. Judges are
given a pool of items and a set of instructions that requires
them to estimate the degree of desirability of the trait implied by the item.

In the literature of the past few years a number of individual difference measures of the response styles of social
desirability and acquiescence have appeared, employing,
explicitly or implicitly, the concepts of controversiality,
communality, and rated social desirability. Hanley (1961)
has recently suggested a classification scheme for social
desirability scales based on whether response frequencies
played a role in item selection and whether the social
desirability of the items was determined explicitly or implicitly. Another basis for classifying social desirability
scales, which has been stressed by the present writer
(Wiggins, 1959), is the method of contrasted groups in which
the responses of a group of subjects who, because of special
instructions or special circumstances are considered to be
a group of high social desirability respondents, are compared
with the responses of a control group.

The method of contrasted groups was employed by both
Cofer, Chance, and Judson (1949) and the present writer
(Wiggins, 1959) in the development of two role-playing
scales of social desirability. The responses of a control
group were contrasted with those of subjects instructed to
answer the MMPI in terms of social desirability. In the
construction of the L scale of the MMPI (Meehl and Hathaway, 1946), a group of two clinicians constructed items in
terms of social desirability and guessed at the frequencies
that would occur in a control group. Two groups were contrasted in effect, if not in fact. The K scale of the MMPI
(Meehl and Hathaway, 1946) was constructed by comparing
the responses of one group of presumably non-faking patients with those of another group thought to include a large
number of social desirability respondents. Unfortunately,
the interpretation of the K scale is further complicated by
the fact that an additional set of items was added to the
scale that had been shown not to discriminate between role-
playing and control college groups.

Hanley (1957) has developed a scale with reference to
two groups that were not directly contrasted with one another.
Item controversiality was determined from the Minnesota

college norms (Dahlstrom and Welsh, 1960) and controversial items were given to another group to determine
their rated social desirability values. Items of high and
low rated value were retained and, on rational grounds, it
might be predicted that such items would be answered in
the keyed direction more frequently by social desirability
respondents than by an honest group. In the social desirability scale developed by Edwards (1957a), the response
frequencies of a single group were sufficient to determine
item inclusion. The unanimous agreement of 10 role-playing
judges determined the direction of item keying without reference to a control group. Similarly, the social desirability scales constructed from judges' ratings of the desirability of items from Welsh's A and R scales (Wiggins and
Rumrill, 1959) were based on a single group of judges.

Proposed individual difference measures of acquiescent
response styles have not made direct use of the method of
contrasted groups. Since it is difficult to define acquiescence on other than statistical grounds, appropriate criterion groups do not readily suggest themselves. Scales
measuring acquiescence, in Cronbach's (1946) usage of
the term, should employ items of high controversiality
determined from some normative group. Fricke (1957)
selected items of high controversiality from Hathaway's
normative data (Dahlstrom and Welsh, 1960) and keyed
them all "true" as a measure of acquiescence--the B scale.
This procedure has been recently criticized by Hanley
(1961), who argues that if acquiescence scales are to be
considered as different from social desirability scales, they
should contain items of neutral social desirability values as
well as high controversiality. Hanley (1961) has, in fact,
obtained social desirability ratings on Fricke's B scale
items and found an imbalance of socially undesirable items.
Fortunately, there were 32 items judged to be of neutral
social desirability by Hanley's raters, and these items are
employed later in the present study as a revised B scale
(Bn) of neutral social desirability value. In a similar vein,
Fulkerson (1958) has developed an acquiescence scale with

items of high controversiality that do not discriminate between high and low adjustment groups.

Table 7-1 presents data on four characteristics of
social desirability scales that are relevant to our discussion
of communality and rated social desirability. These characteristics are (a) communality of items in the scale; (b)
rated social desirability of items in the scale; (c) endorsement vs. rated social desirability of items in the scale; and
(d) the success achieved by the scale in identifying subjects
instructed to answer the MMPI in terms of social desirability. A brief description of these social desirability
scales is given in Table 7-2.

Scale communality is defined as the average proportion
of subjects in a normative group who answered the items in
the direction in which the scale is keyed (in this case social
desirability). The communality values in row one of Table
7-1 were computed from item frequency counts of the
records of 140 Stanford students (55 men, 85 women). The
social desirability scales have been ordered, in terms of
their average communality values, from high (on the left)
to low (on the right). In the bottom row of the same table
are the phi-coefficients reported in an earlier study of the
predictive efficiency of social desirability scales in separating a group of 250 social desirability role-players from a
group of 190 controls (Wiggins, 1959). It can be seen that
the average communality value of a scale places a definite
limitation on the extent to which it is sensitive to the communality shifts produced by role-playing instructions.
Thus, with a scale such as Edwards' SD, in which the average scale communality is close to 80 percent, even slight
shifts in the direction of social desirability would approach
the limit of maximum communality. The social desirability
scales with lower average communality values, on the other
hand, are potentially sensitive to a much wider range of
communality increases, and this, among other things, is
reflected in the relative success of these scales in identifying social desirability role-players.

The average social desirability scale values given in
the second row represent the averaged median ratings for

TABLE 7-1. CHARACTERISTICS OF SOCIAL DESIRABILITY SCALES

	SD	Sd-A	Sd-R	K	Ex	Cof	Sd	L
Communality[a]								
Mean	.79	.66	.55	.53	.50	.35	.30	.20
S.D.	(.13)	(.18)	(.24)	(.22)	(.19)	(.17)	(.16)	(.16)
Social Desirability[b]								
Mean	5.70	5.47	5.20	4.65	5.23	4.69	4.72	4.39
S.D.	(.50)	(.65)	(.24)	(1.20)	(.62)	(.66)	(.74)	(.84)
Endorsement vs. Social Desirability[c]								
r	.91	.55	.56	.46	.05	-.33	-.17	.58
Screening Efficiency[d]								
Phi	.330	.386	.395	.217	.461	.619	.721	.539

[a]140 college subjects
[b]50 college raters
[c]Group a vs. Group b
[d](Wiggins, 1959)

TABLE 7-2. SOCIAL DESIRABILITY SCALES

SD: Ten judges were instructed to answer 149 items from L, F, K, and MAS scales in such a way as to give the most socially desirable picture of themselves. Unanimous agreement on 79 items which were reduced to 39 items by item analysis. (Edwards, 1957a)

Sd-A, Items from Welsh's (1956) Factor Scales A (39 items) and R (40
Sd-R: items) were rated for both "true" and "false" responses on a seven-point scale by a total of 181 judges. Sd-A is a pool of low rated items and Sd-R is a pool of moderate items. (Wiggins and Rumrill, 1959)

K: Twenty-two items which differentiated patients with high L scores and normal MMPI profiles from a comparable group of patients with abnormal profiles plus eight items which remained unchanged under role-playing instructions in normals and also differentiated severe disturbance from normality. (Meehl and Hathaway, 1946)

Ex: Fifty-three items of high controversiality (Hathaway norms) were rated by 92 judges on a nine-point scale of social desirability. Twenty-six high and low rated items constitute scale. (Hanley, 1957)

Cof: Thirty-four reliable items which were unchanged under fake-bad instructions but changed under fake-good instructions in a role-playing study utilizing 81 subjects. (Cofer, Chance, and Judson, 1949)

Sd: Records of 178 social desirability role-players were contrasted with 140 controls to yield 40 differentiating items. (Wiggins, 1959)

L: Two judges made up 15 socially undesirable items that they felt would be frequently endorsed by normals. (Meehl and Hathaway, 1946)

Sx: Eight items were eliminated from Ex (see above) to make a balanced scale of nine "true" and nine "false" items. (Hanley, 1957)

TSD: Using Heineman's data (1952) on five-point favorability ratings for all MMPI items by 108 subjects, all items less than 2.5 and greater than 3.5 were keyed for favorability. (Present study)

ESD: Using Heineman's data (1952), the 39 items of "extreme" favorability value (less than 1.5 or greater than 4.5) were keyed for social desirability. (Present study)

all items in the scale when answered in the keyed direction
(social desirability). Ratings of the item pool that contained all the social desirability scales were obtained from
50 college students (24 men, 26 women) who rated the
social desirability of a "true" answer on a seven-point
scale. Since the ratings were for the desirability of a
"true" answer, it was necessary to reflect the ratings for
items keyed "false" in the social desirability scales. This
reflection must be considered as only an approximation to
the rated social desirability of answering "false" since
previous research (Wiggins and Rumrill, 1959) suggests
that empirical values will often differ from reflected
values. When these median ratings and reflected median
ratings are averaged across a given scale, an index of the
intensity of a social desirability scale is provided. A close
correspondence can be seen to exist between the communality values and the social desirability values which range
from "moderately desirable" in Edwards' SD to "neither
desirable nor undesirable" in the L scale. Despite this
apparent variation with communality values, the actual
range of social desirability values is quite small, all
scales being within 1.31 points of each other. The communality values, on the other hand, cover a range of 59 percentage points.

The third row presents the correlation between the
rated social desirability of a "true" answer and the number
of subjects in an independent group of 140 college men and
women who actually endorsed the item. This was calcu-
lated in the now standard method for estimating the extent
to which social desirability considerations influence responses to items in a given scale. It can be seen that
despite the limited variability in average social desirability
value, there is considerable variation among the scales in
the relationship between endorsement and rated social
desirability. This ranges from a near-zero correlation in
Hanley's Ex to a .91 in Edwards' scale. It can also be seen
that as the communalities approach controversiality, there
is a corresponding decrease in the endorsement-favorability

relationship, and that as the communalities drop below 50 percent, the relationship becomes negative--with the notable exception of the L scale. It should be recalled that the rationale behind Hanley's Ex scale was such that he predicted a near-zero correlation in an "honest" population (Hanley, 1957). To the extent that this population of students is honest, we must conclude that the pool of high communality items that constitute Edwards' SD scale would tend to make us suspicious of almost everyone.

All this, of course, raises the general issues of what properly constitutes an individual difference measure of social desirability and what would be the expected behavior of such a measure under role-playing instructions. Edwards is quite explicit about this in his monograph on the social desirability variable (1957a). It is his contention that since social desirability is a relatively all-pervasive influence in determining inventory responses, the majority of normals should be considered as possessing a substantial amount of the trait to begin with. Under social desirability instructions, he reasons, scores of the minority who are usually uninfluenced by social desirability will shift in the direction of the majority whose faking scores remain unchanged, and all scores become more homogeneous (Edwards, 1957a, pp. 55-56).

In the role-playing study already mentioned (Wiggins, 1959), the dissimulation measures (including that of Edwards) exhibited increased rather than decreased variability under desirability instructions. More important than this, however, is the actual distribution of scales under the two sets of instructions. Figure 7-1 presents these distributions for two scales of markedly different effectiveness in differentiating the two instructional groups. The upper part of the figure shows the distribution of the writer's Sd scale under the two conditions. This scale, of course, was more or less custom-made for this type of discrimination, and it is not surprising that satisfactory separation of the two groups is achieved. Under standard instructions, the Sd scale is seen to be relatively normally distributed at the

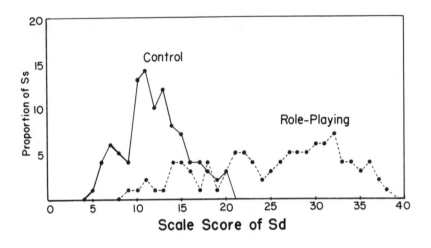

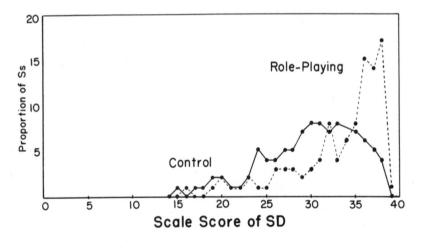

FIGURE 7-1. Distribution of Two Social Desirability Scales in Role-Playing and Standard Instruction Groups (from Wiggins, 1959).

lower end of the possible range of scores. This reflects, among other things, the low communality values of the items in the scale. Under fake instructions, it can also be seen that the faking group takes full advantage of the room for shifting in the direction of social desirability by distributing itself along the entire length of the scale, with a median score at a comfortable distance from that of the control group.

The social desirability scale of Edwards (SD), at the bottom of the figure, presents a somewhat different picture. The control group does, as Edwards predicts, show a marked piling up at the upper end of the scale, and this would be anticipated by the high average communality value of the scale itself. Under role-playing instructions, shifts in the direction of hypercommunality appear to be limited by the already high communality value of the scale.

I would like to make it clear that I am not espousing the role-playing experiment as the ultimate criterion for social desirability scales. I readily concede that there is a certain amount of artificiality to such a procedure that limits its generalization (Hanley, 1961). However, if social desirability is conceived of as a tendency toward communality which at its extreme end exceeds the communality of the average group member, then social desirability scales must themselves be of sufficiently low communality value to allow for detection of this extreme. If we take a pool of items of high communality value scored in the direction of social desirability and administer them to a standard group and a role-playing group, we would not expect large shifts to occur under the two conditions. However, we should not interpret this to mean that the instructions did not produce the style if the particular item pool did not provide sufficient opportunity for the style to be detected. Finally, if social desirability response style is considered to be a style that virtually everyone possesses to a relatively invariant high degree, it is difficult to see its relevance to the study of individual differences in general or stylistic tendencies in particular.

Stylistic Tendencies on the MMPI

At this point, I would like to return to a consideration of the MMPI as an occasion for the emergence of stylistic tendencies. The MMPI is a large pool of items, a substantial majority of which describe psychiatric symptoms, feel-

ing states, and social attitudes which are not common to the
general population. Of the items, 63 percent reflect a lack
of communality with the population at large when answered
"true," while only 37 percent indicate a divergence from
population norms when answered "false." This generalization is somewhat modified by the existence of so-called
"O-items" which, in certain scales, are keyed in the direction of communality. However, the fact that 86 percent of
all "O-items" are keyed "false" on the standard clinical
scales provides opportunity for the emergence of still
another stylistic tendency.

The use of psychiatric criterion groups in the development of the MMPI clinical scales reflected the intent of the
test authors to develop indices of the extent to which a given
individual possessed traits or test-taking attitudes, or both,
which are more typical of a psychiatric group than the population at large. The middle range of such scales may be
thought of as reflecting the degree of communality an individual possesses with the Minnesota normals on whatever
trait or set of circumstances is involved in the scale. This
middle range of the MMPI clinical scales has never been
seriously proposed as a definitive criterion of "normality,"
nor have very fine discriminations been expected of it. We
would expect a certain amount of "conformity" to be operative here in the statistical sense that the majority of normals
will endorse what is considered the acceptable response by
the majority of normals. This tendency toward conformity
becomes of special interest when it appears in the exaggerated
form of hypercommunality, that is, when the individual's
responses become determined almost exclusively by efforts
to match anticipated cultural patterns of acceptability rather
than by honest assessment of his own position on the trait
continuum. As we have already pointed out, certain kinds
of item pools are necessary for the differentiation of this
extreme tendency from the statistical "conformity" that is
implicit in our definition of normal groups.

Individuals who ascribe socially undesirable statements
to themselves are deviant; although this alone does not iden-

tify the psychiatric patient, it is inextricably involved in such predictions. The Deviation Hypothesis of Berg (1955) suggests that we capitalize on the statistical concept of communality in constructing instruments to identify members of deviant groups. However, a complicating factor imposed by the MMPI item format is that the individual is given the option of responding deviantly or non-deviantly to an inventory of symptoms by answering "true" or "false" as the occasion calls for it. The responses of interest to those subscribing to the Deviation Hypothesis would be deviant ones, which are sometimes "true" and sometimes "false," depending to a large extent on the direction of item phrasing. If the number of "true" and "false" deviant answers were neatly balanced in each scale, it would be possible to speak of relatively pure measures of deviance or noncommunality which could in turn, perhaps, be related to certain deviant criterion groups. Unfortunately, most MMPI scales reflect the scoring asymmetry of the original item pool. Thus, we are immediately faced with the possibility that individuals may respond with stylistic tendencies to answer deviantly "true" or deviantly "false" that may be independent of, or at least different from, communality on a given behavior dimension. This presents no particular obstacle to theorists such as Berg and Barnes, who are inclined to take their deviance where they find it. Barnes (1956a), for example, has shown that the tendency to answer deviantly "true" is a good predictor of the MMPI "psychotic scales" while the tendency to answer deviantly "false" is substantially related to the MMPI "neurotic scales." However, those whose interest goes beyond capitalizing on whatever predictive variance is available are inclined to wonder just what is going into these gross predictive measures. The response style of acquiescence which has been shown to be operative in other tests (Jackson and Messick, 1958) is no doubt partially involved in Deviant True measures. Acquiescence, as originally defined by Cronbach (1946), involves the tendency to answer "true" when the issue is unimportant, that is, a Non-Deviant True tendency. Similarly, tendencies to be overcautious in committing oneself to relatively innocuous,

or "non-deviant," statements may be involved in Deviant
False measures. Whatever the relationships of these possible styles to each other and to the dimension of communality, progress in determining the structure of the MMPI
as a measuring instrument awaits their differentiation.

The format of the MMPI, with its imbalance of deviant
"true" answers, makes this an ideal to be approximated
rather than an easily attainable goal. It occurred to the
writer, however, that a very primitive step in this direction
would be to examine the relative contributions of each of
these two possible deviant styles to existing measures of
other stylistic dimensions and to the MMPI clinical and
special scales themselves. With this in mind, a 356-item
Deviant True key and a 210-item Deviant False key were
constructed in a manner analogous to the scoring method
used by Barnes with individual record forms (Barnes, 1956a).
The item scoring direction or direction of noncommunality
for normative groups is given by the authors of the MMPI
for all items (Hathaway and McKinley, 1951). Items were
keyed Deviant True and Deviant False on this basis.

When scores from these two keys were correlated in a
sample of 100 college students (50 men and 50 women) the
correlation between them was found to be .0001. A tendency
to favor "true" answers as such would elevate the Deviant
True score and depress the Deviant False score, creating
a negative correlation. A tendency to favor unpopular
answers would increase both scores, creating a positive
correlation. A zero correlation is therefore not something
to be expected on the basis of either of these single tendencies. The correlation found is almost exactly zero. This
striking result fully supports Barnes' contention that two
independent deviant response styles are operative in the
MMPI (Barnes, 1956b). In addition, the fact that these two
possible stylistic determinants of MMPI responses are completely uncorrelated leads to a satisfying clarity of conceptualization in viewing their relative contributions to other
stylistic dimensions and to the various MMPI scales. Figure
7-2 presents this conceptualization. The abscissa represents

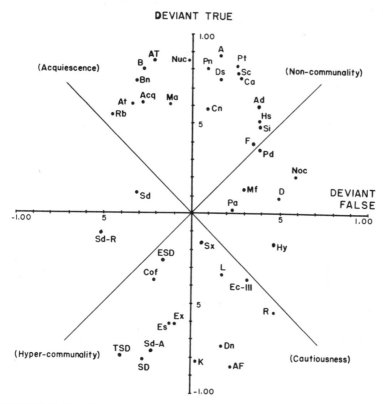

FIGURE 7-2.   Correlations of MMPI Measures with Deviant True and Deviant False Keys.

degrees of correlation of a given scale with the 210-item Deviant False key, ranging from -1.00 to +1.00.   The ordinate represents degrees of correlation of a given variable with the 356-item Deviant True key, from -1.00 to +1.00.   The justification of this orthogonal plotting of the two response measures is the zero correlation that exists between them in this group of 100 college students.   A brief description of the scales represented in Figure 7-2 is given in Table 7-3.

A relatively pure measure of Deviant True style is provided by Block's (1953) Neurotic Undercontrol Scale (Nuc)

TABLE 7-3. ACQUIESCENCE AND MMPI SPECIAL SCALES

B: Using Hathaway's data on endorsement frequencies for a combined college and normal group, 63 items of high controversiality (40-60%) were keyed "true." (Fricke, 1957)

Bn: Using groups of raters totalling 151, Hanley (1961) obtained nine-point desirability ratings on the 63 items from B above. The 32 items judged to be of "neutral" value (4-6) were keyed "true." (Present study)

Rb: Eighty-four items of high controversiality (40-60%) in a group of 190 college subjects were rated on a seven-point scale by a different group of 50 subjects. The 27 items of "neutral" value (3.5 - 4.5) were keyed "true." (Present study)

Acq: From a group of 472 aviation cadets who had been rated for adjustment, 46 items of 40-60% controversiality were found which did not discriminate between adjusted and non-adjusted subjects. This pool was reduced to 24 items by internal consistency and they were keyed "true." (Fulkerson, 1958)

At: Keying was changed on half the items in Sx (see "Social Desirability Scales") to yield an 18-item "all true" key. (Hanley, 1957)

AT̂:   The number of items, out of 566, that are answered "true" by a subject taking the MMPI.

MMPI SPECIAL SCALES

	SCALE	NO. OF ITEMS	AUTHORS
A	First factor anxiety scale	39	Welsh (1956)
Ad	Admission of symptoms	32	Little and Fisher (1958)
AF	Number of "false" responses	566	(Present study)
Ca	Caudality (cerebral lesions)	36	Williams (1952)
Cn	Control of personality	50	Cuadra (1956)
Dn	Denial of symptoms	26	Little and Fisher (1958)
Ds	Dissimulation of neurosis	74	Gough (1954)
Ec-III	Ego control	23	Block (1953)
Noc	Neurotic overcontrol	18	Block (1953)
Nuc	Neurotic undercontrol	33	Block (1953)
Pn	Psychoneurosis	33	Block (1953)
R	Second factor repression scale	40	Welsh (1956)

which appears at the top of the y-axis. This measure of
deviant undercontrol may be thought of as reflecting the
"yea-saying" character style described by Couch and Keniston (1960). Welsh's (1956) Factor I or A scale is another
strong candidate for inclusion as a measure of Deviant True
style, as has been emphasized by Messick and Jackson (1961b).
It is of interest to note that while the K scale (at the negative end of the y-axis) is a strong measure of the extent to
which a person does not respond in the Deviant True direction, it is unrelated to the tendency to respond with a Deviant
False style. Pure measures of Deviant False style are not
as easily identified among the scales included in this analysis. However, it should be noted that Block's (1953) Neurotic Overcontrol Scale (Noc), which is presumably orthogonal to his Undercontrol Scale (Nuc), and which might be
thought of as a "nay-saying" scale, is highly related to the
Deviant False dimension.

Perhaps the most interesting feature of this scatterplot
is that the scales that fall within each of the four quadrants
have a definite logical relation to one another. Quadrant I
contains the MMPI clinical scales of the first-factor variety.
Quadrant II contains six different measures of response
acquiescence. Quadrant III contains seven measures of
social desirability; and Quadrant IV contains five scales
that are presumably related to repressive overcontrol or
denial.

The scales within a quadrant can be seen to vary in the
extent to which they are related to Deviant True, Deviant
False, or both response styles. The 45-degree lines extended out through the quadrants in a manner analogous to
"fusion factors" represent points of balance or symmetry
between the two main hypothesized response styles. Scales
which fall along or near these lines may be considered to be
equally influenced by both Deviant True and Deviant False
styles. Although the format of the MMPI and the purposes
for which it was constructed make it unlikely that any relevant stylistic dimensions will be isolated that are unrelated
to Deviant True and Deviant False, scales to which these

styles contribute equally have some potential for measuring other stylistic dimensions. Consequently it is of interest to consider the scales that fall along these balance lines.

In Quadrant I, the MMPI Pd and F scales are quite close to the balance line. The F scale, which has been referred to as the "screwball scale" is a relatively powerful measure of noncommunality. It consists of items of highly asymmetrical endorsement frequencies which are keyed in the direction of deviance. In this particular college population, Pd is seen to be an even better-balanced measure of noncommunality. In Quadrant II, the distance of the various acquiescence scales from the balance line seems to reflect the extent to which care was taken in their construction to take out the effects of adjustment or communality variance. The most successful of the scales, in this respect, seems to be the Rb scale developed by the writer from a pool of items of both high controversiality and rated neutral social desirability. This scale is interpreted as reflecting the tendency to answer "true" to indifferent items, i.e., "acquiescence" in Cronbach's (1946) sense of the word.

In Quadrant III, the social desirability scales tend to be heavily influenced by the tendency to respond in the opposite direction from Deviant True (as represented by the K scale). Consequently, most of them are some distance from the line that would represent a balanced measure of hypercommunality. The ESD scale contains items of extreme social desirability value, and it would probably be difficult to find individuals who did not score high on this scale. Cofer's scale (Cof), with its interesting item pool, already discussed, falls farther from the origin, but cannot be considered a "balanced" scale. The Quadrant IV balance line is well represented by Welsh's (1956) second factor "repression" scale, Scale R. Block's (1953) Ego Control Scale (Ec-III), which is presumably a fusion factor of the Overcontrol (Noc) and Undercontrol (Nuc) scales, also falls near this balance line. Scales which fall along this balance line are interpreted as having potential for measuring the tendency to deny relatively neutral or non-deviant statements.

The foregoing discussion of the various stylistic scales in relation to Deviant True and Deviant False may have given the impression that Deviant True and Deviant False are the most psychologically significant styles present in the MMPI. It seems more likely, however, that they reflect method variance peculiar to psychiatric inventories rather than stylistic dimensions of broad theoretical significance. The stylistic dimensions of acquiescence and its complement, denial, do seem to have some precedence as theoretical constructs. Likewise the concept of communality, which stems from the generally useful Deviation Hypothesis, would seem to be worthy of further exploration. If the MMPI method imposes limitations on the development of stylistic measures that are independent of Deviant True and Deviant False, then I would suggest that efforts be directed toward the development of balanced or equally influenced measures of other styles--particularly that represented by the concept of hypercommunality.

Douglas N. Jackson

Pennsylvania State University

and

Samuel Messick

Educational Testing Service

8

Response Styles and
the Assessment of
Psychopathology

The problem of discriminating powerfully between
psychopathological syndromes with scores derived from responses to structured personality items is one of the more
challenging unsolved tasks confronting the assessment spe-
cialist. A major impediment in such refined personality
measurement is the existence of substantial sources of response bias pervading wide varieties of item content and
often failing to elicit differential responses in various pathological groups. In an attempt to clarify the role of such response biases, the authors (Jackson and Messick, 1958)
have previously distinguished between the interpretation of
behavior in terms of content and of style, and have suggested
that stylistic response determinants, such as the tendency to
respond desirably or to acquiesce to heterogeneous or neu-

The present research is part of a series of studies on stylistic
determinants in personality assessment supported by the National
Institute of Mental Health, United States Public Health Service,
under Research Grants M-2738 to Pennsylvania State University
and M-2878 to Educational Testing Service. Portions of this material also appear in Jackson, D. N., and Messick, S. Acquiescence and desirability as response determinants on the MMPI,
Educ. psychol. Measmt, 1961, 21, 771-790; and in Jackson, D. N.,
and Messick, S. Response styles on the MMPI: Comparison of
clinical and normal samples, J. abnorm. soc. Psychol., 1962, in
press.

tral item content, might not only be considered as sources
of systematic error, but as reflections of predispositions
in the respondents which possibly represent important personality traits.

The principal focus of the present paper is upon the results of a series of investigations into the internal structure
of the MMPI. In the discussion of these data, three points
which we consider important in the assessment of psychopathology are emphasized: First, we attempt to clarify the
distinctions between variance associated on the one hand
with content and on the other with response style, and we
describe a factor analytic method for deriving relatively precise estimates of the contributions of each of these components to total variance. Second, we evaluate and contrast
content and stylistic response determinants on the MMPI in
three widely varying populations--prison inmates, hospitalized neuropsychiatric patients, and college students. Third,
using these analyses as a point of departure, we draw some
general inferences about the differential assessment of psychopathological conditions using structured questionnaires.

While the title of the present paper reveals accurately
enough our emphasis on identifying stylistic determinants
in structured personality inventories, it might have equally
well been called, "The Quest for the Elusive Content."
Actually, we are very much concerned with measuring content, but content--like a tarpon being hunted by a spear fish-
erman at 10 fathoms--usually appears somewhat closer,
larger, and more easily captured than is actually the case.
Our research has convinced us that questionnaire items
which ignore response-style effects in the quest for content
will leave the investigator with very little more than two or
three scales from the tarpon that eluded him. While he
might be able to convince his colleagues that tarpon really
exist from the scales that he has found, they may remain
unconvinced that tarpons can be reliably differentiated from
sharks (that is, response sets), that they take on any particular form, that they are as large as claimed, or that the
quest for them is worth the trouble, especially in shark-
infested waters.

We do believe that the quest for content in structured personality questionnaires is well worth the trouble but that, to avoid adding to fish stories, one must learn to fish selectively for tarpon and for sharks--to differentiate clearly between content and stylistic determinants in the assessment of psychopathology and to appraise each separately. However, even sharks have economic value, and response style scores may tell us something of interest about the respondent; but to make such a determination it is all the more essential to differentiate clearly what is being assessed--content or style.[1]

Distinctions Between Components of Content and Style

Wiggins (1962b), in a careful analysis of response consistencies in personality inventories like the MMPI, has suggested a further distinction between components of response variance--a distinction between strategic, method, and stylistic variance. By strategic variance, Wiggins refers to response variation which reflects a subject's similarity to a normative group in contrast with some criterion group. The nature of such variance depends upon the strategy of constructing scales to discriminate between criterion and normative populations and upon the nature of the criterion groups. By method variance (cf. Campbell and Fiske, 1959), Wiggins refers to response consistencies attributable to constraints imposed by the available response options and to the idiosyncratic nature of particular item pools with respect to such characteristics as the proportion of true and false items and the variation in item popularity. By stylistic variance, Wiggins refers to ex-

---

[1] However, this tarpon metaphor should not be interpreted too literally. In particular, it should not be taken to suggest that you have to decide whether an item is a content item or a style item. The problem is not one of assigning instances to classes; it is one of disentangling components and assigning relative responsibilities. There are many factors--some content, some style, some set-- that lead to the response outcome, and the major problem in the present context is to separate out these factors and determine their appropriate weights.

pressive response consistencies, independent of specific
item content, having relevance not only to the particular
test format but to more general modes of commerce with
the environment. Wiggins' analysis cuts across previous
separations of response variance into content and stylistic
components, and in the interest of clarity we should like to
explicate further our distinction between content and style,
with particular reference to personality questionnaire data.

In the present context, variance associated with content is considered to refer to response consistencies in
certain defined assessment situations which reflect a particular set of broader behavioral tendencies, relatively enduring over time, having as their basis some unitary personality trait, need state, attitudinal or belief disposition,
or psychopathological syndrome. The item content used
to elicit such behavioral predispositions may be developed
initially on theoretical or on a priori grounds, may be obvious or subtle, may be direct or indirect, and may be highly
relevant or only slightly relevant to some particular prediction criterion. The initial defining property of content
assessment is some form of response consistency, for if
one cannot establish this primary requisite, then certain
mathematical operations upon the response data, such as
adding item endorsements to yield a total score, cannot
with impunity be interpreted in terms of a particular latent
dimension (cf. Messick and Jackson, 1958). Of course,
consistency is not the sole criterion for defining meaningful
response content; it might be shown, for example, that certain traits which are trivial both theoretically and practically
could be assessed reliably. Before the "meaning" of a test
score can be understood, it is necessary to consider its
linkages with theory (Hempel, 1955) and to validate the test
and the construct with any and all methods at the disposal
of the investigator (Cronbach and Meehl, 1955; Loevinger,
1957), of which the differentiation of criterion samples from
normative groups is but one. While agreeing with Wiggins
(1962b) and others (Dahlstrom and Welsh, 1960) that the
empirical differentiation of pathological from normal samples is an important strategy in validational research, the

value of experimental, physiological, cross-cultural, sociological, psychopharmacological, role-playing, judgmental, performance, behavior rating, clinical and biographical, anthropometric, and dream process studies, among others, should also be carefully considered as possible sources of evidence bearing upon construct validity.

The separation of response style from content can be made more clearly at the conceptual level than at the level of data for two important reasons: (a) a given response can be considered a function of each, in some proportion, but in any case confounded to a degree difficult to determine; (b) stylistic consistencies, such as the tendency to acquiesce, may reflect or be related in some degree to personality characteristics and need states. Thus, while the response style to endorse desirable personality items may not in itself be classifiable simply as conformity, the fact that a relation exists between some aspects of conformity and a desirability response style (Marlowe and Crowne, 1961) serves to illustrate that these styles may be related to, and sometimes moderate, content effects. Other examples of interactions between content and style may be found in the measurement of authoritarian attitudes, where it has been suggested that an all "true" item format (Gage and Chatterjee, 1960) or an extremely-worded item style (Jackson and Messick, 1958; Couch and Keniston, 1960; and Clayton and Jackson, 1961) may have greater empirical validity for appraising authoritarian behavior.

There is a further problem in defining response style, namely, that of differentiating trivial response biases, or method variance, from valid variance reflecting important behavioral predispositions. Wiggins (1962b) has approached this by defining method variance in distinction to stylistic variance. There is a serious difficulty in clearly separating these at the level of data, however, despite the importance of this distinction conceptually. If one confines an analysis to the internal structure of a single test, there is little basis for distinguishing response style from method variance. In any event, the interpretation of stylistic consistencies as method variance or bias on the one hand, or as valid indicators of personality traits on the other, depends as much upon the aims of the investigator and his preferred strategy of assessment as upon the potential validity coefficients obtained with diverse criteria for the particular response style in question. Whether interpreted as bias or as valid variance, accumulating evidence supports the view that where response style variance is pervasive and intimately associated in varying degrees with content, as it is in the MMPI, only the most careful analysis and separation of these components will allow inferences to be drawn regarding responses to items, particularly inferences regarding response content.

Subject to the above qualifications, variance associated with response style has reference to expressive consistencies in the behavior of respondents which are relatively enduring over time, with some degree of generality beyond a particular test performance to responses both in other tests and in non-test behavior, and usually reflected in assessment situations by consistencies in response to item characteristics other than specific content. These characteristics may include the following:

(a) Some aspect of the form or tone of item structure, such as difficulty level (Gage, Leavitt, and Stone, 1957), positive or negative phrasing (cf. Bass, 1955; Jackson and Messick, 1957; Chapman and Bock, 1958; Elliott, 1961), style of wording (Jackson and Messick, 1958; Hanley, 1959; Buss, 1959), ambiguity or specificity of meaning (Bass, 1955; Nunnally and Husek, 1958; Stricker, 1962), and extreme generality vs. cautious qualification (Clayton and Jackson, 1961); and

(b) Some general aspect of the connotations of the items, such as desirability (Edwards, 1957a), deviance (Berg, 1955; Sechrest and Jackson, 1961), controversiality (Fricke, 1956; Hanley, 1957), communality (Wiggins, 1962a; 1962b), subtlety (Edwards, 1957a; Hanley, 1957), or some perceived difference between communality and desirability, as revealed in the MMPI Lie scale or

in scales derived empirically to detect malingering
(Cofer, Chance, and Judson, 1949) or defensiveness
(Hanley, 1957).

Consistencies in response to formal item properties
that are restricted in time to a single test session and recurrent consistencies observed only on a specific test
form are referred to as response sets (Cronbach, 1946;
1950).

Response Styles on the MMPI

In an attempt to evaluate on the MMPI the respective
contributions of consistent responses to item content on the
one hand and of stylistic determinants on the other, three
factor analytic studies were undertaken on three diverse
samples--prison inmates, hospitalized neuropsychiatric
patients, and college students. In these studies the two response styles of acquiescence and desirability were high-
lighted, and in order to appraise their relative effects new
measures of both styles were constructed. Five desirability
(Dy) scales, with all of their items keyed true, were developed to obtain scores reflecting acquiescence at systematically varying levels of item desirability (Jackson and
Messick, 1958; 1961). Construction of the Dy scales was
accomplished by dividing all MMPI items into five levels of
judged desirability in terms of Heineman's (1952) scale
values and using a table of random numbers to select items
within each level to comprise a "scale." Item overlap between keys for Dy and MMPI clinical scales was systematically limited by substituting additional randomly selected
items for those initial Dy items found to be keyed also for
clinical scales. The five scales developed in this manner
were labeled Dy1 for the scale having the highest judged
item desirability through Dy5 for the scale with the lowest
judged item desirability; Dy3 was composed of items judged
neutral in desirability. Each desirability scale contained
60 items except Dy1, which, because of the relative scarcity
of extremely desirable items on the MMPI, contained only
50 (Jackson and Messick, 1961).

By obtaining Dy scale reliabilities, intercorrelations, and relationships with MMPI clinical scales, it is possible to estimate the degree of response consistency due to the generalized stylistic components of acquiescence and desirability, as contrasted with variance attributable to responses to specific item content.

Prison Sample

The booklet form of the MMPI was administered under standard instructions to 201 male inmates of a state correctional institution (Jackson and Messick, 1961). Clinical and validity scales were scored in the usual way with one important exception: In order to appraise acquiescence variance systematically, separate scores were obtained for items keyed true and for items keyed false, thus producing two scores for each scale, the sum of which would generate the usual total scale score. This permitted an evaluation of the possibly differential influence of acquiescence on "true" and "false" items. In addition, Welsh's (1956) "pure factor" scales, A and R, believed to reflect different combinations of desirability and acquiescence variance (Jackson and Messick, 1958; Wiggins and Rumrill, 1959), were also scored.

Intercorrelations were obtained among 30 MMPI variables (true and false parts of 11 clinical and validity scales, five Dy scales, and the K, A, and R scales), and the resulting matrix was factor analyzed by the method of principal components. Communalities were estimated by the highest correlation in each column. An examination of the relative sizes of the 30 latent roots led to the retention of eight factors, which together accounted for 69.7 percent of the total variance. These factors were rotated analytically to a modified quartimax criterion of orthogonal simple structure (Saunders, 1960).

The rotated factor loadings, together with the percentages of variance accounted for by each factor, are presented in Table 8-1. Two very large factors emerged, accounting for 45 and 31.3 percent of the common variance, respectively. The next six factors were extremely small in mag-

TABLE 8-1. FACTOR LOADINGS FOR THE PRISON SAMPLE[a]

(N = 201)

| Variable | | Factors | | | | | | | h² |
	I	II	III	IV	V	VI	VII	VIII	
1. F_t	31	57	-02	11	48	01	-01	04	.67
2. F_f	-37	40	10	-07	-00	19	-23	33	.51
3. Hs_t	23	50	-46	-06	-10	-23	12	-02	.59
4. Hs_f	-06	66	-08	07	-06	-44	08	06	.66
5. D_t	50	51	-37	-12	02	09	-28	-12	.75
6. D_f	-61	35	04	-03	-13	-31	-25	06	.68
7. Hy_t	34	48	-55	00	02	-10	-02	-04	.66
8. Hy_f	-60	14	-13	-17	03	-51	01	14	.71
9. Pd_t	60	42	-22	-11	11	12	-13	20	.68
10. Pd_f	-51	03	08	-07	-06	-06	-10	45	.49
11. Mf_t	69	09	-07	-17	08	-26	-22	-10	.64
12. Mf_f	-46	17	-04	-50	-04	-12	01	12	.53
13. Pa_t	45	54	07	-07	42	-03	00	-01	.68
14. Pa_f	-61	-10	-11	-30	09	-30	-12	-03	.60
15. Pt_t	64	57	-25	-30	-05	-07	-05	-05	.91
16. Pt_f	04	59	-14	04	-29	-23	-14	11	.55
17. Sc_t	57	66	-11	-13	24	02	-05	01	.85
18. Sc_f	-10	52	07	01	-11	-03	-12	45	.52
19. Ma_t	79	21	-04	01	05	05	20	08	.73
20. Ma_f	-23	-22	-01	-02	06	-09	12	59	.47
21. Si_t	60	60	-01	-06	-16	14	-18	-27	.87
22. Si_f	-70	40	04	-11	-09	14	-07	-12	.71
23. K	-78	-37	00	05	17	-19	05	20	.85
24. Dy1	36	-79	-01	-01	08	03	00	01	.76
25. Dy2	55	-62	-08	-02	08	02	-04	-05	.71
26. Dy3	88	00	-00	05	-04	-07	00	-03	.78
27. Dy4	78	49	06	-05	-03	09	03	08	.86
28. Dy5	53	71	-09	-01	18	03	-04	-05	.82
29. A	71	56	-08	-28	-04	-05	-05	-09	.91
30. R	-82	21	04	-15	11	04	02	-02	.76
% Tot. Var.	31.4	21.8	3.0	2.3	2.5	3.4	1.5	3.8	69.7
% Com. Var.	45.0	31.3	4.3	3.3	3.6	4.9	2.1	5.4	

[a]Loadings above .25 are underlined for factors III - VIII.

nitude, together accounting for a portion of common variance less than one-fourth that explained by the first two
factors. This finding is consistent with other factor analytic
studies of MMPI scales, which have also usually yielded
only two or three large common factors (cf. French, 1953;
Messick and Jackson, 1961b).

The interpretation of these first two large dimensions
is facilitated by examining a plot of their test vectors
(Figure 8-1). Since the Dy3 scale was composed entirely
of "true" items of moderate desirability and heterogeneous
content, it was considered to be a possible criterion measure of acquiescence. Hence the first axis was placed directly through the Dy3 vector by means of Saunders' (1960)
pattern quartimax procedure, the second axis being oriented
orthogonal to the first in the plane of the two major dimensions. The first factor seemed clearly identifiable as
acquiescence, since not only did Dy3 receive the highest
loading on it, but all of the "true" scales had positive loadings and all but one of the "false" scales had negative loadings; the one exception, Pt_f, received an essentially zero
coefficient. Thus, by differentiating true and false keys
for MMPI scales, a complete separation of their loadings
was obtained on the first factor. There were also marked
tendencies for scales moderate in desirability, rather than
those extremely desirable or undesirable, to show the highest positive and negative loadings on this factor.

The second factor displayed a marked separation in
loadings for scales with high and low desirability values.
This dimension was interpreted as a clear reflection at one
extreme of the tendency to respond desirably and at the
other extreme of the tendency to respond undesirably, as
evidenced by a correlation between loadings on this second
factor and the mean judged item desirability of each scale
(with "false" items appropriately reflected) of .95.

Although the obtained pattern of test vectors on the
first two factors is easily interpreted, it does not meet
criteria for simple structure, nor was this to be expected.
Rather, with scales varying on a continuum of average

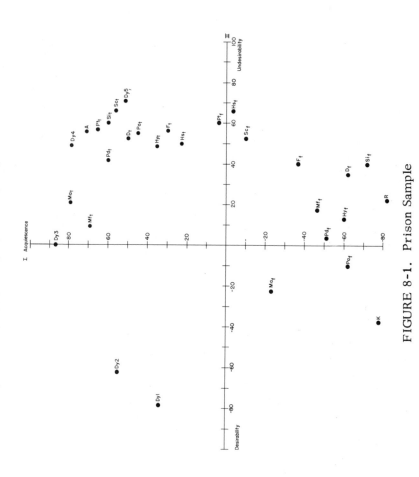

FIGURE 8-1. Prison Sample

judged desirability and with an inseparable dependence in the same set of items of various levels of acquiescence-eliciting potential, we would expect the scale vectors to form a circle (cf. Schaefer, 1959). Such a circular array is evident in Figure 8-1, indicating a kind of reciprocity between acquiescence and desirability for a given scale-- as desirability or undesirability of content increases from neutrality, the acquiescence component becomes smaller. The relative lack of vectors in the two left quadrants of Figure 8-1 is attributable in this battery to the poor representation of both "true" and "false" scales of highly desirable content. Inclusion of such scales would be expected to fill out the circle, with quadrants consisting of items keyed (a) desirable "true," (b) undesirable "true," (c) undesirable "false," and (d) desirable "false."

The remaining six factors taken together accounted for only 16.5 percent of the total variance and 23.6 percent of the common variance. Since they were individually quite small, explaining from 2.1 to 5.4 percent of the common variance each, interpretation was sometimes difficult. Interpretation was made particularly complicated by the fact that considerable item overlap exists between many of the scales with high loadings on these small factors. By eliminating from consideration factors probably attributable to item overlap, three dimensions (IV, VII, and VIII) remained which seemed to warrant psychological interpretations (see Jackson and Messick, 1961), for a discussion of item overlap factors and their appraisal).

Factor IV received moderate loadings for Mf_f, Pa_f, Pt_t, and A. From an examination of relevant item content of these scales, it would appear that high scorers would reject content suggestive of hyper-masculine "toughness" and cynicism, in denying, for example, that "most people are honest chiefly through fear of being caught" (common to Mf_f and Pa_f). They would also tend to admit more freely to diverse symptoms of anxiety. One might speculate that such persons would be deviant in a prison. It is notable that while Mf_f is highly loaded on this factor, Mf_t is not, which is consistent with their -.15 correlation but inconsistent with the MMPI practice of adding the two scales together. It also argues against a simple identification of Factor IV as femininity.

Factor VII, although quite small, provides a rare instance in which the true and false keys of a given scale, in this case D, appear on the same factor. Thus, there indeed appears to be some consistent responses to content in items characteristic of depressed persons when the major stylistic determinants are first partialled out by factor analysis. It is necessary, however, to take these stylistic determinants into consideration, since the original correlation between D_t and D_f was only -.11.

Factor VIII appeared to be a combination of correlated independent responses and item overlap. Although Ma_f and Pd_f on the one hand and Sc_f and F_f on the other have common items, there is little item dependence between these two sets of scales. All loadings, however, are in the false direction, and the item content associated with these scales would suggest that subjects scoring high on them might be reflecting tendencies to deny certain classes of deviant material. Clinically, high scores on the above (complete or total) scales are commonly associated with alcoholism (cf. Meehl, 1956), impulsivity, chronic trouble with the law, an amoral outlook, rebellion against established authority, a degree of social brashness, and employment instability--characteristics which might be represented in the aggregate with greater than average frequency within a prison inmate population, but which were also found in the following study to be of more general relevance.

Hospital and College Samples

Because the sample of prison inmates used in the above study might be deviant and might permit only limited generalization of the results, it was considered important to ascertain the relevance of the conclusions to other populations. The following investigation (Jackson and Messick, 1962) seeks to replicate and amplify the previous study with both a wider sampling of populations and a broader array of MMPI scales.

Two different samples were employed, with separate analyses being performed for each. The first of these, the "hospital" sample, consisted of 194 patients--119 males and 75 females--from a state neuropsychiatric hospital. The second group, the "college" sample, was composed of 334 undergraduates--160 males and 174 females--all paid volunteers from introductory psychology classes at a state university.

As in the preceding analysis, separate scores were obtained for each subject on true- and false-keyed items of MMPI clinical and validity scales, along with scores on the five Dy scales. Separate "true" and "false" scores were also obtained for the following additional MMPI scales: J. A. Taylor's (1953) Manifest Anxiety Scale (MAS); Barron's (1953) Ego Strength Scale (Es); Edwards' (1957a) Social Desirability Scale (SD); Hanley's (1957) scale of test-taking defensiveness (Tt); the Cofer, Chance, and Judson (1949) positive malingering scale (Mp); and Fulkerson's (1958) acquiescence scale (Aq). Single scores were derived for Welsh's (1956) MMPI pure factor measures, the predominantly true-keyed A scale and the all false R scale.

The two matrices of intercorrelations among these 40 MMPI variables (true and false parts of 15 MMPI scales, five Dy scales, and the L, K, A, R, and Aq scales) were factor analyzed separately for the hospital and college samples by the method of principal components. Communalities were estimated by the highest correlation in each column. An examination of the relative sizes of the 40 latent roots for each matrix led to the retention of nine factors in the hospital sample and 11 in the college sample, such a large number being deliberately chosen in an effort to clarify rotations (Cattell, 1958).

The factors in each of the present groups were separately rotated analytically to an orthogonal patterned quartimax criterion (Saunders, 1960), with acquiescence and desirability as the hypothesized large factors. An additional orthogonal rotation was applied to the first two factors in each sample to balance the loadings of Dy1 and Dy5 and of

Dy2 and Dy4 on the first factor, as opposed to the alternative position obtained by making factor I co-linear with Dy3. (There was little difference between these alternative alignments in the foregoing analysis of the prison data.) The rotated factor loadings for the hospital sample are presented in Table 8-2 and those for the college sample in Table 8-3.

Plots of test vectors on the first two large dimensions in each sample provide a clear basis for their interpretation (Figures 8-2 and 8-3). It should be noted that for each group there is again a complete separation of true- and false-keyed subscales on the first factor, so that in no case does a "true" scale have a negative loading or a "false" scale a positive loading. Accordingly, this factor may be interpreted relatively unequivocally as acquiescence, a consistent tendency on the part of subjects to endorse or reject items. It should be noted that all of the Dy scales received positive loadings on this factor, a finding predictable from their all "true" keying, but that Dy3, a scale of items neutral in desirability, received the highest loading. As scales depart from neutrality in becoming either more desirable or more undesirable, their loadings on factor I become more moderate.

In both the hospital and college samples, as in the prison sample previously discussed, the second factor is clearly identifiable in terms of individual differences in the consistent tendency to endorse desirable item content, as indicated by correlations above .90 in both samples between loadings on the second factor and independently obtained average desirability values for each scale (Messick and Jackson, 1961a). For both samples the scales having the largest loadings on this factor included Dy1 in the desirable direction and Dy5 in the undesirable, both of which had been especially designed to be extreme in desirability but heterogeneous in content. Also obtaining high loadings in the desirable direction were the Edwards SD "true" and "false" subscales, which had been similarly selected for their extremeness in judged desirability (Edwards, 1957a). Most of the MMPI clinical scales, reflecting as they do deviant and

TABLE 8-2. FACTOR LOADINGS FOR THE HOSPITAL SAMPLE[a]

(N = 194)

Variable		Factors									
		I	II	III	IV	V	VI	VII	VIII	IX	h²
1.	F$_t$	31	71	-26	-08	06	-04	21	09	27	.81
2.	F$_f$	-29	64	-12	01	-16	-01	05	29	-20	.66
3.	Hs$_t$	07	65	-07	04	65	01	00	-04	02	.85
4.	Hs$_f$	-20	68	05	-06	47	26	05	10	-04	.81
5.	D$_t$	18	75	00	47	25	12	-01	-05	-02	.90
6.	D$_f$	-53	52	04	23	21	49	-05	04	-03	.70
7.	Hy$_t$	13	69	-01	30	52	-01	-05	03	-03	.86
8.	Hy$_f$	-61	04	04	11	43	32	-04	28	06	.76
9.	Pd$_t$	44	68	-01	11	-08	03	-06	19	20	.77
10.	Pd$_f$	-40	15	07	-05	-07	09	-18	46	06	.44
11.	Pa$_t$	39	70	-02	08	04	-06	24	07	38	.85
12.	Pa$_f$	-59	-23	03	17	13	18	-17	16	23	.60
13.	Pt$_t$	27	81	00	41	18	04	-03	-08	06	.95
14.	Pt$_f$	-16	70	-02	16	23	35	-02	07	-07	.73
15.	Sc$_t$	30	84	-16	17	09	-09	09	06	19	.93
16.	Sc$_f$	-16	73	-18	-09	02	07	09	26	02	.70
17.	Ma$_t$	60	61	-06	-07	03	-17	01	12	13	.80
18.	Ma$_f$	-34	-45	-03	-10	10	-04	15	57	01	.68
19.	Si$_t$	33	79	02	24	-10	02	05	-32	-02	.93
20.	Si$_f$	-69	29	02	08	-16	-02	-05	-31	00	.69
21.	K	-55	-68	-07	-09	06	03	03	24	13	.87
22.	Dy1	30	-84	-04	03	03	-03	01	-04	-03	.80
23.	Dy2	60	-61	00	05	-02	02	05	04	07	.75
24.	Dy3	79	39	06	00	04	05	-10	03	03	.80
25.	Dy4	58	73	-09	07	-01	00	06	-04	-02	.89
26.	Dy5	30	87	-08	20	03	-01	14	-02	10	.94
27.	A	36	79	07	39	05	08	-02	-12	06	.95
28.	R	-81	01	-10	05	09	16	10	-21	-05	.77
29.	MAS$_t$	27	79	11	43	16	08	-05	-11	04	.94
30.	MAS$_f$	-16	76	35	15	27	07	-14	00	02	.86
31.	Es$_t$	63	-02	00	12	-19	-39	-20	20	-09	.69
32.	Es$_f$	-45	-64	-02	-25	-28	-07	-17	12	-17	.85
33.	SD$_t$	14	-76	-35	-11	-19	08	01	08	04	.78
34.	SD$_f$	-28	-85	02	-30	-03	-03	-06	14	-06	.93
35.	Tt$_t$	47	-18	-13	-06	00	-10	36	-07	-09	.43
36.	Tt$_f$	-50	-56	-05	02	04	08	07	07	31	.69
37.	Mp$_t$	59	-24	04	-26	-04	05	34	12	09	.62
38.	Mp$_f$	-47	-56	04	-16	-05	-01	50	00	-01	.82
39.	Aq	73	49	06	-17	-04	-05	-03	01	-06	.81
40.	L	-39	-39	-02	05	-00	02	72	03	03	.83
% Tot. Var.		20.0	39.0	1.2	3.7	4.2	2.2	3.4	3.3	1.6	78.6
% Com.Var.		26.0	49.0	1.6	4.7	5.3	2.8	4.4	4.2	2.0	

[a]Loadings above .25 are underlined for factors III - IX.

TABLE 8-3. FACTOR LOADINGS FOR THE COLLEGE SAMPLE[a]

(N = 334)

Variable	I	II	III	IV	V	VI	VII	VIII	IX	X	XI	h^2
						Factors						
1. F_t	35	57	-18	08	-09	-16	13	02	-17	24	00	.62
2. F_f	-26	44	02	-45	-11	-01	00	09	-03	-01	-12	.50
3. Hs_t	10	39	00	15	27	-06	-19	16	03	05	-38	.47
4. Hs_f	-11	67	-08	17	-04	20	-20	26	28	-01	-03	.72
5. D_t	17	69	-03	-09	46	18	04	-06	04	01	-13	.79
6. D_f	-61	28	-01	00	08	33	-04	22	09	-03	06	.62
7. Hy_t	14	58	-11	14	19	01	06	05	02	-01	-45	.63
8. Hy_f	-49	-11	-17	10	09	14	-13	55	20	-06	-03	.68
9. Pd_t	38	69	-14	-15	10	-18	06	19	-15	-05	-03	.77
10. Pd_f	-26	11	05	-02	-08	00	11	69	-02	-05	-01	.59
11. Pa_t	25	70	-12	10	22	-22	00	02	-07	-04	06	.68
12. Pa_f	-50	-28	-46	01	11	-01	-03	12	11	-05	-09	.59
13. Pt_t	31	79	-08	04	42	-04	-03	-08	04	-04	-03	.91
14. Pt_f	-07	63	-03	01	12	31	-04	13	04	-11	-03	.55
15. Sc_t	34	80	-15	-04	24	-13	-01	08	-11	-04	-13	.88
16. Sc_f	-12	60	-09	-19	-15	03	-12	11	-11	09	-30	.58
17. Ma_t	66	50	03	03	-09	-23	-07	04	-10	-06	-08	.78
18. Ma_f	-01	-37	03	-13	-03	-07	-04	55	-05	17	-02	.50
19. Si_t	21	76	12	-04	33	12	11	-36	02	09	06	.91
20. Si_f	-68	32	14	-04	03	-04	13	-27	-02	04	04	.67
21. K	-56	-65	-15	-04	-09	04	05	23	-03	04	-04	.82
22. Dy1	28	-79	07	01	11	-05	01	-04	-02	-05	06	.72
23. Dy2	50	-60	-12	-01	-02	-01	04	09	00	13	-08	.65
24. Dy3	79	31	-07	04	-01	12	09	-02	11	01	-08	.77
25. Dy4	51	76	02	-04	08	-10	-01	01	-03	-04	05	.86
26. Dy5	29	81	-05	02	22	-07	11	06	-04	13	-03	.84
27. A	32	80	00	-04	43	04	03	-06	07	01	02	.94
28. R	-80	01	-03	02	02	04	-07	-13	-04	01	19	.69
29. MAS_t	26	78	02	07	43	-03	-02	-04	17	-05	-04	.91
30. MAS_f	-19	71	02	11	14	02	-01	07	52	-08	-02	.85
31. Es_t	55	-09	05	-01	-04	-15	32	-04	09	-11	-23	.51
32. Es_f	-37	-60	10	-08	-45	07	10	04	-11	-06	00	.75
33. SD_t	39	-68	06	09	-10	-02	-04	-02	-55	-04	-01	.83
34. SD_f	-27	-82	-04	-12	-32	01	-12	12	-03	-04	08	.87
35. Tt_t	39	-24	-13	-02	-10	-05	-31	-13	-01	24	00	.41
36. Tt_f	-52	-53	-33	-01	16	02	01	12	03	00	-02	.70
37. Mp_t	57	-22	-22	05	-17	07	06	01	-11	34	-09	.59
38. Mp_f	-45	-52	08	07	-08	06	-07	-04	-09	45	-01	.70
39. Aq	74	40	08	-02	-13	-01	-12	-01	-07	-03	05	.76
40. L	-42	-32	03	-06	11	-06	-10	-01	05	54	01	.62
% Tot. Var.	18.0	33.0	1.6	1.1	4.3	1.4	1.2	4.2	2.3	2.2	1.6	70.9
% Com. Var.	26.0	46.0	2.3	1.6	6.1	2.0	1.7	6.0	3.2	3.1	2.3	

[a]Loadings above .25 are underlined for factors III - XI.

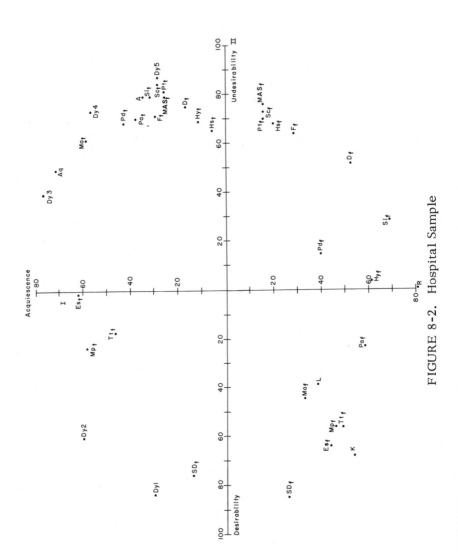

FIGURE 8-2. Hospital Sample

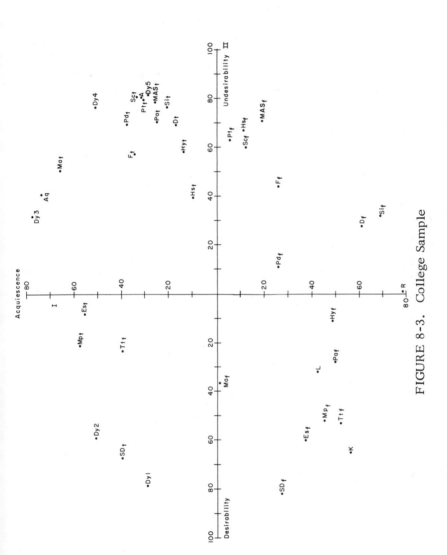

FIGURE 8-3. College Sample

pathological content, received quite high loadings in the undesirable direction.

A remarkable feature of these findings is the high degree of stability obtained across diverse samples. An inspection of Figures 8-2 and 8-3 reveals a strikingly similar
pattern of factor loadings, even though one group was composed of neuropsychiatric patients and the other of superior
young adults. The factor pattern again forms a circular
array of vectors as noted previously in the prison study,
only here the circle is more complete because of the addition of several scales keyed in the desirable direction, such
as L, SD, Es, Tt, and Mp. While the means for the various
clinical scales were quite different in the hospital and college groups, the underlying structure of response consistency was similar. One index of this similarity, the correlation between loadings on corresponding factors for the
two samples, was in excess of .99 for the desirability dimension and was .98 for the acquiescence factor. While
the average degree of undesirable item endorsement was
higher for the hospital group, the general consistencies in
responding desirably or undesirably within each group were
invariant.

In both samples the first two response style factors
accounted for a major proportion of the common variance.
In the hospital sample, the two factors together accounted
for 75 percent of the common variance and 59 percent of the
total variance, and in the college sample they accounted
for 72 percent of the common and 51 percent of the total
variance. The communalities were also quite high, particularly in the hospital sample. Thus, to a substantial degree
correlations between MMPI scales, especially when sub-
divided into true and false subscales, could be reasonably
well reproduced by knowledge of these two factors and without reference to any factors of content. These particular
percentages, of course, reflect the specific method of scoring used--that of dividing standard MMPI scales into true-
and false-keyed parts--a method which reveals the dominant role of acquiescence in influencing responses at the

item level. When "true" and "false" subscales are added
to yield a total score, of course, some of the acquiescence
effect cancels out and the desirability factor should be even
more pronounced (Edwards, 1961). However, imperfect
balancing of "true" and "false" item means and variances
on most MMPI scales still permits substantial generalized
acquiescence effects (Messick and Jackson, 1961b).

In addition to the two large response style factors in
each of the two analyses, seven factors in the hospital sample and nine in the college sample were retained for possible interpretation (Table 8-2 and 8-3). The proportions
of common and total variance accounted for by each of these
factors is quite small, and an appreciable portion of this
common variance is attributable to item overlap between
scales, as distinguished from actual consistencies in responses to related content. The seven small factors in the
hospital sample together accounted for just 25 percent of
the common variance and 19.6 percent of the total variance;
for the nine small factors in the college sample the percentages were 28.3 and 19.9, respectively.

Again eliminating from consideration factors probably
attributable to item overlap, along with specific and inconsistent doublet factors, there remained four dimensions in
the hospital sample (IV, V, VII, VIII) and three in the college sample (V, VIII, X) which seemed to warrant psychological interpretation.

Factor IV in the hospital sample and V in the college
sample were among the largest of the small factors. The
two dimensions are quite similar--each having high loadings
on true-keyed neurotic and anxiety scales (D_t, MAS_t, A, Pt_t,
$-SD_f$, $-Es_f$, Hy_t, Hs_t, Si_t). There is considerable item
overlap among these scales, but the pervasiveness of this
factor and its relative size suggests that it might be interpretable in terms of content. The content of these scales
reflects heterogeneous neurotic symptoms, but the over-all
impression suggests that "anxiety" may serve as a reasonably appropriate label. However, since all the scales load
in the "true" direction, a more precise description would

be "the tendency to endorse diverse anxiety items." A
similar but broader tendency to accept a variety of psychiatric symptoms has frequently appeared as the first dimension in factor-analytic studies of the MMPI (cf. Messick and
Jackson, 1961b), although in the present study such a factor
seems to emerge even after general acquiescence and desirability have been in effect partialled out by orthogonal axis
placement. It may well be, as has been frequently suggested (Barnes, 1956a; 1956b; Jackson and Messick, 1958;
Messick and Jackson, 1961b; Welsh, 1956; Wiggins, 1962b),
that acquiescence interacts with particular content areas
in producing common patterns of responses; but such considerations should not overshadow the possible influence of
item overlap in generating this particular factor.

Both factor VII in the hospital sample and factor X in
the college sample are dominated by a high loading for the
Lie scale and appear to reflect a type of naive test-taking
defensiveness commonly associated with elevated Lie scale
scores. The interpretation of this factor is aided considerably by the inclusion of the positive malingering scale (Mp),
which was explicitly developed to assess faking. Persons
scoring high on this factor would show a common tendency
to respond deviantly in the desirable direction to items with
a substantial disparity between their judged desirability and
their modal probability of endorsement, like the item, "I
read every editorial in the newspaper every day." Such
items would also display large mean differences when answered under standard and faking instructions. This response tendency appears to be relatively independent of
specific content areas and of the response styles of acquiescence and desirability represented in the first two factors
(cf. Voas, 1958). Because responses to such scales may
be interpretable in terms of both a tendency to respond consistently to certain formal properties of items and a mode
of defense involving the maintenance of an excessively
favorable self-concept (Marlowe and Crowne, 1961), these
scales might be considered to reflect stylistic aspects of
responding. It should be noted that the K scale, frequently
interpreted in terms of defensiveness (Meehl and Hathaway,

1946) does not load the present factor, but is instead accounted for in terms of the first two dimensions of acquiescence and desirability.

Another dimension appearing in both the hospital and
college analyses (factor VIII in each case) was also represented in the prison sample. With the exception of Si, both
parts of which load negatively, the high loadings are for
false-keyed scales, with Ma_f and Pd_f prominently represented. Since these scales are usually associated clinically
with impulsivity, alcoholism, rebelliousness, trouble with
the law, employment instability, social brashness, and the
like, we previously suspected this factor to be unique to the
prison inmate population, but its appearance here suggests
a broader relevance.

The hospital sample yielded an additional factor (V)
not obtained in the other two groups. The highest loadings
on this factor were received by both true and false parts of
Hs and Hy. Since this factor provides an all too infrequent
instance of "true" and "false" subscales loading in the same
direction, a direct content interpretation seemed warranted
and the label "somatic complaints" is suggested. The failure of this factor to appear clearly in the younger, healthier,
and generally more highly educated college sample is probably due to a relative lack of variance for such subjects in
reporting somatic preoccupations (cf. Hollingshead and Redlich, 1958).

It is notable that none of the Dy scales were loaded substantially on any of the smaller factors in any of the samples. This finding suggests that the primary aim in developing these scales--that of maximizing MMPI content
heterogeneity while systematically varying desirability
level--was achieved.

The Differential Assessment of Psychopathology

The results from these studies of three diverse samples
reveal a strikingly consistent pattern. In all three analyses,
approximately three-fourths of the common variance and
about one-half of the total variance was interpretable in

terms of the response styles of acquiescence and desirability. Of the remaining very small factors, roughly half
their variance was attributable to item overlap, and hence
is of little or no psychological significance. While consistencies interpretable in terms of reliable responses to item
content did indeed appear in all three samples, with moderate replication in the diverse groups, their aggregate contribution to the total response variance was not great in
comparison with other sources of variance. To interpret
scale scores presumably reflecting such content factors
without taking into account the rather massive response
style effects would be quite hazardous. Because of the
marked influence of acquiescence and desirability on virtually all of these empirically derived scales from the
MMPI, there is a decided tendency for the scales to share
substantial common variance, particularly when "true" and
"false" items are considered separately, causing considerable redundancy and further reducing any unique contribution of a given scale to the assessment of psychopathological behavior.

While our procedure of dividing standard scales into
"true" and "false" subscales admittedly tended to highlight
acquiescence in the response variance of the MMPI, it also
revealed another important property of MMPI scales. Even
after the general acquiescence factor was removed in the
three samples, true and false keys for a given MMPI scale
showed a marked tendency not to load on the same factors.
In the prison sample only the D scale received consistent
loadings for "true" and "false" parts on the same content
factor. Just two of the scales, Si and Mp, yielded consistent loadings for "true" and "false" items in both the college
and hospital samples; whereas Hs and Hy received consistent loadings on a factor found in the hospital sample only.
This unfortunate property of most MMPI scales raises
questions with respect to the logic of adding subscales
which fail to share common variance, and does not add to
the confidence with which characteristics can be unequivocally attributed to individuals on the basis of total scores

obtained by adding true and false items for particular MMPI scales.

The present results therefore raise serious questions concerning the appropriateness and value of standard MMPI keys and scoring methods, and suggest that more efficient and more accurate procedures are possible. As has been pointed out elsewhere (Cronbach, 1958; Jackson and Messick, 1958), the original aim in MMPI construction of developing a method for predicting psychiatric diagnoses has generally not been fulfilled, a failure partially attributable to the heterogeneous and loosely defined Kraepelinian diagnostic criteria. Rather, MMPI scale scores have been increasingly used to draw inferences about traits or characteristics of respondents (cf. Welsh and Dahlstrom, 1956). Unfortunately, this change in practice has been accomplished without a corresponding modification in scoring procedures and without adequate attention to the assumptions implicit in the use of total scores to locate respondents on some latent dimension. Notable among these assumptions is the requirement that scales be homogeneous, that an increasing score primarily reflect a greater degree of only one psychological trait or characteristic. It is evident that the MMPI scales described in the Manual--heterogeneous in content and in stylistic components--are unequal to this task. There is therefore an urgent need to evaluate fresh approaches to scale construction, with emphasis upon homogeneity as well as validity and with adequate consideration given to response sets in scoring and interpretation.

The consistent finding of systematic and very substantial response style effects on the MMPI thus raises important questions as to the conditions, if any, under which responses to structured items can be interpreted in terms of some particular content or criterion relevant to psychopathology. The response styles themselves, of course, may be related to psychopathology, and the search for identifiable personality correlates of these styles (Jackson and Messick, 1958) should certainly continue, for there are already some promising initial results (Bass, 1956; Cattell,

1957; Clayton and Jackson, 1961; Couch and Keniston, 1960; Damarin and Messick, 1962; Frederiksen and Messick, 1959; Jackson, 1959; Jackson and Pacine, 1961; Jackson, Messick, and Solley, 1957; Marlowe and Crowne, 1961; McGee, 1962; and Messick and Frederiksen, 1958). However, with a "true-false" item format as in the MMPI, one rapidly approaches an upper limit on the amount of information elicited by items which permit massive response-style effects like generalized acquiescence and desirability bias. With dichotomous items yielding only "deviant-true" and "deviant-false" responses, one can identify respondents who vary predominantly on only two general stylistic dimensions (Jackson and Messick, 1958; Sechrest and Jackson, 1961; Wiggins, 1962b). If these two dimensions account for a very substantial proportion of the response variance, then the usefulness of the available information for differentiating among respondents with respect to particular psychopathological states or conditions must necessarily be limited. It is true that the presence or absence of various psychopathological conditions might well be reflected in differing weights for the two major response styles. This possibility is consistent with several attempts to differentiate among clinical groups psychometrically which have indeed uncovered only two canonical variates (Rao and Slater, 1949; Beech and Maxwell, 1958; McCarter, 1961). However, the empirical fact that various psychopathological states yield stylistic response patterns on the MMPI which are not distinctive provides a basis for understanding the general lack of discriminant validity associated with MMPI scale scores. To be sure, there are a few other potentially general response styles which might be elicited from MMPI items, such as the differential tendency to endorse deviantly items having high desirability but low communality values, like the Lie Scale (Wiggins, 1962b), or to prefer items with absolutely or probabilistically phrased qualifiers (Clayton and Jackson, 1961). However, it is doubtful that the number of such potential response-style variables is high on the MMPI, nor is their relevance to psychopathology known with certainty.

There is a question then as to whether or not the item format of the MMPI, providing such fertile ground as it does for powerful acquiescence and desirability effects, is the method of choice in the structured assessment of psychopathology. This question naturally devolves upon issues of validity per unit cost (Cronbach and Gleser, 1957). Berg (1955; 1959) has already suggested that it might be more economical to use a small number of items dealing with preferences for abstract drawings--provided one's purpose is to differentiate psychotics from normals (Barnes, 1955; Adams and Berg, 1961a, 1961b). However, in addition to convergent validity, there is a need for discriminant validity (Campbell and Fiske, 1959). We submit that typically the clinician is at least as interested in differentiating a schizophrenic from a depressive as he is in distinguishing hospitalized patients from normals. While massive response sets apparently contribute to the differentiation of normals from mental patients and thus to convergent validity, in most cases such sets will prove to be a definite hindrance to unequivocal and refined differential diagnosis, and therefore militate against discriminant validity. Therefore, where interest is centered upon the differential assignment of characteristics relevant to personality or to psychopathology on the basis of test scores, experimental controls for response set biases are imperative. The particular form that such controls should take in the assessment of psychopathology is a question for further research (Adams, 1960; Messick and Jackson, 1958, 1961b; Messick, 1960, 1962).

9 ║ W. Grant Dahlstrom
University of North Carolina

Commentary:

The Roles of Social Desirability
and Acquiescence in
Responses to the MMPI

Psychologists have long introduced biographical questionnaires or personality inventories to their subjects by
some approximation of "Remember, now, there are no right
or wrong answers to these items." By emphasizing the distinction between this type of test and the familiar ability
scales, they have been making a rather crude attempt to put
their subjects at ease and make them ready to accept these
highly personal inquiries. However, psychologists should
not be beguiled into believing this assertion any more than
the usual test subject is. From the points of view both of
the test subject and of the test interpreter, this statement
is misleading. Each of these points of view will be discussed
in some detail, and I believe I can make clear the need to
keep them separate. Several of the confusions in the three
papers under discussion here (Chapters 6, 7, and 8) can be
traced to analyses and interpretations that switch without
warning from one point of view to the other. Although it is
to be hoped that the two kinds of formulations can ultimately
be synthesized into an elegant theory of why test scales
work (or fail to work) for particular assessment purposes,
I do not think we can do so at this time.

First, the question of right or wrong answers will be
taken up from the point of view of the person taking the test.

For the subject, any one answer, R_a, to some test item, S_i, may be <u>wrong</u> in at least two senses:

(1) S_i-R_a may fail to correspond to some veridical facts in his life history or reactive biography, within the limits posed by the forms of R that are allowed by the test format. Call this standard <u>veridical truth</u>.

(2) S_i-R_a may fail to create some desired impression on the test interpreter, especially when there is some risk involved for the test subject in what he says about himself on the inventory. Call this standard <u>impression formation set</u>.

Clearly these distinctions belong in the context of a theory of test-taking behavior, and Loevinger's (1957) point is well taken in bemoaning the lack of an articulated theory in this area. In Figure 9-1 are schematically represented some of the variables that we can now specify in accounting for responses to items like those in the MMPI.

Under <u>Contextual Conditions</u> are listed some of the major stimulus classes operating at the time the subject takes the test. Differences in the test setting, for example, are important in comparing the testing and rating procedures employed by Wiggins (Chapter 7) or Edwards (Chapter 6) in a college population with the prison testing program which furnished some of the data for the paper by Jackson and Messick (Chapter 8). The contribution of the examiner is generally ignored in inventory work, but he is probably important in and of himself as well as a medium for conveying some of the parameters of the setting. Instructional stimuli vary from the standard ones employed by MMPI users around the country to the role-playing directions employed by Wiggins or the scaling sets employed by Heineman (1953) or Edwards (1957a). Similarly, response to any one item is influenced by the kinds of other items that the subject is asked to answer. Throughout the whole test, the stimuli furnished by the answer sheet and the limited alternatives for responses (True, False, or omission) are continuously operative and controlling.

In Figure 9-1 are also listed some of the <u>Mediating Processes</u> which serve to determine the final choice of R_a

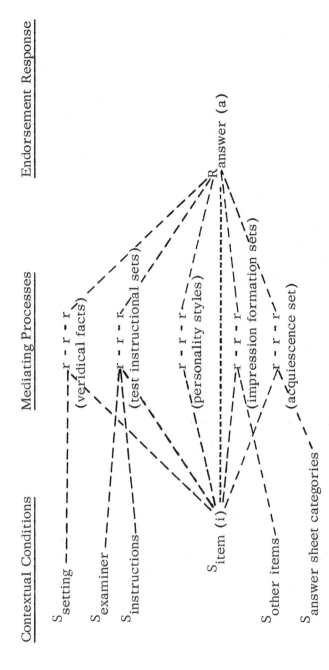

FIGURE 9-1. Schematic Representation of Some Mediating Processes Operating During a Testing Session Through Which Contextual, Contentive, and Stylistic Differences Influence the Response to Individual Inventory Items.

to each S_i. The set to respond to all the items presented in terms of their reference to one's self is presumably operating throughout the whole testing session, although the stimuli inducing this set are introduced only at the start of the session. Correctness of response in either the sense of veridical truth or of impression formation can also be introduced within the framework of the theoretical mediating processes in a subject's repertoire. As will be pointed out below, the uncertainty about the correct answer that is emphasized in Cronbach's (1946) specification of an acquiescence set also requires articulation with the other mediating processes within this same framework.

The test interpreter, however, has a quite different level of interest in the data furnished by the answers to each item, but in the papers under discussion this distinction was often lost or blurred. From the point of view of the psychologist, there are again at least two important ways of designating wrong answers to the test items:

(1) S_i-R_a may fail to describe the test subject, but instead be a description of someone else, or the way the subject would like to be or is afraid he may be. Call this standard test instructional set.

(2) S_i-R_a may fail to correspond to a particular scale key, when it was anticipated to do so from an appropriate prior evaluation based upon non-test evidence and used as validational data. Call this standard valid variance.

For the psychologist, the first kind of wrong answer is obtained when the subject fails to follow the same set of instructions that most of the original subjects obeyed when the derivational data were obtained and the (presumably) valid scales were constructed. We already know of many sources for wrong answers like this, e.g., leaving items out, lying, carelessness, role-playing. In the MMPI, the ?, L, F, and K scores provide crude checks on this kind of wrong answer. The second kind of erroneous item endorsement would occur if the valid variance ordinarily sampled by the unit is obscured by some massive variance in the subject that is uncorrelated with the criterion under consideration. We also

can specify some of these sources of wrong replies, e.g.,
illiteracy, acute delirium, visual defects, clerical ineffi-
ciencies. Both the F and K scores reflect the operation of
these sources of error in MMPI scales.

It must be emphasized that these determinants of test
response can only be meaningfully employed within the
framework of a theory of personality assessment. It should
be clear as well that various combinations of right or wrong
answers resulting from the influence of the four standards
specified above may be possible and are obtained in work
with the MMPI, but that all combinations are not equally
likely. Accordingly, a subject may fail to describe himself
in terms of ascertainable facts about himself, he may fail
to create the particular impression he wanted, and he may
endorse the test item as descriptive or indicative of the way
he would like to be, yet the item may contribute valid variance to a score on some test scale. The way the item-
response unit samples valid variance may lie precisely in
its reflection of this combination of test-taking processes.

Following Wiggins' distinctions in Chapter 7, psychologists have employed, within the theory of personality assessment by inventories, several different means of reducing
data from these S_i-R_a units. These methods include (A)
a priori categorizations, (B) psychophysical scaling of judgments, and statistical treatment of empirical endorsement
behavior on the basis of either (C) a single reference group
or (D) contrasting groups. Each of these procedures will
be briefly discussed in terms of their implications for the
elucidation of problems confronting test users today.

Jackson and Messick (as well as Comrey in Chapter 2)
use Method A in classifying each S_i into different content
groups without regard to R. The rationale appears to be to
assume face validity for endorsements obtained from these
groups that are homogeneous in content. If undesired impression formation errors can be minimized, the reasoning
goes, a utilization of the valid variance of these content
scores can be made. That is, these content scores would
then have veridical truth which would automatically give

them high valid variance for personality interpretations. Without empirical demonstration of such a utility in a given assessment process, however, this is a precarious assumption to make in scale construction. The desired homogeneity does not necessarily reside in contents; it may do so, but the proper criterion lies in the assessment domain, not in the test-taking domain.

Another application of Method A is the a priori classification of the S_i-R_a unit in terms of the form, True or False, of R without regard to the S_i. One purpose has been to get at a style of response to inventories, such as giving a True answer, for example. As Wiggins (Chapter 7) points out, personality style is not a function of S_i features or of R_a features. These characteristics are sampled from subject differences in the stylistic mediating processes in widely varying degrees by different S_i-R_a units.

Edwards (Chapter 6) uses Method A of response classification as a means to characterize the various scales of the MMPI in terms of the proportions of each T or F answer keyed on each scale. However, he considers these tallies a monotonic function of some measure of the role of response acquiescence in each of these scales. It is highly misleading to equate this method of analysis with the acquiescent response set, described by Cronbach (1946). Merely saying "True" (R_a) to a given S_i does not provide evidence that an acquiescent response set was operative in an individual subject or in a statistical summary of a group of subjects. Nor does the total number of items keyed True provide a workable index of the susceptibility of the scale to the operation of such a set. The criterion that is missing in the procedure used by Edwards is the subject's uncertainty about the appropriate answer to the test item under consideration. If the analysis of test-taking behavior discussed above has any worth, there will be at least two criteria of the appropriateness of R_a from the subject's point of view. Both of these standards must be brought to bear upon the R_a in evaluating the role of a subtle construct like response acquiescence. It must be known that the subject is in doubt as to the veridical facts involved in S_i as well as to the appropriate R_a required for the formation of a particular desired impression. Only if both of these considerations are ambiguous would acquiescence come clearly into operation. There may be other criteria of appropriateness of R_a to S_i that will also have to be considered. Certainly, the conditions will vary from one test subject to another.

This need to take into account each subject's state with respect to various controlling sets makes this area a difficult one in which to do unequivocal research. The usual procedure is to try to identify classes of subjects which will generate effectively homogeneous conditions of test response. Thus, persons orphaned from infancy might constitute a homogeneous set of subjects who are in great doubt about the veridical facts in such a statement as MMPI No. 220, "I loved my mother." This hope might be quite forlorn, however, with the vagaries of denotation and connotation accruing to such terms as "love" and "motherhood." One may have to go to the smallest of such classes, the individual subject and his own set of interpretations of veridical facts, interpretations of instructional sets, and wide variety of impression formation intentions. The work of Heilbrun and Goodstein (1961) suggests that this level of analysis may be the most fruitful one to employ in research. Ultimately, however, the hope is that some general features of the subject's repertoire will reveal sufficient common response properties to enable the test interpreter to recognize the operation of momentary response sets. The findings of Messick (1960) encourage one in this hope, at least in regard to favorable impression formation sets.

The whole tone of Edwards' paper (Chapter 6), however, implies that he has adequately dispensed with Cronbach's conditions for acquiescence in his a priori tabulations. He ignores the possibilities that True answers may be veridical facts, may be attempts at various impression formations (including socially favored stereotypes of behavior), or may be acquiescences to a particular pressure explicitly or implicitly conveyed by the instructions, examiner, or test setting. These True answers may even be reactions to the response column of the answer sheet rather than endorsements of each separate S_i. Edwards does not deal adequately with these subtleties in his analyses of item endorsement behavior. He does not seem to heed his own warning in the last sentence of his paper against an approach "which overlooks the complexity of the problem."

In deriving his SD scale, Edwards (1957a) asked his college students to rate the desirability of particular S_i-R_a units. This introduction of Method B is an improvement over the a priori categorizations of the previous approaches in that the data are based upon the behavior of potential test subjects. However, these ratings are only opinions of quite naive judges, and, as such, they are clearly limited in usefulness. As Edwards (1957a) wrote, "If a characteristic is prevalent or dominant in a group, it will perhaps be judged desirable" (p. 85). Now, in Chapter 6 Edwards interprets any item endorsement pattern that shows a moderate to high correlation with his judgmental SD scale as reflecting impression formation variance rather than the variance of veridical truth. Yet it is quite possible that a subject may be, in fact, describing himself on a subset of items and still show a high relationship to the way he would answer them under some favorable impression formation set, as Wiggins' data (Chapter 7) well document. Appropriate here too is the appreciable shift in the desirability of Scale 5 (Mf) from college subjects to prisoners noted in the data of Jackson and Messick (1961). The items are endorsed more frequently by college students (Dahlstrom and Welsh, 1960, pp. 310-316), who also seem to consider them less undesirable in their implications.

Edwards (1957a) asked his subjects to rate how they thought each particular S_i-R_a would reflect upon their personality, not taking into account in any way what they would do in a self-description context. Yet he acts as if he had obtained from them data indicating what they would do when given a conflict between the two sets of veridical truth and (favorable) impression formation. The judges may have rated some items highly favorable because they (implicitly) reflected something they would say about themselves. Edwards now acts as if people endorse these items as True or False because they are favorable. We should not be misled in this kind of discussion; in spite of the use of variance terminology rather than etiological language, correlation is still not causation. In the correlation coefficients relating average rated desirability and self-description there is a strong element of circularity.

When Jackson and Messick (Chapter 8) speak slightingly of the residue of variance left over for their (veridical fact) content groupings after they have extracted the desirability variance in their factor plots, they fall into this same trap. The variance in the MMPI scales appearing in the correlations with their special Dy scales is all called favorability response set information. Only after this information is taken out do they look for veridical fact information in their content groupings. This rotational procedure is based upon the assumption that if the variance resides in the Dy series it is necessarily impression formation error. Therefore, for example, if it is judged undesirable for a test subject to say he has headaches frequently, then if one does deny this kind of disorder it must reflect his unwillingness to look bad to others. Why should these kinds of answers automatically be excluded from content plots as possible veridical facts about the test subject's state of health? He may be responding this way because he does not have many headaches.

The method used to generate the data for the factor plots reported by Jackson and Messick is, of course, the empirical one of Method C, a statistical reduction of endorsements obtained from a single reference group at a time. Less elegant examples of the same sort of procedure are the approaches that generate deviant and conforming S_i-R_a classes, or controversial and non-controversial classes. The methodological advantages are clear here, since the procedures are based upon actual test-taking behavior, not opinions about test-taking. It should also be clear, however, that the findings are most apt to apply to the taking of tests and do not give rise directly to elucidation of the inferences that can be made from test scores.

Jackson and Messick (Chapter 8) make inferences from their factor plots, however, which are far beyond their data and which tend to be misleading. After various large components of the variance of MMPI scales have been assigned to desirability and to response style dimensions, Jackson and Messick conclude that the scales cannot serve as useful bases for personality inferences. That is, impression formation or stylistic sets (which may be inimical to the determination of veridical facts) are judged to be automatically a source of invalid variance for the test interpreter. Discourse about scale validity, however, must be kept distinct from discourse about processes of response mediation until it can be established what processes are in actuality furnishing the variance that is useful in making non-test inferences about test subjects. For example, a major part of the variance in Scale 3 (Hy) (Dahlstrom and Welsh, 1960, pp. 57-60) of the MMPI is based upon the tendency of the criterion test subjects to exceed the normative reference group in endorsing items in the conforming direction. Such replies are highly related to (desirability) impression formation sets: this fact does not reduce the utility of such answers in characterizing the degree of similarity of a given subject to this criterion group. The analyses of Jackson and Messick are excellent contributions to a theory of test-taking behavior. Without a great deal of laborious effort to establish empirical ties with non-test information, however, it is premature to extend their findings to assessment theory. One cannot make the extensions by fiat to the realm of inferences drawn by the test user from the S_i-R_a units.

As implied throughout the discussion above, the most promising method for the further elucidation of both test-taking behavior and personological assessment is Method D, the contrasting of empirical findings from separate groups of respondents. Wiggins' data (Chapter 7) are indicative of the fruitfulness of these approaches. The scales derived

by searching for items which distinguish various clearly
specified groups turn out to do a much better job in identifying and tracing changes in the operation of strong impression
formation sets than do those scales developed by judgments
alone. In our ignorance about test-taking behavior, we need
to proceed empirically for quite awhile yet in working with
such endorsement behavior.

   In the assessment domain of valid variance or practical
utility, no scale can be judged on the basis of its distribution
of True or False responses if the items are validly keyed.
There is little to be gained now from searching for clusters
of items that are homogeneous in terms of someone's a priori
opinion of the content reference of the items. What is needed
for correct personality inferences is evidence that the scales
have a single source of valid variance. Homogeneity in this
sense cannot be determined by judgment or by inter-item
correlation on single groups. This kind of uniformity must
be demonstrated by the usual procedures for establishing a
scale's construct validity. Since single items are almost
certain to be multiphasic in their variance contributions,
any cluster of items is also likely to be. No item cluster
can be expected to be entirely homogeneous, either in the
mediating processes it samples or in the inferential implications it bears in personality assessment. Such scales will
probably always have to be used in combination with other
measures specifically designed to check on various extraneous, undesired sources of response variance.

   I have little faith, either, in the judgments of even well-
trained psychologists, let alone naive subjects in a psychophysical scaling study. In my opinion, people judge people
better than they do S_i-R_a units. Witness the faulty construct
validity of Taylor's Manifest Anxiety Scale (Dahlstrom and
Welsh, 1960, pp. 290-294), where experienced clinicians
did a poor job in identifying items reflecting this none too
subtle personality attribute. Employing college undergraduates as judges does not do much to enhance the validity of
such judgments. They still do not distinguish between
answering and evaluating an answer. On the other hand,

college undergraduates have proven to be useful judges of
each other in providing criterion groups for many of the
scales in Gough's California Psychological Inventory (1957).

The difference in the utility of the other methods discussed above and that of the method of contrasting groups is
the hold on non-test variance supplied by the procedures
used to form the groups. Sometimes these procedures are
not very powerful, as reflected in some studies of the
changes induced by role-playing instructions. At times the
separations do not prove to be very reliable, as in some
judgments of improvement under various therapies. Within
a theory of personality assessment, however, we can still
profit a great deal from the careful utilization of judged differences in groups of test subjects and the leverage these
extra-test differences give in elucidating the personological
implications of test item endorsements. Better yet, when
the reference groups can be formed by stable, response-
product criteria rather than the usual fallible human judgments, we will be even further along the road toward depend-
able, workable measuring instruments in the personality
area.

PART III

Stylistic Consistencies in Cognition

10

Hanna F. Faterson

State University of New York
College of Medicine
at New York City

Articulateness of Experience:
An Extension of the Field-
Dependence-Independence Concept

When individual differences in mode of orientation in the tilting-room-tilting-chair and on the rod-and-frame tests were first observed and investigated (Witkin, Lewis, Hertzman, Machover, Meissner, and Wapner, 1954), the contrasting modes of orientation identified in these experimental situations were conceptualized as involving primarily visual or primarily postural experiences. In these test situations, designed to create a contradiction in the way the body feels and the way it looks, some subjects relied primarily on postural experiences and others primarily on the surrounding visual field as the standard of reference in making their judgments of the vertical. Most subjects fell somewhere in between in the continuum defined at one end by extreme reliance on the body and at the other end by extreme reliance on the visual field.

As further evidence accumulated, it became apparent that the "postural vs. visual" interpretation was too limited.

This paper is based on parts of a forthcoming book (Witkin, Dyk, Faterson, Goodenough, and Karp, 1962). The work was supported in part by a research grant (M-628) from the U. S. Public Health Service, National Institute of Health. H. A Witkin is the Principal Investigator for this grant. Equipment used in the tilting-room-tilting-chair test was made available by the Office of Naval Research, equipment-loan contract Nonr-1175(00).

171

Subjects with contrasting modes of orientation were also found to differ significantly in their performance on tasks which in no way involved posture or body position, for example on the embedded-figures test. Persons who, on the space orientation tests, used the body as a base of reference in judging the vertical against the counter-pulls of the visual field were also more adept at finding a simple geometrical figure hidden in a complex figure on the embedded-figures test. It was at this point that the term "field-dependence-independence" came to be used. Thus the original postural vs. visual distinction was modified so as to include in the broader concept the requirements common both to performance on tests not involving spatial orientation and to performance on tests which did involve it. This was an early step in taking account of the psychological consistencies which were beginning to emerge.

What the three perceptual tests--the tilting-room-tilting-chair, the rod-and-frame, and the embedded-figures test--have in common is, following Witkin's well-known formulation, the necessity to keep an item separate from a field or embedding context. The item might be the subject's own body, as in the body-adjustment part of the tilting-room-tilting-chair test, or an external object, as a stick in the rod-and-frame test, or a geometrical figure in the embedded-figures test. In these situations, for the relatively field-dependent subjects, object and field tend to "fuse," so that the separation called for by the task cannot easily be made. In this sense, the more field-dependent subjects' experience can be characterized as global. In contrast, the performance of a relatively field-independent person, who is able to keep object and field separate, can be termed analytical. It should of course be noted again that the terms "global" and "analytical" refer to extremes of a dimension represented by a continuous distribution of scores on perceptual tests.

The next question which arose was whether the distinction between global and analytical styles of functioning on perceptual tests is specific to perceptual situations, or whether it extends to intellectual functioning as well. We knew from our own work and the work of others that persons with a relatively more field-independent, analytical mode of approach tend to make higher total scores on conventional intelligence tests; moreover, an early study by Woerner and Levine (1950) indicated that for the WISC the relationship is higher for the non-verbal than for the verbal sections. Examination of the content of certain performance subtests suggested that successful performance on them involved an analytical mode of approach, or analytical ability. These relationships required further exploration.

Accordingly, a factor-analytic study, based on a group of 10-year-olds and one of 12-year-olds, was carried out by Goodenough and Karp (1961). The variables in the correlation matrix included scores on the three perceptual tests, the 12 WISC subtests, and selected special tests.

Three major factors, consistent for the two groups, emerged. Factor I is of special interest in relation to the extension of the field-dependence concept. The three perceptual tests had their highest loadings on this factor, along with only three of the WISC subtests. These were Block Design, Picture Completion, and Object Assembly. According to our conceptualization, performance on these three subtests, as well as performance on the three perceptual tests, have in common the requirement that the influence of an embedding context be overcome. It is this capacity to overcome an embedding context which seems to underlie performance on all six tests loaded on Factor I, and which makes possible an analytical way of experiencing. The "global vs. analytical mode of field approach" thus becomes a designation for a cognitive style which expresses itself in both perceptual and intellectual functioning. What we have been calling "field-dependence-independence" is thus in effect the perceptual manifestation of this more general cognitive style. Factor I may thus be designated as the "analytical vs. global field approach" factor. Factors II and III appeared to be interpretable as the verbal factor and the attention-concentration factor respectively, similar to those reported in other factor-analytic studies of the WISC (Cohen, 1959).

The scores on the three WISC subtests which appeared on Factor I--Block Design, Picture Completion, and Object Assembly--have been combined into a single score by summing for the individual the weighted scores on these three subtests. These summed scores, which we have called intellectual index scores, showed a high correlation with scores on the three perceptual tests combined into a perceptual index. By contrast, groupings of the WISC subtests on the basis of Factor II (Vocabulary, Comprehension, and Information subtests) and Factor III (Digit Span and Arithmetic) fail to show a significant correlation with the perceptual index. Thus the higher WISC IQ's of the relatively more field-independent children appear to be accounted for in large part by their superior performance on those subtests which seem to require the ability to overcome an embedding context.

It is even more impressive that the cognitive style designated as analytical also seems to underlie performance on the classical Duncker-type problem-solving situations. The essence of such problems is, of course, the requirement that the material presented to the subject be restructured, and that an item be taken out of the context in which it is embedded. The structure of the task is thus similar to the structure of the task in the perceptual tests. A study by Harris,[1] and one done in our laboratory, in which insight problems and perceptual tests were used, suggest that ability to solve such insight problems is related to measures of field-dependence. In a series of studies by Guilford, Frick, Christensen, and Merrifield (1957), performance on insight problems was found to be related to performance on the Thurstone-Gottschaldt, a test similar to the embedded-figures test.

This brief reference to substantial data from these three sources suggests, then, that the cognitive style in question-- the global vs. analytical style of experiencing--extends to a wide variety of intellectual tasks.

---

[1] Personal communication.

Degree of ability to break up an existing structure, which underlies the global vs. analytical style of experiencing, may be thought of as one aspect of a broader dimension. We hypothesized that children who, in structured situations, show an analytical mode of approach would, in unstructured situations, be better able to impose structure on a field. On the other hand, children with a global field approach, who passively accept the prevailing organization of a structured field, would tend to leave "as is" stimulus material that is unorganized, and thus would experience it as poorly structured. While it is, experimentally, difficult to separate the ability to analyze from the ability to impose structure, the experimental situations to be described were designed to feature primarily the ability to impose structure on an inherently unstructured field.

Two situations used to test the hypothesis that ability to break up an existing structure and the ability to structure an unstructured situation tend to go together were the Rorschach and a specially designed interview. The subjects in both situations were 10-year-old boys.

The Rorschach, in this context, was used to assess a child's perceptual experience with respect to the vagueness-clarity dimension, regardless of the adequacy or accuracy of the resulting percepts themselves. A child unable to impose structure on the stimulus material would tend to experience his percepts as vague and confusing; one able to impose structure would experience his percepts as clear, and would not be confused or overwhelmed by the task. We have considered that, though the child's experience in interpreting ink-blots is a private one for him and cannot be directly assessed, it can nevertheless be inferred or gauged from a variety of observable manifestations. For example, is the child willing to leave his percepts vague and ill-defined, or does he achieve or strive to achieve precision and articulateness by anchoring his percepts to the stimulus material in appropriate detail? Is he able to respond differentially to the succession of stimuli presented to him, or do the blots tend to fuse and "look alike" for him? Is he actively able to utilize, or eliminate, aspects of the blot which do not

fit with an intended organization, or does he allow them to
register passively, so that they interfere with his thought
process and confuse him? Differences in perceptual experience are illustrated in the following pair of examples: one
child says, "bat--its got wings on the side, and the little
things in front like they have." Another says, to the same
blot, "butterfly--no, no, change that to part of a design of
a butterfly--no, no, it has wings--no, it was just an impression." We never did find out what it was this child saw. He
did not know what he saw. The experience, for him, was
both confused and confusing.

It was possible to define 10 clues to the clarity of the
child's experience. These clues were used as guides to
over-all Rorschach percept ratings on a five-point scale.
In a cross-validation group, Rorschach percept ratings
were significantly correlated with perceptual index scores.

We then turned to the child's manner of experiencing
his real-life, everyday situation. In a tape-recorded interview, which usually opened with "Would you begin by telling
me a bit about yourself?", we sought evidence of the extent
to which the child could articulate his experiences of himself
and of his world. We explored, by means of open-end questions ("What is your mother like?" "How is school this year?"
"What do you do in your spare time?"), school life, friend-
ships, interests, life at home, plans for the future. We have
come to use the term "cognitive clarity" as descriptive of
the dimension being evaluated. A pair of contrasting examples will perhaps best convey the kind of differences in cognitive clarity we have encountered. One child, who said he
wanted to be an engineer, gave this reason for his choice:
"My brother wants to be one, and he thinks that's why I do.
But I don't think so, I think it is because I like to tinker."
At the other extreme, a 10-year-old gave this as his reason
for wanting to be a doctor: "See, because my two grand-
mothers...they were both in the hospital...once my grand-
mothers almost died--the other one, she went three times,
only the third time she died."

A child who shows a high level of cognitive clarity experiences himself and his world in a way which is both clear

and organized. Events are experienced as discrete but also
in relationship to other events. He is aware both of himself
and other persons as individuals with distinguishing characteristics and with definite roles. He is able to view events
in relation to both past and future. On the other hand, a
child with a low level of cognitive clarity is very different
in these regards. Events, for example, are experienced
neither as clearly segregated from other events, nor as co-
herently related to each other. His account of situations is
likely to be--as in the case of the dying grandmother--con-
fused, circumstantial, and overconcrete. Again, definite
clues to the judgment of cognitive clarity shown by children
in the interview were formulated, and used as guides for an
over-all rating of each interview. These ratings, for a
group of 10-year-old boys, correlated significantly with perceptual index scores. This study, as well as the Rorschach
study, remains yet to be cross-validated.

We now turn from articulateness of experience in situations which are primarily perceptual and intellectual to
articulateness of experience in relation to oneself and one's
body. The body-adjustment series of the tilting-room-tilting-
chair test, as stated earlier, had suggested wide differences
in the ability to keep the body segregated from the surrounding field. Moreover, the way in which the children described
themselves in the interview when asked, "What are you like?"
suggested differences in the articulateness with which children experienced themselves. Extremes of articulateness
of self-concept are illustrated by two contrasting answers
to this question. One replied, "I am a good boy"; another
said, "I like to work hard, I am very quiet when I work, I
don't cry when things don't go my way." There was also
the impression from the interview that children who were
able to structure the world around them also tended to have
a clearer sense of their own identity and of their role in the
family, and a clearer and more articulated self-concept.

In one study, we turned to a more probing investigation
of the body concept, conceived of as an organized impression
of the body in its experiential and symbolic as well as physical aspects. Our special interest was in the degree of

articulateness of the body concept, that is of the extent to
which the body is experienced as having limits or boundaries,
and discrete yet interrelated parts within those boundaries.
The medium through which we sought some insight into the
degree of articulateness of the body concept is human figure
drawings.

Figure drawings had been used in earlier work (Witkin
et al., 1954). A scale for the evaluation of drawings, developed by Karen Machover, stressed several aspects of
personality organization. What was needed was a method of
evaluating drawings which would concern specifically the
degree to which a drawing of the human figure conveys the
impression of a global vs. an articulated body concept. A
five-point scale, designed to yield a single over-all rating
based on specific drawing features, was formulated. To
give some indication of the basis for judgment, drawings
were rated as showing a high level of articulation when
trunks and limbs were realistically represented, when ap-
pendages were successfully integrated with the trunk, when
detailing was appropriate, when the sex identity of each
figure was clearly recognizable, when the kind of person
portrayed was indicated (e.g., a child, a soldier, a glamor
girl in evening dress). A rating of low level of articulation
was assigned to drawings in which body parts were represented by primitive ovals or rectangles, with limbs in the
form of sticks or more ovals, the parts merely stuck on to
each other, in which there was little evidence of the role or
sex of the figures, so that the male and female figures
looked essentially interchangeable.

It should be noted that while on first view the poorly
articulated drawings may appear impoverished, they apparently are not necessarily associated with over-all intellectual inferiority. On the WISC, in a group of 30 ten-year-old
boys, drawing ratings correlated significantly only with
performance on the Block Design, Picture Completion, and
Object Assembly subtests, but were not significantly related
to scores on verbal subtests. Thus, articulateness of body
concept, as reflected in drawings, is significantly related

to only those parts of an intelligence test which involve the global-analytical dimension.

The figure-drawing scale has been the most extensively applied of our rating techniques, and its relation to measures of analytical ability has been repeatedly demonstrated with groups of children, college students, and psychiatric patients.

An entirely different approach to body experience in relation to mode of field approach was used by Epstein (1957). He found that subjects who are perceptually field-dependent underestimate their body-height more than field-independent subjects and are less accurate in using their hands in a finger apposition test. Performance in these special tests may be considered to reflect articulateness of body concept. In a factor-analytic study reported by Epstein, the Finger Apposition Test, height estimation, a variable derived from the figure-drawing test, and perceptual tests all appeared on the same factor.

Articulateness of body concept may be thought of as only one aspect, although a crucial one, of the broader experience of oneself as a separate person, or what we have been calling a sense of separate identity. A sense of separate identity implies both clear boundaries that segregate one from others in the environment and a well-developed inner structure. It implies, among other things, the existence of internalized frames of reference, something like an "inner center of gravity," which helps to maintain the self as segregated from the environment. Such internal frames of reference provide a basis for interpreting and reacting to the world. We anticipated, for example, that a person with a well-developed sense of separate identity would have relatively less need for guidance and support from others; would show relatively greater "individuality" in his attitudes, judgments and values (as contrasted with unquestioning conformity); would maintain more firmly his orientation and direction in the face of outer pressures; and would be better able to maintain a stable self-view in social contexts, since he needs social contexts less for self-definition.

When analyzed conceptually in this way, the sense of separate identity lends itself to experimental investigation.

Two examples of such investigations may be cited. In one study from our laboratory, a child's task attitude while taking the TAT was analyzed, and certain manifestations of his sense of separate identity were singled out. One manifestation was the ability some children showed to define for themselves the task and the procedure, in contrast to other children who sought to force the examiner to define the task and procedures for them, thus showing their dependence on him. Another manifestation was what we have called the "evidence of an I," of a story-teller in action, going about his task of developing and organizing a sequence of ideas with a sense of his own role as a story-teller. For example, a child might state in advance his general plan for a story, might comment on problems he encountered in developing a story, might suggest in his remarks that he is able to stand aside from the story he had created and offer an evaluation of it. As anticipated, ratings on task attitude correlated significantly with perceptual index scores.

A study by Rudin and Stagner (1958) deals with a very different manifestation of separate identity. They investigated the stability of the self-concept in varying social contexts. A subject was given descriptions of four situations, was asked to imagine himself in each, and to describe himself on semantic differential rating scales as he thought he might be in each situation. The amount of variation in self-description from situation to situation served as an index of stability of self-view. As hypothesized, subjects who were more field-dependent in perceptual tasks showed larger fluctuation than field-independent subjects. Incidentally, one of our 10-year-olds neatly illustrates the link between mode of field approach and the need for outside context for self-definition. On the body-adjustment test he said he was sitting straight up-and-down when actually he was tilted by 30 degrees and thus was almost aligned with the tilted room around him. In interview, when asked, "What are you like?", he replied, "Other people say I am nice."

Thus individual consistency in functioning extends from body orientation tests to tests which require the overcoming of an embedding context but do not involve body position, to parts of conventional intelligence tests which require an analytical approach, to insight problems which require re-structuring, to clarity of experience in unstructured situations like the Rorschach and the interview, to articulateness of the body concept, and to various manifestations of a sense of separate identity. We have used the term "articulateness of experience" as descriptive of the dimension that underlies functioning in this variety of situations. According to this formulation, the field-dependence-independence dimension may be thought of as a manifestation, in specifically perceptual situations, of a more general style of experiencing. In considering this variety of situations to which the concept of articulateness of experience applies, it is obvious that it is impossible to say where perception, or intelligence, ends and personality begins. But it is precisely because field-dependence reflects so broad a dimension and lends itself to objective measurement that it is a useful tool in the assessment of personal organization.

11 $\|$ Riley W. Gardner
The Menninger Foundation

Cognitive Controls in Adaptation:
Research and Measurement

During the past 12 years, members of the "Perception Project" at The Menninger Foundation have engaged in an investigation focused upon individual consistencies in certain aspects of cognitive functioning. Broadened conceptions have long been needed of the aspects of cognitive organization that lead to individual consistencies in perception, thinking, remembering, concept formation, attention deployment, etc. Beginning with studies of "perceptual attitudes" by Dr. George S. Klein and his associates, members of the Menninger research group are among those who have demonstrated this need. These principles of cognitive organization have been termed "cognitive attitudes," or "cognitive system principles," but the apparent mediational and delay functions of these principles in respect to the expression of drives suggest that the terms "cognitive controls" or "cognitive control principles" may be more appropriate. We have spoken of different patternings of control functions as components of the over-all cognitive style of the individual (Klein, 1958; Gardner, Holzman, Klein, Linton, and

These studies have been supported in part by research grants from the National Institute of Mental Health, Public Health Service. The current work referred to is being conducted under grant M-2454.

183

Spence, 1959). In the present volume, I shall attempt to sketch our current theoretical and methodological position and its exemplification in our recent experimental work.

Some of us see our studies as an attempt to fill in, or articulate, certain as yet undifferentiated areas within the broad general framework provided by psychoanalytic theory. Although our results can be conceptualized in other ways, it may be that psychoanalytic theory is the only current behavioral theory that provides an adequate place for all the facets of human behavior and its organization that must ultimately be dealt with in such research. To take but one example, psychoanalytic theory has, from the beginning, made a place for enduring structural arrangements of complex mental functions that can lead to individual consistencies in cognitive behaviors. In this respect, we have been much concerned with relations between cognitive controls and the structures referred to as the mechanisms of defense. To take a second example, psychoanalytic theory makes an adequate place for the facts indicating qualitatively different levels of organization of cognitive functions. There is not time here to dwell upon such complex issues in detail; suffice it to say that some of us conceive of our investigations as experimental-clinical studies of secondary-process functions (or if you will, ego organization) and the arrangement of these functions in individuals. More specifically, the principles of cognitive organization we have tentatively defined may help to articulate a previously undifferentiated area or aspects of ego functioning--the "conflict-free" sphere pointed to at various times by Freud (e.g., 1950, pp. 316-357) and elaborated upon by Hartmann (1950; 1958) and others. The major point to be made here is that the structural arrangements of cognitive processes we have concerned ourselves with must be "emergent" structures, in the sense that they become relatively autonomous in the course of development and are shaped by both constitutional and experiential factors. Some of the controls we have studied may begin to emerge from the interaction of these two sets of determinants in the earliest phases of experience and, we think, could serve as pre-conditions for defense (Gardner et al., 1959; Holzman and Gardner, 1959). We hope to explore some of these difficult questions in detail in the not too distant future. In the course of this work we hope also to learn more precisely how some of these controls determine the ways in which drives are expressed through various cognitive behaviors at different levels of psychological differentiation.

The dimensional principles of cognitive control cannot be defined solely in terms of the individual. To observe these principles in operation, one must establish both the individual's intention (e.g., as induced by experimental instructions) and the stimulus conditions in which he attempts to execute this intention. Klein's demonstration (1954) that an experimentally intensified need has different effects upon the cognitive functioning of individuals who differ on a relevant dimension of cognitive control, for example, has provided rather dramatic evidence of the ways in which cognitive controls modulate the expression of a drive.

The Cognitive Controls Studied

The hypothesized dimensions of cognitive control that I shall refer to here do not, of course, represent anything like the entire sphere of such principles of structural organization. Rather, they represent certain broad areas of ego organization that seem to be important to the individual's efforts to achieve his own particular style of adaptive coordination to his world. These principles have each been studied as a separate entity in several investigations. Each has also been studied in relation to the others in one or both of two exploratory studies (Gardner et al., 1959; Gardner, Jackson, and Messick, 1960). These preliminary studies of relationships between controls have provided both some evidence of the independence of these dimensions of ego organization and some of the working hypotheses that guided the initial phases of our current work. One of these studies, done in conjunction with Jackson and Messick (1960), was focused upon relations between several cognitive control

principles and a variety of specific intellectual abilities
isolated by Thurstone and others in factor analytic studies
employing paper-and-pencil tests. Suffice it to say here
that anticipated links were apparent between the dimension
of Field-Dependence, or Field-Articulation as we termed it,
and several intellectual abilities. As for the other controls
involved, the results generally confirmed our assumption
that they may represent aspects of ego organization not
sampled in the usual ability tests. The process interpretation of Field-Articulation outlined earlier by Gardner et al.
(1959) seemed to be fruitful for predicting performance in
these several types of ability tests. The process hypothesis
employed involves interpretation of performance in Witkin's
Embedded Figures and Rod-and-Frame Tests in terms of
individual differences in selectivity of attention and response
to relevant vs. irrelevant material. The common variance
among these measures and the ability tests used was great
enough to submerge the individual abilities involved, making
them largely unrecognizable as separate entities. This was
true, at least, for our relatively small sample of female
subjects, but the study deserves replication with a sample
of men. In our culture, men as a group show more evidence
of structural differentiation in respect to this form of "active,
analytical" behavior, to use one general term Witkin has
adopted. It may be, therefore, that an hierarchical arrangement of a cognitive control and specific intellectual abilities
linked to it may appear in a study with male subjects. Messick has proposed to test this hypothesis, among others, in
a study under way at ETS.

Current Research Strategy

Following the two exploratory studies of relations between controls, the Menninger research group agreed that
further understanding of the complex cognitive processes
involved in the hypothesized control dimensions, which I
shall describe in more detail later, was the first order of
business. In pursuit of this general aim, we have engaged
in a series of experimental and experimental-correlational

studies of individual controls, a series designed to refine
our understanding of the functions involved and to provide us
with more and better measures of these functions. In some
cases this work has, of necessity, included basic experimental tests of hypotheses concerning certain cognitive
functions. In one such instance, for example, we have performed an experiment relevant to Leveling-Sharpening con-
trols--which appear in consistent individual differences in
process-trace interaction--that illuminates for the first
time the role of attentional intensity in determining assimilative interaction among new perceptual processes and memories or memory schemata representing related earlier
experiences. In another experimental study, we have successfully demonstrated that even slight shifts in a subject's
set toward selectivity in attending to relevant cues can have
highly significant effects on his experiencing of the Müller-
Lyer illusion, which we have used in our studies of individual differences in selectivity of attention. In another experimental study we are exploring relations between scanning behaviors and experienced magnitude under systematically varied stimulus conditions in size-estimation tests.
These are but examples of a research program that includes
a series of correlational studies designed to provide differential tests of hypotheses concerning the cognitive processes
involved in certain behaviors sampled only superficially
under the usual clinical or laboratory test conditions. Some
of these we call "generality" studies, since they bear on
the situational ecology of the individual consistencies involved. Included in some of these studies are samplings
from apparently related procedures used by others. A
recent study of the dimension we have called Equivalence
Range included procedures developed by Clayton and Jackson (1961), Rokeach (1951), Kelly (1955), Pettigrew (1958),
Fillenbaum (1959), Frederiksen and Messick (1959), and
others. In the course of these studies we are giving considerable attention to the psychometric properties of the
measures we are now developing, but the essential problem
may still be one of finding optimally effective methods of
observing certain facets of cognition.

At this point I should like to make some comments on our recent experiences in sampling. Whenever possible, we have been avoiding pre-selected samples of subjects, such as college students, and have been drawing our subject groups from the general population. One of these groups is drawn from a stratified random sample of the population of Topeka and serves as a model for our future work. Several of our recent studies that included replications of work done elsewhere with restricted populations have re-impressed us with the obvious need for adequate sampling to demonstrate the full range of individual differences in these behaviors. To take one example from our own work, we recently tested a special group of subjects, only to find later that one whole extreme of the distribution of scores--as indicated by previously obtained normative data--simply did not appear. These results point to some rather bitter truths about possible errors in inferring "personality variables" from work with restricted populations.

Lest you think that we are too little concerned with measurement in the more common sense of the term, let me comment on some of our minor achievements in this area in the course of this work. In our recent studies of scanning controls we have, we believe, achieved the first valid measures of the inverted-T illusion obtained in this country. We succeeded in this not by applying more refined psychometric methods to the kinds of data we obtained earlier, however, but by a new approach to the measurement of this illusion, pointed to by Jean Piaget and his co-workers on the basis of a study that included only a handful of subjects (Piaget, Vinh-Bang, and Matalon, 1958). Our work has shown the correctness of his statement that one must control for errors of the standard in measuring this illusion. In fact, our subjects showed roughly three times as much error when the error of the standard complemented the illusion effect as when it worked against the illusion effect. My own paper (Gardner, 1961) on individual differences in these errors takes advantage also of two experi-

mental studies of errors of the standard that were done in
our laboratory (Gardner and Long, 1960a, 1960b). In discussing the fruitfulness of this approach to the inverted-T,
which I use simply as an example, I am reminded that the
largest study of the inverted-T I know of employed over
1,000 subjects but failed to contribute anything important
to our understanding of the functions involved. In fact, this
study did not contain a useful measure of the illusion itself.
In other work, we have made the first attempts at control
judgments in the measurement of other illusions, and have
developed residual measures of aftereffects that may represent a distinct improvement over earlier scoring schemes.
We have also explored the potential usefulness of variations
in measures from several of the tests employed in earlier
studies in our laboratory.

If we soon have improved criterion procedures for
evaluation of these hypothesized control functions, it is our
plan to begin some large-scale studies focused, for example,
on relations between three-dimensional variables that seem
relevant to attentional behaviors: Scanning, Field-Articulation, and Leveling-Sharpening. We plan to combine these
into developmental studies that include assessment of defense mechanisms and other aspects of ego organization,
including various aspects of what is usually termed "intelligence." We are currently engaged in a pilot developmental study that may prepare us for this work. Exploration of the origins and the developmental emergence of
cognitive control structures presents a series of difficult
problems to the investigator who hopes for more than
simple age curves for performances in various criterion
tests. Since we deal with a variety of control principles
and with arrangements or patternings of these controls, it
may be necessary to achieve simultaneous evaluation of
the nature and stability of both defensive and adaptive control structures at selected points in development. The need
for such studies and the general nature of the approach we
must take is fairly clear. We hope that our current pilot
study will both illuminate some aspects of the development

of these controls and serve as a springboard for our future developmental studies.

Let me turn now to a brief description of a part of our current work dealing with studies relevant to three hypothesized dimensions of cognitive control: Scanning, Field-Articulation, and Leveling-Sharpening. Outlining a few of our current studies will illustrate our employment of the general strategy I have described.

Some Studies of the Scanning Principle

Two of the control principles we have studied--Scanning and Field-Articulation--seem directly relevant to attentional behaviors. The Scanning principle was originally inferred primarily from individual consistencies in response to size-estimation tests (Figure 11-1). The indi-

FIGURE 11-1. A Size-estimation Test Including Electronic Recording of the Subject's Eye Movements.

vidual consistencies observed in simple size judgments
also seemed apparent, however, in other situations tapping
the extensiveness with which persons sample both external
stimuli and internal memory schemata under relatively
"free" conditions. Some persons seem to sample extensively, whether or not this degree of sampling is necessary
for effective performance in the task at hand. Such sampling may even be a handicap under certain circumstances
in that it increases decision time. Others seem to attend
primarily to "dominant" objects in the field and in other
ways to scan in a relatively restricted manner.

It was obvious that the constant errors subjects make
in special size-estimation tests at best represent potential
consequences of scanning strategies. This hypothesis,
derived in part from the results of the first 32 experimental
studies of perceptual development by Jean Piaget and his co-
workers, required verification. We therefore set ourselves
the task of developing measures of scanning per se in such
situations and of exploring relationships between scanning
strategies and the apparent magnitude of different classes
of stimuli. In this we were guided in part by Piaget's suggestions about the developmental emergence of schemata
of attention deployment and their effects on apparent relative magnitude. Our experiments could not, however, be
considered a direct test of his general hypothesis.

In this study we tested 70 subjects with a battery of
potential tests of extensiveness of scanning. The study included (a) an investigation of the relationships between
scanning patterns and experienced relative size in a series
of size-estimation tests, and (b) a study of the generality
of operation of the scanning principle. The former problem was approached through electronic recordings of subjects' eye movements during size judgments. A variety
of scanning measures was obtained. This study yielded
impressive evidence of individual consistency in scanning
patterns across situations and over time. It also yielded
evidence that the relationship between scanning and apparent
magnitude is a complex one. In the size-estimation test we

had used to provide indirect measures of scanning there was
a relationship between extensiveness and apparent magnitude, a result we subsequently replicated. In simpler size-
estimation tests, however, no such relationship appeared.

Earlier results (Gardner et al., 1959) suggested that
persons for whom isolation is a predominant defense--that
is, persons who are unusually obsessive or compulsive--
are among the most extensive scanners. Ratings of Rorschach protocols of 20 extreme subjects seemed to confirm
this hypothesis. In the light of this finding, the electronic
records of eye-movements are particularly intriguing.
Simple inspection of these records shows the wide range of
sampling behaviors in our 70 subjects. The extensive
scanners, for example, look back and forth many, many
times in making even simple judgments. The "obsessive"
quality of their scanning is also apparent in the highly significant correlation between the number of scanning movements and the amount of time subjects spend "checking"
their settings of the comparison stimuli after completing
their judgments.

A current replication and extension of this study includes other measures of the degree to which an individual
scans a situation before committing himself to a decision
about what he has seen. We are also exploring relations
between extensiveness of scanning in size-estimation tests
and performance in (a) other judgmental tasks of varying
degrees of difficulty, and (b) the amount of stimulus information a subject demands before committing himself to a
response. Decision time is also represented in our battery.
This further study is also designed to shed new light on
relations between these controls and the controls previously
referred to as Field-Articulation and Constricted-Flexible
Control, both of which may involve other aspects of attentional strategies.

Some Studies of the Field-Articulation Principle

Klein (1954) employed measures of individual consistencies in "constricted-" and "flexible-control" to show that

a strong need has different influences on cognitive behavior in persons who vary along this dimension. The experiment seemed to provide direct evidence of the mediational properties of a cognitive control principle.

Also in 1954, Witkin, Lewis, Hertzman, Machover, Meissner, and Wapner published their first major study of "Field Dependence-Independence." This dimension of individual consistency was apparent in responses to an embedded figures test, to a rod-and-frame test--in which the subject attempts to adjust a rod to the true vertical although the rod is contained in a tilted frame and the subject may be tilted in the same or opposite direction--and to a variety of other tests. From responses to clinical tests and interviews it was inferred that "field-dependent" subjects--in Witkin's terms, those unable to extract the relevant item from the surrounding field (Witkin, 1959; Witkin, Karp, and Goodenough, 1959; Witkin et al., 1954)--were relatively passive, unable to introspect, etc.

Whether or not these two dimensions are actually one is a question we are attempting to answer in our current study. Whatever the outcome of this study, our attempts to develop process rationales for response in these situations have led us to a tentative interpretation of performances in embedded figures tests and the Rod-and-Frame test somewhat different from that of Witkin. To us, Witkin's tests and related procedures may sample, first and foremost, individual differences in the capacity to attend and respond selectively to relevant (vs. irrelevant) cues. Thus, in such laboratory tests, the Field-Articulation principle seems to govern the selectivity of hypercathexis.

I have used this process rationale in a study showing that Field-Articulation controls govern individual differences in the ability to overcome illusions requiring selective attention, whereas the independent Scanning principle governs one aspect of response to another type of illusion (Gardner, 1961).

Refinement of selectivity in attention deployment is obviously a developmental phenomenon. Piaget's studies of perceptual development, for example, are replete with evidence of a progression from "passive" and "global" perception and perceptual activity to more refined patternings of attention deployment (see Piaget, 1950, Chapter 3). Witkin's (1959) own studies show the expected kinds of developmental curves for performances in his tests and also show that mothers who encourage active exploration tend to produce field-independent (high in Field-Articulation) children, whereas children of growth-inhibiting mothers tend to be field-dependent (low in Field-Articulation).

Our current studies of this important dimension of cognitive control are aimed at confirmation or rejection of our tentative process interpretation of certain of these test performances. This working hypothesis was originally formulated because of our doubts concerning the definition of Field-Dependence in these situations as the ability to extract an item from its surround. Results of our studies suggested that persons who are adept at differential response to embedded items are also adept at response to surrounds themselves, when the surrounds are relevant and the embedded items irrelevant to response. These results suggested to us that the general active, analytical orientation so well described by Witkin and his co-workers actually implied superiority in selectivity of attention to relevant vs. compelling irrelevant cues no matter what the relationship between these two sets of cues. In one recent study referred to earlier, we first measured individual differences in response to the Müller-Lyer illusion, then gave brief instructions as to how one might concentrate to improve performance. The results seem to support our assumption that selectivity of attention is an important determinant of response. In addition, we have used a size-estimation situation to provide a test of our working hypothesis. We set up a test employing the concentric circles illusion of Delboeuf and some related figures. We reasoned that if embedded figures performances represent the ability to extract items from compelling surrounds, subjects who find embedded figures quickly would be superior to other subjects only in selective response to the inner circles.

If a more general principle of selectivity of attention is involved, however, subjects adept in the Embedded Figures Test should show less illusion both when asked to respond to the embedded circles and when asked to respond to the surrounds. Our results provide clear evidence in favor of the latter hypothesis.

Some Studies of the Leveling-Sharpening Principle

Further exemplification of our current research strategy can be gleaned from a brief sketch of our studies of Leveling-Sharpening. The Leveling-Sharpening principle is currently defined in terms of individual consistencies in the degree to which new experiences and memory traces of related earlier experiences interact or "assimilate." Subjects at the sharpening end of the continuum are those who show a minimum of such mutual assimilation, subjects at the leveling end show relatively great assimilation. Among people in general, the degree of assimilation is a function of the "similarity" of the new experience to the earlier experience(s). The built-in similarities between new and earlier experiences for our subjects in laboratory tests of Leveling-Sharpening have ranged from the obvious similarity between projected squares of different sizes in the original criterion test to "clang" (sound) similarities between words in learning tests and to meaning similarities between elements sequentially presented in stories.

First studied by Holzman and Klein (1954; Holzman, 1954), this control principle has been explored in a number of subsequent experiments. Two studies have shown links between extreme repression and extreme leveling (Holzman and Gardner, 1959; Gardner et al., 1959). These results may help to spell out some of the processes involved in repression. They seem to bear out Freud's (1925, pp. 84-97) contention that repression involves not only the "pushing" or "holding" of ideas out of consciousness, but also the assimilation of new experiences to unconscious, drive-related constellations of memories at the very moment the person has a new experience.

Leveling-Sharpening may also be amenable to another level of explanation: that of attentional intensity. Extreme levelers may show maximal "assimilation" because of weak initial cathexes of new stimuli. That is, extreme levelers may have unusually limited quantities of neutralized energy for spontaneous cathexis of new stimulus events, just as everyone may "level" more when the new experience is peripheral, rather than central, in the attentional field. The point of view that individuals may be strikingly differ- ent in their quanta of deployable cathectic energy is com- patible with the psychoanalytic view of attentional energies, but has not yet been explored in detail.

If it is true that intensity of attention is one of the determinants of assimilative interaction, artificial reduc- tion of stimulus intensity and duration in our earlier cri- terion test of this variable should provide better measures of Leveling-Sharpening. But as far as we knew no one had tested the basic hypothesis. We therefore set up an experi- ment employing assimilation-prone pairs of designs used earlier by Gibson. We presented members of each pair briefly, in sequence, and then asked our subjects to draw that pair as accurately as possible. One group of subjects did this with four pairs of designs. A second group viewed the last two pairs of designs while counting backward by two's in unison--a crude but effective means of reducing attention to these designs. Analysis of covariance of ratings of assimilative interaction showed an increase in assimilation in the distracted group at the .002 level of significance.

While we do not assume that intensity of attention is necessarily the only factor contributing to Leveling-Sharp- ening, we have nevertheless developed a modified version of the criterion test of Leveling-Sharpening that takes advantage of these findings. We hope that these or other current modifications of the criterion test will yield meas- ures that are more highly saturated with assimilation, less saturated with extraneous factors; and we are preparing a small study to test this assumption.

A major current study of Leveling-Sharpening was designed to explore possible links between this dimension and assimilation-proneness in classical laboratory tests of learning and recall (Gardner and Long, 1960c), some of these based upon earlier work by Siegal (1957); proactive inhibition, retroactive inhibition, and "importation," as shown in the recall of stories (cf. Paul, 1959); and a variety of possibly related behaviors, including other tests of assimilative interaction. Three variations of the criterion test are being included in this study.

Other Recent and Current Studies

These groups of studies of Scanning, Field-Articulation, and Leveling-Sharpening are paralleled by a similar group of studies of the generic properties and situational generality of the previously hypothesized control dimension referred to as Equivalence Range. A comparable study of a control dimension we have conceptualized as Tolerance for Unrealistic Experiences will soon follow. These brief sketches of some of our studies will serve to exemplify the general strategy we have been pursuing in our efforts (a) to understand some of these behaviors, (b) to develop more adequate criterion measures, and (c) to learn more of the kinds of situations that elicit these behaviors.

We are also engaged in some other kinds of studies that represent our special interest in clinical phenomena. In one of these we are administering a battery of these experimental procedures to persons who have already participated in five-hour batteries of clinical psychological tests, including intelligence tests. Some of these subjects have undergone intensive psychiatric evaluation. The control dimension conceptualized as Tolerance for Unrealistic Experiences, for example, may have rather wide-ranging clinical implications. We have already evaluated it in terms of approaches to the Rorschach test. We intend to seek out its correlates in response to the Thematic Apperception Test and other clinical situations in which the relative autonomy of the ego (Rapaport, 1951; 1958) from drives and their lower-order ideational derivatives on the one hand and reality considerations on the other can perhaps be evaluated.

Summary

In summary, I have tried to sketch the general outlines of a program of research intended to increase our understanding of several areas of cognitive functioning and of individual differences in adaptive strategy that are expressed through particular structural arrangements of these functions. I have emphasized the need for the development of methods by which these functions may be adequately observed, and I have outlined groups of recent studies relevant to some of these areas of cognitive behavior as a means of exemplifying the strategy of this research. I hope that in doing these things I have given a meaningful look into our approach to some of the unsolved problems concerning the ways in which individuals achieve their particular styles of adaptive coordination to the world about them.

12

Michael A. Wallach
*Massachusetts Institute
of Technology*

Commentary:
Active-Analytical
vs. Passive-Global
Cognitive Functioning

Over the last few years we have witnessed a growth in
concern with individual differences in cognitive processes.
The word "style" has entered psychology's technical vocabulary to signify certain kinds of generality--that someone
who reacts in one manner in one situation will react in a
particular characteristic way in another. The essential task
of a psychologist who wishes to explore style is to understand
this generality--to learn the basis for predicting how the
same person will react in different situations. To achieve
this, one must fashion an interpretation or theory concerning a particular style's defining attributes; knowledge of
such attributes then tells one where and how to look for other
manifestations of this "same" style.

Much of the recent research activity on cognitive styles
has been concerned with these crucial phases of interpretation or theory-construction and with the search for empirical
correlates that will test the adequacy of a proposed interpretation. Two of the foremost research sequences exemplifying

The preparation of this paper was supported in part by a
research grant (M-2269) from the National Institute of Mental
Health, Public Health Service, conducted under the auspices of
The Age Center of New England, Inc. The writer is indebted to
Nathan Kogan for critical comments.

199

this kind of work are the investigations by Witkin and Faterson and their associates, and those by Klein and Gardner and
theirs, as represented by papers in this volume. Extensive
related studies also are being carried out by Bruner (1960),
Kagan and Moss (1960), and others. The reader who tries
to assimilate these researches may, when viewing this tradition of work in perspective, find himself prey to the uneasy
feeling that certain issues have not been dealt with sufficiently.

The present paper calls attention to two problems concerning an interpretation or theory so attractive that it appears in the construct vocabulary of almost every psychologist concerned with problems of style in cognition--the interpretation that contrasts active, analytical, articulated,
specific, critical cognitive functioning with cognitive functioning that is passive, global, vague, diffuse, uncritical.
The two problems are: (1) Different groups of operations
have been given this same theoretical interpretation but do
not turn out to correlate fully with each other relative to
their reliabilities; (2) essentially the same correlational
test yields evidence for this theoretical interpretation on one
occasion but not on another.

Two suggestions seem in order toward the solution of
these problems. Regarding the first problem, the articulated-vague or analytical-global label may well be hiding
two or more somewhat different constructs; or, in other
words, the construct of articulated-vague or analytical-
global cognitive functioning may stand in need of refinement.
The second suggestion relates to both problems. In the case
of the first as well as the second problem, it may be that the
variables in question actually are related even when one fails
to find a correlation between them. This can happen when
the subjects vary on some other factor such that some of
them actually exhibit the relationship in question while others
show some other kind of relationship. Lumping both subgroups together thus leads to a cancelling out of contrary
effects. Differentiating factors of this kind have been called
"moderator variables" (Saunders, 1956).

We shall take up first the problems and then the suggestions.

Problem I: Partially uncorrelated operations have been given the same theoretical interpretation

Two spheres of operations--one more perceptual and the other more verbal--recently have been conceptualized by their respective investigators in terms of the analytical vs. global style of cognitive functioning. The first sphere is that of Witkin, Faterson, and their associates, originating in work on field independence-dependence (see Witkin, Lewis, Hertzman, Machover, Meissner, and Wapner, 1954; Faterson, this volume). These same operations have been conceptualized by Gardner, Klein, and their collaborators (Gardner, Holzman, Klein, Linton, and Spence, 1959; Gardner, this volume) in terms analogous to those recently used by the Witkin team as represented by Faterson's paper. The research of the Witkin group originated with tests that required the subject to orient himself to apparent verticality in a tilting-room or to orient a rod to apparent verticality in a tilting-frame. The extent to which such orientations resisted influence from tilting the room or the frame (i.e., the "field") tended to correlate (more strongly for men than for women) with ease of finding a simple visual figure embedded in a more complex pattern. The instructions for the task just mentioned encouraged an analytical attitude in the subject: he was to extract the embedded figure and disregard its confusing context.

Perceptual constancy was proposed as a further correlate of field dependence and was found, for females, to be related in the predicted manner. A brightness-constancy test was arranged in which a square of gray paper served as a standard stimulus within a given field of illumination or shadow, while on the other side of a partition were a series of comparison stimuli under direct light--papers ranging from white to black. The subject was asked to make a retinal match--i.e., to choose that comparison stimulus which matched the gray of the standard stimulus, disregarding the given field of illumination or shadow in which the standard stimulus was placed. A retinal match, i.e., non-constancy, thus required that the subject "analytically" deal with the standard stimulus apart from contextual information concerning the degree of illumination in the field--information that would be taken into account in a judgment that maintained constancy. For women, individuals who were field-dependent in terms of the embedded-figures and tilting-room procedures described earlier tended toward greater brightness constancy, and hence were thought of as using a more global, non-analytical approach, than the field-independent subjects, who in turn were more likely to achieve a retinal match.

In studying more general behavioral correlates, Witkin et al. found that field-dependent persons tended toward passive dependence on, and absence of initiative in relation to, the social and non-social environment; while field-independent subjects tended toward an active, initiating, and organizing role in relation to social and non-social environmental forces.

The original interpretation by the Witkin group of this series of findings was in terms of the effects on judgment of the tendency to segregate stimuli in an active, analytical manner from irrelevant contextual or "field" influences vs. the tendency to let these stimuli blend or merge in a passive, sloppy, or global manner with these irrelevant field influences. It later became apparent to the Witkin group, however, that the distinction between figure and field actually was a relative one, the crucial consideration being the subject's ability to resist influence from any cues which were irrelevant to the task but nevertheless compelling. Thus, Faterson in this volume offers a conceptualization in terms of analytical vs. global cognitive functioning in general, contrasting the extent to which the individual is able to articulate, specify, and delineate his experience--with the tendency to leave it diffuse, hazy, and ill defined in an uncritical manner. This broadening of the Witkin group's original conception has also been noted by Messick (1961).

Faterson's paper in this volume cites a number of further correlates in support of this more general conceptualization of field independence-dependence. Thus, greater success on the picture-completion, block-design, and object-assembly subtests of the Wechsler was found in field-independent boys. These subtests require a critical, analytical performance from the subject: he must analyze a picture of a familiar object in order to find a missing part, dissect a design into its components in order to reproduce it, break down a given configuration and integrate its parts into a new whole. It was pointed out by Faterson that while the three preceding performance subtests of the Wechsler were related to field independence, none of the verbal subtests bore any relation to it. This difference was taken as evidence consistent with the generalized analytical vs. global conceptualization of field independence-dependence presented in the preceding paragraph. Also correlated with field independence was the subject's degree of clarity and specificity in describing Rorschach ink blots, and the subject's degree of clarity and articulateness in describing his environment and himself in an interview situation.

We turn now to a somewhat different sphere of operations that has also been conceptualized in terms of an analytical and articulated vs. global and diffuse style of cognitive functioning. This work was reported by Kagan and Moss (1960). These investigators began with a task that required the adult male subject to group or sort a large array of human figure stimuli in any manner desired, and contrasted individuals who sorted on the basis of carefully defined descriptions of the physical qualities of the stimuli with those who sorted on the basis of ill defined, sloppy, thematic groupings. These two types of sortings--the carefully defined and the sloppy--were favored by different individuals. Correlates of this stylistic difference in sorting were found in many of the same kinds of tasks that have been described as differentiating field-dependent and field-independent perceivers. For example, the analytical sorters were clearer and more exact in their descriptions of Rorschach ink blots, and were rated as better able to describe their experience of inner states in an interview situation. Relationships between field independence and such Rorschach

and interview tasks were reported by Faterson. In addition,
the analytical sorters, rated without knowledge of their sorting behavior, were found to be more active and striving,
less dependent. We recall that these same variables were
found to be correlates of field independence by Witkin et al.
(1954).

This emerging cluster of relationships led Kagan and
Moss (1960) to hypothesize a stylistic dimension conceptualized in the same terms as Faterson has proposed: on
the one hand, cognitive effort, articulation, and analysis;
on the other, cognitive passivity, diffuseness, a more
global reaction. Interestingly enough, Kagan and Moss
went on to talk about their analytical subjects as better able
to differentiate information which is relevant from that
which is irrelevant, and hence as better able to differentiate
figure from ground--thus using the relative rather than
absolute sense of the terms "figure" and "ground" and ar-
riving thereby at what would appear to be the same understanding of analytical vs. global cognitive functioning as
had been reached by Faterson and by Gardner. Kagan and
Moss also hypothesized that their analytical subjects would
perform more effectively than the global individuals at the
kind of problem-solving task that requires one to "see the
crucial element" within the field and avoid the influence of
irrelevant but possibly compelling aspects of the situation.
Faterson suggested the same hypothesis and described evidence in support of it.

In contrast with results presented by Faterson, however,
Kagan and Moss found their active-analytical subjects to
achieve higher scores on the Wechsler vocabulary and information subtests than did their global-passive subjects.
Kagan and Moss took this outcome as consistent with their
definition of the analytical vs. global cognitive style, arguing that this style concerns degree of clarity and critical-
ness in one's analysis of the world, and implying that the
vocabulary and information subtests of the Wechsler concern the same function at least in part. Examination of the
scoring criteria used in Wechsler's (1949, 1955) vocabulary

subtest, for example, would seem to bear this out. In both children and adult forms, full credit is given for responses indicating, among other things, "one or more definitive or primary features" of objects; half credit, for such responses as "a vague or inexact synonym"; and zero credit, for responses which, among other things, "are very vague even after questioning."

To summarize the first problem: Witkin, Faterson, and their colleagues find relationships among such indicators as field independence in the rod-and-frame test; field independence in the tilting-chair-tilting-room test; ease of extracting embedded figures; retinal matching in a perceptual constancy situation; general activity, striving, and independence; clarity in Rorschach descriptions; clarity in an interview situation; and proficiency on certain perceptual subtests of the Wechsler but not on the Wechsler verbal subtests. Kagan and Moss find relationships among such indicators as carefully defined rather than thematic sorting; general activity, striving, and independence; clarity in Rorschach descriptions; clarity in an interview situation; and proficiency on certain verbal subtests of the Wechsler. Both clusters of correlates have been conceptualized in terms of an analytical vs. global dimension of cognitive style, and the kinds of correlates held in common indicate why the same interpretation might be favored in the two cases. The two clusters seem differentiated, however, in that one does not correlate with verbal subtests of an intelligence test battery, while the other does correlate with verbal subtests of the same battery.

The slippery quality of the analytical-global distinction is suggested by the fact that the two research teams could accept the outcome that verbal subtests of the Wechsler did not or did correlate with their other measures as consistent with their analytical-global interpretation. Both teams couch their interpretation of these somewhat different sets of findings in terms of the same stylistic contrast: on the one hand, subjects who actively differentiate and segregate experiences; on the other, subjects who passively permit experiences to fuse and enmesh in a confused, non-differentiated manner.

Problem II: Essentially the same experiment yields a relationship upon one occasion but not upon another

A second type of problem which has arisen in connection with the analytical-global cognitive construct concerns failure to replicate a previously obtained relationship even though nothing essential has been altered. Consider, for example, some of the findings recently reported by Gardner and Klein and their associates (Gardner et al., 1959). In addition to using the rod-and-frame and embedded-figures tests that constituted two of Witkin's original indices of field dependence, Gardner et al. (1959) also administered a size-constancy procedure which was strikingly similar in design to the brightness-constancy situation used by Witkin et al. (1954). We recall that the Witkin group had found this brightness-constancy situation to be related to field dependence for women, and had interpreted this result in terms of the view that a retinal match, or non-constancy, requires the subject to perform an "analytical" separation of the standard stimulus from its contextual field. In a retinal match the standard stimulus is judged in terms of its own "local" qualities, without being influenced by environmental cues as to field illumination and hence "object" brightness, in the case of brightness constancy, or by environmental cues as to distance and hence "object" size, in the case of size constancy.

In the size-constancy experiment by Gardner and his colleagues, the subject first was trained to understand the difference between real and apparent size--i.e., between preserving constancy and making a retinal match. He then was shown a standard stimulus cardboard circle and was required to match variable stimulus circles against it, the variable stimuli being arranged in a series ordered by size. As in the experiment by Witkin et al., the subject was required to judge in terms of a retinal match: i.e., to ignore any contextual cues whose utilization would make for constancy (in this case by providing indications as to distance).

Gardner et al. (1959, p. 44) point out that "Effective retinal matching requires the subject to reflect critically

and analytically upon his own experience." Analogous or
identical terms are used by Gardner and by Faterson in
characterizing field-independent behavior (see their papers
in this volume). From the earlier results by Witkin and his
collaborators, and from the conceptualization of field independence vs. dependence in terms of analytical and articulated vs. global and passive modes of experiencing as presented by Faterson and by Gardner, it would seem reasonable to expect a relationship between the tendency toward
a retinal match in this constancy situation and field inde-
pendence--at least for women and at least in the case of
the embedded-figures procedure. It was for this sex and
for the embedded-figures and tilting-room measures of
field independence that Witkin et al. obtained such a relationship. (Since the tilting-room task was not included
among the procedures used by Gardner et al., the predicted relationship between that task and the size-constancy
index cannot be tested with the Gardner et al. data.)

Unequivocal evidence for a relationship between retinal
matching and field independence is not, however, found regarding either the embedded-figures or the rod-and-frame
measures of field independence in the case of either sex.
The correlation matrix in Appendix A of Gardner et al. (1959)
indicates the following: Of the 18 correlations computed between size-constancy measures and embedded-figure solution time measures (nine in the case of each sex), only one
is significant for women and only one for men. The two
significant correlations only reach the .05 level, and they
are between different measures in the case of each sex. Of
the 18 correlations computed between size-constancy measures and rod-and-frame error measures, none is significant
for either sex. Of the six correlations computed between
size-constancy measures and an over-all field-dependence
score based on a combination of embedded-figure and rod-
frame indices, none is significant.

In sum, then, the kind of problem exemplified by the
preceding comparison of results from the Witkin and Gardner research teams is that of non-replication of a relation-

ship predicted and previously obtained on the hypothesis of an analytical-global cognitive style.

Having studied examples of evidence suggestive of two kinds of problems concerning the analytical-global conceptualization, we shall turn now to suggestions of paths along which solutions of these problems may lie. In doing so we also will be led to consider some further data. The first suggestion pertains to Problem I, while the second may well be applicable to both the problems we have considered.

Suggestion I: Refinement of the analytical-global construct through multidimensional rather than unidimensional strategies of research

We have found that a more perceptual and a more conceptual group of operations have both been interpreted in terms of a dimension of active and analytical vs. passive and global cognitive functioning. The two groups of operations seemed indeed to possess some overlap, but to be differentiated in terms of their correlation with verbal subtests of the Wechsler battery. That these differential correlates could occur and yet the two groups of operations be given the same theoretical interpretation may very well lead one to question the interpretation's adequacy.

To conceptualize cognitive functioning as being more active or passive, more analytical or global, more articulated or vague, is to invoke a construct that has been highly popular in the history of Western thought. The construct's ancient and honorable heritage has been evident not only in such dichotomies as have already been noted, but also in the form of roughly parallel distinctions drawn between rational vs. intuitive thinking or scientific vs. artistic ways of knowing. The common presence of these dichotomies in our culture's psychological vocabulary makes it easy for us to utilize, with a conviction of its correctness, the analytical-global or active-passive dimension as a way of characterizing a broad array of behaviors. Perhaps the very ease of falling into this interpretation should make us especially wary of it. At any rate, the strong historical sanction that exists for this interpretation seems to encourage investi-

gators to render the construct in as general a form as possible. Faterson's paper in this volume, for example, is an
instance of just such further generalizing of the construct.
We have seen both the Witkin team and Kagan and Moss invoke the same highly general form of this construct as an
interpretation of their findings, though these findings are
actually contradictory in part.

We would suggest that the more appropriate direction
of theoretical development for analytical-global conceptualizations is not toward greater generality and extension--if
you will, a kind of "imperialism" which leads one to view
all phenomena as exemplars of one conceptual dichotomy;
but rather, toward greater specificity of meaning. Thus
Witkin, Faterson, et al., for example, actually seem to
think of the analytical style more in terms of the separation
or grouping of parts of the phenomenal field in perception,
while Kagan and Moss seem to conceive of the analytical
style more in terms of the labeling and tagging of stimuli
after perception has occurred. This difference in shades
of meaning--one more perceptual, the other more concep-
tual--renders it understandable that each team would accept
relationships with different parts of the Wechsler as consistent with its construct, but also underlines the danger in
each team's overgeneralizing its interpretation. It is reasonable to expect clarity in the Rorschach and interview
tasks, and inclinations toward activity and independence in
general behavior, to be related both to perceptual segrega-
tion abilities and to tendencies to provide conceptual labels
whose definitional applicabilities are clear. But it also is
reasonable to expect the operational resemblance of these
conceptually different interpretations to break down in other
areas.

These considerations call into question a research strategy that puts all its resources behind one construct and seeks
to find evidence for that construct's influence in as wide a
range of tasks as possible. The effect of such a plan could
be to generate an interpretational common denominator
whose vagueness and scantiness of properties at the theoretical level render it of little explanatory significance. A

multidimensional approach would seem more appropriate, an approach wherein one works simultaneously with several constructs and seeks to find their relative contributions to the variance of numerous empirical tasks. We learn more, for example, by comparing the similarities and differences in the research results described by Faterson and by Kagan and Moss, than we do by picking one or the other team's approach as closer to the "essence" of analytical vs. global cognitive functioning, thereby lowering our level of interest for whatever turns out to be inconsistent with the approach on which we are betting.

The need for such a multidimensional strategy becomes even more apparent when we consider a recent report by Kagan, Moss, and Sigel (1961). In this study these investigators report work with children where two measures are referred to interchangeably as criterion indicators of what is presumed to be the "same" construct of analytical vs. global cognitive functioning. One of these measures is a children's version of the sorting procedure from the Kagan-Moss study with male adults described earlier, and it once more shows a trend, for male sixth-graders, toward higher correlation with verbal than with performance scales of an intelligence test--although this differential was more marked for the adults. This serves to replicate with male children the Kagan-Moss finding with male adults that we have discussed. The other measure, unlike the sorting procedure, shows a trend, for male sixth-graders, toward higher correlation with performance than with verbal scales of an intelligence test. The two measures show different rather than similar patterns of relationships with other variables too. Yet both measures are referred to in different parts of the report as criterion tests for the "same" construct, and the construct in question is presumed to be the very one that Witkin and his collaborators are studying.

One final indication of the conceptual confusion that can arise from a unidimensional approach may be mentioned. Kagan, Moss, and Sigel (1961) cite the construct of "leveling-sharpening" that is used in the study by Gardner et al.

(1959) as another variant of the "same" analytical-global construct that Kagan et al. are considering. This despite the fact that measures of leveling-sharpening and measures of field dependence-independence have been found by Gardner et al. (1959) to load on different orthogonally rotated factors in the factor analysis that they report.

The point of view advocated here thus is closer to the method of work adopted by Gardner, Klein, and their colleagues, than to that of Witkin, Faterson, et al., or Kagan et al. Indeed, Gardner et al. (1959) even note that the same task may share some of its variance with one cognitive style dimension and some of its variance with another. To investigate such a task as an exemplar of only one or the other of these stylistic dimensions thus would lead to a distorted understanding of the processes at work. To avoid the possible pitfalls of excessive commitment to one organizing principle at the expense of another, therefore, it seems advisable to adopt a multidimensional rather than unidimensional strategy of research at the outset.

Suggestion II: Consideration of moderator variables

The investigations by Gardner et al. (1959), by Witkin et al. (1954), and by Kagan et al. (1961), seem to share an assumption to the effect that, with the possible exception of sex differences, any particular type of stylistic consistency ought to manifest itself in the same way in the behavior of all persons. Individual differences are expected in regard to the position occupied by one or another subject along the stylistic dimension in question, but the dimension itself is expected to be equally applicable to all. Thus, some subjects may perform at the "analytical" end of various indices while the performances of others may lie at the "global" end of these indices, but the consistency among the performances being correlated is expected to be of the same nature for one person as for another.

This kind of assumption with respect to stylistic consistencies made its first psychometric appearance, perhaps, in the early work on expressive behavior carried out by Allport and Vernon (1933), who, indeed, are acknowledged

by Gardner et al. (1959) as pioneers in the tradition of research on cognitive styles that we are considering and as
influential in determining the type of method that Gardner
et al. have followed. Given this assumption, the proper
way of exploring individual differences in cognitive styles is
to determine, for a sample of individuals taken as a whole,
the degree of association between performances on one test
and performances on another different test. To the extent
that the two tests are associated for the sample as a whole,
these tests define a common stylistic dimension along which
individuals differ. This basic approach, used in Allport and
Vernon's work, has been applied without substantial modification in the various studies commented upon in this paper.

There is evidence that this assumption is not true, however, in the realm of expressive behavior. Recent studies
by Wallach and his collaborators (Wallach, Green, Lipsitt,
and Minehart, 1962; Wallach and Greenberg, 1960; Wallach
and Gahm, 1960) have revealed individual differences not
only in subjects' positions along one dimension of stylistic
consistency, but also in the kind of consistency exhibited by
various subjects. Consider an investigation by Wallach et al.
(1962) on relationships between overt assessment of social
interaction vs. isolation and covert, expressive assessment
of needs for social interaction vs. isolation. Allport and
Vernon's original view would imply that persons who overtly
manifest social interaction should covertly indicate needs
for social interaction, while persons who overtly manifest
social isolation should covertly indicate needs for social
isolation. In fact, however, only people low in tendencies
toward denial or defensive inhibition behaved this way.
Among those high in the tendency to inhibit or deny awareness of certain feelings and thoughts, on the other hand,
persons who overtly manifested social isolation covertly
indicated needs for social interaction, while persons who
overtly manifested social interaction covertly indicated
needs for social isolation. For the deniers or inhibitors,
in other words, overt social interaction or isolation seemed
to function as a means of hiding or disguising needs which

were contrary to the manifestations permitted on the surface. The deniers or inhibitors, therefore, showed a direction of relationship between the overt and covert indicators that was the inverse or contrary of the direction exhibited by persons who did not deny, but was no less consistent.

It is evident that computation of an over-all correlation coefficient between overt and covert indices for the sample as a whole in a study such as the above would not be meaningful, because the direction of relationship between these indices differs for the two types of persons. These contrary directions of relationship would tend to cancel each other out.

The investigation just described considered indicators that were more overt vs. covert, direct vs. indirect, as regards the ease with which the subject could comprehend their significance in terms of the kinds of feelings and thoughts they reflected. The experiment demonstrated that, to the extent that the subject was trying to inhibit or deny awareness of certain feelings and thoughts, the more overt assessor, being subject to influence from such inhibition or denial, tended to indicate the opposite of what was revealed by the more covert assessor. A predictable contradiction between measures thus was found--one which psychoanalysts have referred to with such terms as displacement, compensation, and reaction formation. In this study we were able, therefore, to isolate denial or defensive inhibition as a moderator variable predicting, in the realm of expressive behavior, which of two forms of stylistic consistency would be manifested by different individuals. The pervasive role of this variable in clinical study is evident from the multiplicity of terms that refer to it in the literature: "defensive inhibition" (White, 1956), "defensiveness" (Rogers, 1959a, 1959b), "repression," and "denial" (S. Freud, 1925; A. Freud, 1946), to mention a few. It should be noted that the point under discussion here is not that defenses correlate with styles--both the Gardner and the Witkin research groups have begun work exploring this possibility. Rather, defenses are being considered as variables that may influence the patterns or kinds of stylistic consistency that will emerge.

While expressive styles and cognitive styles presumably pertain to somewhat different domains, information about moderator variables learned in the former area may well be applicable to the latter. At the very least, the idea of seeking moderator variables ought to be transferable from the area of expressive styles to that of cognitive styles. We may recall in this context that Gardner et al. (1959) saw Allport and Vernon's research on expressive behavior as one source of their own concern with stylistic consistency in cognition, and even went so far as to suggest that questions of style in expressive behavior and in cognitive processes may really be forms of the same basic inquiry.

Both the Witkin-Faterson and the Gardner-Klein research groups, as well as Kagan et al., have entertained the idea that sex may function as a moderator variable of the sort described above. In addition, however, it may be necessary to distinguish, within sex, other moderator variables concerning aspects of personality and motivation. Let us briefly explore some ways in which the undetected action of one or more moderator variables might lead to the types of problems concerning "analytical" vs. "global" cognitive performances that we have considered in this paper.

Concerning the first problem, it is possible that the more perceptual and more conceptual forms of the analytical-global construct actually do have a common basis for some but not all individuals, and hence that the different patterns of results reported by Faterson and by Kagan and Moss in connection with the Wechsler are accidents of a failure to separate each sample into subgroups on the basis of a relevant moderator variable in the area of personality or motivation. The perceptual and conceptual forms of analytical vs. global functioning may constitute a unified stylistic dimension applicable to one subgroup but not to another. The effect of using a sample unsegregated into relevant subgroups thus would be to cancel out the appearance of correlations for the sample as a whole, or to render their occurrence precarious at best.

Turning now to the failure to replicate discussed as our second problem, we noted an instance where one experiment

revealed a particular relationship between perceptual constancy and field dependence for the sample as a whole, while
an attempt at replication found no relationship. Suppose the
type of stylistic consistency described by this relationship
were directly relevant to one of two or more subgroups
segregated on the basis of a particular moderator variable,
but not relevant to the other subgroups. It may be that the
replication sample failed to contain a sufficient representation of that subgroup for which the stylistic consistency in
question is relevant.

The crucial task now, of course, is to delineate moderator variables that may influence relationships in the realm
of analytical vs. global cognitive functioning. A first attempt
to explore moderator variables in another sphere of cognitive activity--decision making--has been carried out in
recent work by Kogan and Wallach (1961), where application
of a moderator variable revealed the presence of a particular type of cognitive consistency in one subgroup and its
absence in another. Perhaps the best research strategy for
the domain of analytical vs. global cognition is, once again,
the multidimensional approach: locating, with the help of
factor analysis, dimensions of personality functioning--such
as denial--which turn out to be orthogonal to performances
on those procedures that define analytical vs. global cognitive approaches. Subgroups then can be segregated in terms
of values along such dimensions, and one can proceed to
explore patterns of stylistic consistencies in the analytical-
global area that may differentiate one subgroup from another.

In conclusion, the present paper has considered certain
problems connected with research on analytical vs. global
cognitive functioning, and has offered some suggestions
which may aid in their resolution. Underlying these suggestions is the view that in order to gain a full understanding of
some domain of cognitive functioning one must study it in
the context of (1) other cognitive dimensions with which it
may be partially related, and (2) variables of personality
and motivation that may cause differences in the patterns of
relationships within the domain for different subgroups of
persons.

PART IV

Social and Situational

Influences in

Personality Assessment

13 ‖ Edward E. Jones
Duke University

Some Determinants of Reactions to Being Approved or Disapproved As a Person

I should like to present some selected results of a rather complicated experiment illustrating the joint manipulation of situational and individual difference variables. Although the experiment was not initially designed with the goal of validation uppermost in our minds, the study can be viewed as an attempt to validate, experimentally, an attitude measure about which little information is available in the published literature, that measure being the Mach or Machiavellianism scale of Richard Christie. Since, in the present case, our validation attempt ended by confirming the opposite of our predictions to a significant extent, it requires a fair amount of masochism for me to outline what our expectations were and then to present the uncooperative results. But, in addition to the fact that I think the results are intrinsically interesting and potentially important, I think that the study illustrates some of the many difficulties faced by the experimenter who wishes to predict from individual difference measures to behavior in complex social situations, and I should like to concentrate on some of these difficulties in discussing the experiment.

Permission to reproduce this paper, which discusses the experiment reported in Jones, E. E., Gergen, K. J., and Davis, K. E. (1962), has been granted through the courtesy of Norman L. Munn, Editor, Psychological Monographs.

In planning the present study, we were interested in exploring some of the variables which condition reactions to being approved or disapproved as a person. We were especially interested in the dependent variable of self-presentation: Does a person change the way he presents himself immediately following disapproval as compared with approval? Is his tendency to change a function of the conditions under which he presented himself in the first place? Finally, are there measurable personal characteristics which affect reactions to approval or disapproval?

In an attempt to shed some light on these questions, we designed the following experiment. Each of 80 female undergraduate subjects was briefly interviewed by two different persons. Although essentially the same questions were asked in each interview, the subjects were differentially pre-instructed concerning their own roles. Half of the subjects were told to be completely accurate in talking about themselves in the first interview. They were instructed to suppose that this was a student counseling interview in which it would be very important to be completely candid and honest. They were told "If you mislead the interviewer... he might end up giving you the wrong advice." I shall call this the accuracy set. The remaining half of the subjects were urged to make a special effort to create a favorable impression. They were instructed to suppose that the interview could be an important factor in determining whether they were qualified for a traveling fellowship to Europe. They were told to "try to create the most favorable picture you can...one which is likely to appeal to the interviewer, even though it does not accurately reflect the picture you have of yourself." This I shall call the hypocrisy set. In all cases, the subjects were led to believe that the interviewers were unaware of any special setting instructions, and the subjects were urged to conceal from the interviewers any cues about the instructions under which they were operating.

Instructions were reversed for all subjects in the second interview. That is, those under accuracy set in the first interview were given the hypocrisy instructions preceding the second interview. The interview itself was brief and highly standardized. The main feature of the interview was an orally administered triads test. Each subject was handed 16 cards by the interviewer, each of which contained three self-descriptive phrases. The phrases had been preselected to tap different areas of the self-concept such as warmth, tolerance, motivation, activity level, dependability. Each of the phrases on a particular card referred to a different one of these areas. One phrase had been judged by several graduate student raters to be a very positive, self-accepting statement (example: "People invariably find me easy to meet and talk to."); one had been judged to fall in the range between slightly positive and slightly self-critical (example: "I usually try to be as sincere with others as I can."); the final phrase was definitely self-derogating in content (example: "In most respects I am a weak and compliant person.") The subject was to examine the phrases on each card and to indicate the one she considered most characteristic of her and the one least characteristic. From the responses to the triads test it was possible to assign each subject a score representing the degree of her tendency to present herself favorably or unfavorably.

In between the first and the second interview, each subject received a standard appraisal sheet from the first interviewer indicating either that the interviewer was quite favorably impressed or quite unimpressed by the subject. For convenience, I shall call these two treatments positive and negative feedback. Subsequent to this differential feedback and some ratings by the subject of the interviewer which will not concern us here, the subject was given instructions for either accuracy or hypocrisy in the second interview and then introduced to the new interviewer. The second interview was identical to the first except that a different, but closely matched, form of the triads test was administered. All subjects received form I during the first interview and all received form II during the second interview. (The Kuder-Richardson reliabilities were I = .801, II = .853, change = .725.)

Our interest here is in the effects of the three independent variables--set, feedback, and Mach score--on self-presentation scores. Having outlined the experimental design, let me now try to explain why we thought Machiavellianism was a relevant variable.

Richard Christie has developed several attitude scales based on concepts taken from the writings of Niccolò Machiavelli. One of these scales, designated Mach IV by Christie, was used in the selection of subjects for the present experiment. According to its author, the items of the scale "express a conception of human nature as fallible and weak, a lack of affect (i.e., the value of detachment in dealing with other people), and the use of expedient procedures in social relations. Those making a high score on the scale endorse such items and reject items of opposed kind, such as those portraying human nature idealistically, emphasizing the need of warmth and affective involvement with other people, and holding that social relations should always be governed by strict adherence to ethical norms." (Christie and Merton, 1958.) In brief, high scorers on the Mach scale tend to be cynical and harsh in their view of human nature and seem willing to tailor the means of social intercourse to the end of augmenting their own power and status.

The Mach scale was chosen as a selection device because it seemed reasonable that high scoring subjects would be more affected than the lows by feedback that they weren't going over so well. We also expected that the highs would tend to blur the distinction between accuracy and hypocrisy sets. Both of these tendencies, we felt, would be reflected in the self-presentation data. Specifically, the lows were expected to vary their behavior as a function of set, but less so as a function of feedback. The highs, on the other hand, were expected to respond about the same way to hypocrisy and accuracy instructions but to modify their self-presentation upon learning that they had created a poor impression in the first interview.

Let us turn to the results, as they are graphically depicted in Figure 13-1. The ordinate of this graph is the

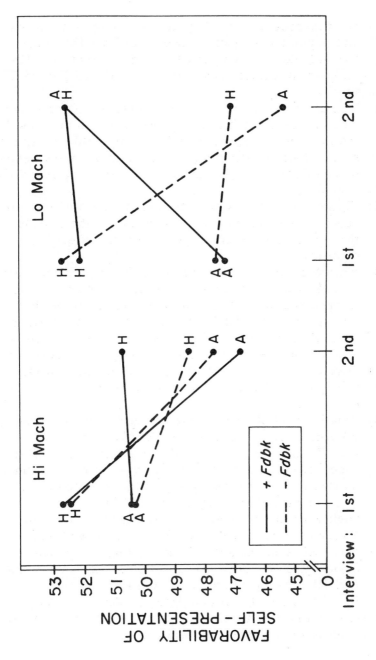

FIGURE 13-1. Favorability of Self-Presentation in First and Second Interviews.

degree of favorability of self-presentation and represents the tendency of the subject to choose positive and reject negative self-descriptive phrases on the triads test. The most important features revealed by this figure are the following:

(1) It is clear that there is a direct effect of instructional set. Those in the hypocrisy set--trying to impress the interviewer that they are of fellowship calibre--tend to stress their good points and play down any weaknesses more than do those in the accuracy set. ($F_{1,72} = 9.59$, $P < .01.$)

(2) These direct effects of instruction in the first interview seem to be more striking with regard to the low-Mach than to the high-Mach subjects, but this effect is not significant.

(3) While this is not too easy to judge by inspection, there is a significant tendency for the scores to change more in the direction of self-criticism after negative than after positive feedback. In other words, there was a main effect on self-presentation of the feedback received, and we can conclude that people in general are affected by approval vs. disapproval in subsequently telling about themselves to others. ($F_{1,71} = 9.27$, $P < .01.$)

(4) Finally, it is clear that high and low scorers responded differently to the receipt of feedback. It is also clear that our expectations about the direction of this difference were dramatically disconfirmed. One may summarize the differences by saying that the lows are much more clearly affected by feedback than the highs. After positive feedback, their self-presentations are quite favorable; after negative feedback, the lows become quite self-effacing and self-derogating. The highs obviously do not show this reaction to the same extent. ($\pm$, HL: $F_{1,71} = 6.50$, $P < .02.$)

For the remainder of this paper I should like to concentrate on this last result and explore the problems which such "negative" findings make salient.

The first problem suggested by the study just described is the difficulty of establishing the validity of a measure when the referent of that measure has no clear conceptual context. In the present study, to speak defensively for a moment, we had little more to work with than intuitions based on a careful reading of item content. I think that such a procedure may be justified on the grounds that validation attempts must start somewhere, but working from face validity is fraught with dangers. Almost all scales which are aimed at important personal dispositions are multidimensional in structure. While one dimension or component may generate a relationship in situation A, perhaps another component will generate a different relationship in situation B. In the present case, our predictions were based on extrapolations from such items as "Never tell anyone the real reason you did something unless it is useful to do so." The results, however, seem more in keeping with a different facet of Machiavellianism, which is tapped by such items as "Anyone who completely trusts anyone else is asking for trouble." In other words, the results suggest that the high scorers are cynical, unaffected by praise or blame from others, and perhaps more than a little suspicious. They give no support to the thesis that high-Mach subjects seek power through gaining the favor of others and attempt to gain this favor by ingratiating changes in self-presentation.

Second, there is the pesky problem of a restricted range of Mach scores in the population from which the high and low samples were drawn. I know that those of you who have worked with the F scale on sophisticated samples are familiar with this kind of problem. Before conducting the present study we knew that the norms for female college students are considerably lower than those for male college students on the Mach IV scale. We also were convinced that female subjects would be more responsive in general to indications that they were approved or disapproved as persons. Since we were actually more interested in the situational variables, we decided to use a female sample.

However, the consequence of this was that our "high-scoring" subjects had an average item score of 4.07 on a seven-point scale. In other words, our "highs" really did not endorse the Machiavellian sentiments expressed on the scale, they merely felt neutral about them or agreed and disagreed in equal parts. It is obvious that we should be very cautious in generalizing the present results to samples of high-scoring males.

Third, there is the question of the possible contribution of social desirability to Mach scores on the one hand and self-presentation scores on the other. Christie informs me that he has found correlations in the 60's and 70's between social desirability (Edwards, 1957) and score on the Mach IV scale for female subjects. In fact, the correlation tends to be considerably higher for females than for males. In our own sample of experimental subjects, we found a correlation of -.50 between Mach IV scores and a measure of social desirability developed by Christie. This correlation was based on 70 out of the 80 subjects. It seems quite reasonable that the low-Mach subjects, since they also tend to be high on social desirability, are the ones who are sensitive to differential feedback. This is consistent with the generally held belief that those persons who tend to endorse socially desirable items do so because they are anxious to make a favorable appearance. Unfortunately for our peace of mind, however, this correlation alone does not solve the mystery represented by our findings on self-presentation. When we partialled out the contribution of social desirability scores, the interaction between Mach score and feedback was slightly reduced, but still statistically significant. Thus the Mach score has a contribution to self-presentation variations which is to some extent independent of the social desirability variable.

Finally, we must face the possibility that the observed interaction, though statistically significant, was actually the result of chance or coincidence. There are two reasons why I think we can have confidence in the descriptive empirical meaning, if not the underlying explanation, of the observed interaction. The first of these reasons comes from the analysis of additional data collected during the experiment. In all of the interviews, before taking the triads test, the subjects were asked to tell which of their personal characteristics they would change if they had a chance, and were also asked to indicate their strong points as a person. Answers to these questions were recorded verbatim by the interviewers and later subjected to content analysis along a five-point scale ranging from extremely other- to extremely inner-directed. The instructions for the inner-directed anchor emphasized the concern with personal integrity, honesty, and independence of judgment. The inner-directed person was described as one who has stern and demanding ideals, the realization of which must be evaluated in terms of his own internalized standards. At the other extreme of the scale, the other-directed person was described by the coding instructions as placing extreme importance on getting along with others. Conformity and the development of an agreeable, inoffensive personality was stressed.

The content analysis was restricted to those protocols of the 40 subjects who responded under accuracy instructions during the first interview. Working without knowledge of Mach scores, three independent coders each judged the protocols of the highs to be significantly more inner-directed than the protocols of the lows. Such a finding seems very much in line with the main results, which emphasize the lows' concern with the opinions of others.

A second reason for having faith in the present results stems from the findings of a recently completed experiment by Exline, Thibaut, Brannon, and Gumpert (1961). These investigators contrived a situation in which subjects were induced by a confederate to cheat while the experimenter was out of the room. The subjects were then confronted by the experimenter and accused of cheating while their reactions to this confrontation were recorded by motion picture and hidden observer. One of their findings was that the higher the subject's score on the Mach scale, the less inclined he was to become implicated in the cheating. Once implicated, furthermore, the highs were much more poised and composed than the lows during the confrontation by the experimenter. In their experiment as in ours, therefore, the low-Mach subjects seemed to be more sensitive to social pressures and their behavior was more markedly influenced by the nature of the social situation in which they found themselves.

In conclusion, it seems to me that we may have shed some light on one aspect of Machiavellianism at the expense of another. Christie and Merton (1958) describe the high scorer on Mach IV as being tough-minded, cynical, and as valuing detachment in dealing with other people. The lows invest more affect in social relations and emphasize the need for warmth and affection. I would say that our results are quite consistent with this emphasis. However, the high's presumed opportunism and drive toward power are certainly not represented in our data. The high Machiavellian female may desire to influence others, but she apparently does not do this by trying to get others to like her.

14 | James Bieri
New York School of Social Work
Columbia University

Analyzing Stimulus Information
in Social Judgments

The behavior of the other person is a very powerful
stimulus condition in social behavior, and has been recognized theoretically. Such formulations as Murray's (1938)
concept of <u>press</u> recognize the importance of what might be
called "content" variables in analyzing the social stimulus
value of another person. A domineering person could provide press for evoking submissive or rebellious behavior
in someone else, depending on the particular content of
that someone's needs. In the present paper I would like to
examine the possibility of still a different conception of the
stimulus value of another person's behavior in terms of
certain formal properties or parameters within which behavior may be construed. To particularize the question:
If we hold constant the <u>type</u> of behavior exhibited by another,
be it dominance, affection, or aggression, does the <u>form</u>
of expression of this behavior serve a stimulus function?
If forms of expression do in fact influence behavior, they
might be expected to affect the social perceptions or judgments one develops about the other. The three formal

The research discussed in this report is supported by grant
M-3611 from the National Institute of Mental Health, U. S.
Public Health Service.

229

properties of any given behavior I wish to explore are its
intensity, its frequency, and its consistency. Before elab-
orating these properties, I would like to consider briefly
the nature of the social judgment process.

　　We may consider the process of perceiving another
person as a series of inferential stages starting with the
other person as a stimulus and culminating in a more or
less organized conception of that person. This inferential
process is mediated through these stages by the cognitive
system or construct system of the perceiver, which may
have certain characteristics in its own right, including
some degree of differentiation or complexity and some degree of integration or organization. It may be helpful to
isolate arbitrarily three points in this process of perceiving another. At point one we have the presence of the other
person's behavior, either directly observed or reported.
Obviously, the nature of the interaction situation can structure and partially determine this behavior, but the behavior
per se provides the primary cues which concern us. At
point two this behavior stimulus becomes "encoded" or
"construed," through the cognitive system, into the formation of a trait impression or personal construct. Note
that an inferential process has already occurred between
points one and two. While the conceptual gap between these
points may not be great, individual differences in the judgments formed can be expected as a result of the perceiver's
personality, cognitive system, and role set. Finally, as
we move to point three, further inferences are made about
the personality of the person being judged. The move to
this third point involves trait integration at some level.
The integration reflects how the person observed fits into
the construct system of the perceiver, or what some call
his lay "theory" of behavior.

　　The preceding analysis permits us to order some of
the research concerning the social perceptual process.
For example, the work of Jones and Thibaut (1958) on
inferential role sets involves the manipulation of situational factors at point one, holding the behavioral stimuli

constant in order to determine the effects of these role sets on the process between points one and three. The work of Asch (1946) and of Bruner, Shapiro, and Tagiuri (1958) on the effects of various trait configurations on other impressions appears to center on the relationships between points two and three. Our present concern centers most nearly upon the relationships between points one and two, i.e., how variations in observed behavior lead to differences in trait judgment. This calls for more specific analyses of the behavior itself, so that its effect on judgment may be more precisely delineated. We begin, then, with discrete behavioral acts of the other person as the starting point in this cognitive process. We propose to analyze the three properties of behavior mentioned above in terms of their influence on the judgment process and to present some initial empirical evidence.

The three properties of behavior we have mentioned-- intensity, frequency, and consistency--are certainly common distinctions which intrude upon the formulations of the personality theorist, the researcher, and the clinician alike. For example, how do we determine how dependent a person is? Let us assume that we have reached some agreement on a class of behaviors as signifying dependency. Now, do we look first at the intensity of the behavior? Or is frequency a more important factor? That is, are we more likely to judge someone "a dependent person" if he is extremely dependent in a few given situations (an intensity statement), or if he is dependent only moderately but in many situations (a frequency statement)? Perhaps there is some subtle joint use of both properties as criteria when we apply a trait label to a person. For example, it is possible that a person must manifest a given intensity of response in a given situation before he meets the criterion of being dependent. Once this threshold has been reached, it may be that we infer that the person will be dependent frequently, i.e., in many different situations. Conversely, it may be that if we observe a person behaving dependently in many situations, we judge him to be an intensely depend-

ent person because we infer that situations do not call for
a dependent response this frequently. As Heider (1958)
has suggested, explanation of behavior by a trait of the
individual must take account of situational demands, and
knowledge of either the intensity or the frequency of behavior, or both, may be necessary in order to isolate situa-
tionally-appropriate from personality-characteristic behavior.

Something like the possible confusion of frequency and
intensity statements by the layman can be found in our
scientific attempts to measure personality constructs such
as dependency. We often measure the "strength" of a need,
an intensity function, on the basis of a frequency assessment, e.g., how often a person selects a certain type of
response on a personality inventory. The person is, in
effect, reporting that he acts dependently in many situations or that he acts dependently more frequently than he
acts in some other way. On the other hand, we may attempt to assess dependency from the Thematic Apperception Test, where intensity may be a more salient factor.
Thus, the degree to which the person's TAT story develops
and elaborates a dependency theme is considered to reflect
the strength of this need. We may then proceed to sum
these intensity judgments on a frequency basis to obtain an
index of motive strength. Perhaps this confusion between
the frequency and the intensity of a response in our assessment helps explain the very low correlations we so often
find between two measures of the same personality variable.

Returning to the role of these properties of behavior
in trait impressions, we may raise the general issue of
whether people can discriminate between the frequency of
a given behavior and the intensity of that behavior in their
judgments of others. We are currently engaged in studies
which we hope may provide some answers to this question.
As one approach to this problem, we presented subjects
with behavioral information about a person and asked for
two types of judgment, one an intensity judgment and one a
frequency judgment. We found that identical scale ratings

were made under each judgmental set. By controlling the amount or frequency of behavioral information and varying its intensity, a more definitive answer to this cognitive problem may be obtained.

Another approach we took to this problem was to determine the relationship between the frequency of behavior information available to a subject and the degree to which he would judge traits related to the behavior to be characteristic of the individual. Two types of behavioral information were studied: information concerning dominance behavior and information concerning love behavior. On the basis of a factor analysis of the Leary (1957) interpersonal checklist, we found that judgments of these two kinds of behavior were substantially independent of each other. Further, dominance and love are important behavioral dimensions which can be used readily to construct specific items of social behavior for stimulus information. A list of eight behavioral acts in each of these two categories was constructed. Behavior was sampled in different interpersonal settings, including family relationships, job relationships, and general social situations. Subjects were given one, two, four, six, or eight items of this stimulus information, all items being consistently either dominance or love behavior. Using a modified rating scale version of the checklist, subjects were asked to rate their impressions of this person on the basis of the information provided. By combining the ratings of the three octants (subscales) of the checklist which had been found to be most heavily weighted on dominance, and by combining the two octants found to be most heavily weighted on love, judgment scores for dominance and love were obtained. For the five groups of subjects who received varying frequencies of dominance information, analysis of variance yielded a significant F value for judged dominance. Similarly, a significant F value was obtained in the analysis of love judgments across the five conditions of frequency. The curves generated on both the dominance and love judgments indicated a linear relationship between increasing frequency of information and the degree to which the requisite trait was judged to be characteristic of the individual up to four items of information. Beyond that point, increasing the frequency of information had little effect.

These findings suggest that a "minimal frequency" principle may mediate trait judgments. That is, trait impressions appear to become locked in on the basis of relatively minimal information, beyond which point additional information is redundant. Our data suggest that for the type of information we are using, this locking-in point occurs at four items of information. These results bear upon the assumption made by Heider (1958), G. A. Kelly (1955), and others that people tend to infer traits immediately from a particular observation of behavior, rather than gradually build up the inference over a series of observations. Our results suggest that while a trait inference can develop from one item of information, increasing the frequency of stimulus information up to a point does affect the certainty with which this judgment is held.

We turn next to the more complicated condition in which the stimulus behavior is not consistent. This third formal property of behavior with which we are concerned refers to the tendency for persons to manifest contradictions in their behavior, to act one way now and in quite the opposite way at another time. We are familiar with the constructs personality theorists have invoked to account for these inconsistencies, such as reaction formation, repression, and compensation. Theoretical distinctions between latent and manifest behavior, or genotypes and phenotypes, also often represent attempts to deal with behavioral inconsistencies. How, we may ask, do persons in their social judgments deal with contradictions in others' behavior? In particular, to what extent does the comparative frequency of a given behavior and its opposite affect the intensity judgments of traits closely allied to the behavior in question? Does the person respond to behavioral contradictions in another person on an undifferentiated, all-or-none basis, or are these contradictions perceived in terms of a continuous function relative to the amount of behavioral inconsistency? Is the form this judgment process assumes specific to the type of behavior involved, or are these judgments general across different behavioral categories?

Our method of approaching these problems called for providing all subjects with the same total amount of information, while varying among groups the degree of contradiction, based upon the relative frequency of information concerning a given behavior and its opposite. For each of the behavioral categories we presented four degrees of contradictory information to the subjects. For example, one group, the 4-4 group, received equal amounts of dominance and submission information, while six groups received either more dominance than submission information or more submission than dominance information, in the proportions of 5-3, 6-2, and 7-1. The order in which either dominance or submission information was presented was counterbalanced to control for any ordering effects on judgments. No such effects were observed except for occasional slight and insignificant primacy effects on some of the judgments. The subjects in these studies came from two groups which will be treated separately in our analyses. One group consisted of about 280 social work graduate students, a predominantly female group, and the other consisted of about 70 Army reserve personnel, a predominantly male group. The subjects were asked to read all the stimulus information and then rate the person, a man, on the modified checklist mentioned above.

The mean trait ratings were plotted against a seven-point scale of contradiction, each point representing the ratio of information given about one of a pair of traits to total information given. For instance, in the case of dominance-submission, the top of the scale represented seven bits of dominance information and one of submission, the midpoint equal amounts of both, and the bottom point one bit of dominance information and seven of submission. The scale was thus linear in terms of the difference in the amount of information given about each trait.

The results for the group of social work students will
be discussed first. Here we find that their judgments of the
love-aggression and aggression-love contradictions conform
fairly well to a linear function. As we plot the amount of
love inferred in the trait judgments against the seven-point
scale, a linear relationship is found, with the intensity of
trait judgments increasing as the scale values representing
the proportion of love information increase. Very similar
results emerge when we plot the intensity of dominance
judgments based upon the dominance-submission contradictory information. Here again, as the scale value of the
difference between dominance and submission behaviors increases, the degree of judged dominance increases. These
results suggest that for these subjects a rather simple cognitive process mediates the perception of an inconsistent
behavior and the ensuing trait judgments. This process is
a weighting of the relative amounts of each type of information and appears to be general across both types of behaviors
studied.

In an initial attempt to determine the generality of this
cognitive judgment process in another population, we presented the same dominance-submission information to a
group of Army reserve personnel. Here we find a somewhat different picture. The gradually increasing linear
judgments of the social workers gives way to what appears
to be a step-wise function for the Army subjects. Thus,
these subjects made judgments of degree of dominance at
both 7-1 conditions and the 4-4 condition practically identical with those of the social workers. However, under the
5-3 condition of predominantly dominance information,
Army subjects sharply increased their judgments of dominance from the 4-4 condition. There was a step-wise
gradient that remained at the same level for the 6-2 and
7-1 judgments. Further, as these subjects received predominantly submission information under the 5-3 and 6-2
conditions, there was only a slight drop in the curve, followed by a significant decrease in dominance judgments
between the 6-2 and 7-1 conditions. Here we have tenta-

tive evidence suggesting that the cognitive process mediating the judgment of inconsistent behavior varies across
populations. Exactly what personality variables may account for such differences we cannot say. However, the
differing sex composition of the two groups suggests that
males' judgments of contradictory dominance behavior
may reflect a need to maintain an enhanced estimate of
dominance in the face of evidence to the contrary. Thus,
males may accept more equivocal evidence than females in
judging a man to be dominant, but require relatively unequivocal evidence before they will tend to judge a man as
submissive. Perhaps we have here a rare example of a
cognitive behavior in which women are less variable or
erratic than men. In any event, a relationship between
need states of the person and judgment patterns is suggested.

If we return to judgment differences across behaviors,
one final set of observations can be made. This concerns
the question of the relative <u>slope</u> of the judgment gradients
for each type of behavior. One way to approach this problem is to ask at what two scale points, equidistant from the
scale midpoint, do significant differences in judged intensity of a trait first occur? For example, do the judgments
based upon a 5-3 predominance of dominance behavior differ significantly from those based upon a similar proportion of predominantly submission behavior? Or does such
a significant difference not occur until the more extreme
6-2 versus 6-2 comparison? Here we find that the type of
behavior judged may determine the scale points at which
judgments differ. Thus, for the love-aggression behavior,
a significant difference in trait judgment is not reached
until the 6-2 ratios are compared. Subjects who receive
5-3 information which is predominantly love do not judge
the person as significantly more loving than persons who
receive 5-3 information which is predominantly aggression.
In regard to dominance-submission behavior, a significant
difference in judgments is made between the two 5-3 groups
in both subject groups studied. We are inclined to believe

that such differences across behaviors may be due to such factors as the relative social desirability of the traits being judged.

These initial analyses of the results obtained to date suggest the fruitfulness of this method in the analysis of cognitive processes which mediate the relationship between certain formal aspects of observed behavior and trait judgments. Our results suggest that a small minimum amount of behavioral information evokes judgments which are relatively constant as further consistent information is provided. This "locking-in" effect does not provide a basis for predicting the judgments when contradictory information is also present. Instead, we find that the judgments reflect a weighting of the relative frequency of each type of contradictory behavior. Important, perhaps, is the suggestion that varying modes of judgment resolution of conflictual information can be observed both as a function of the behavior being judged and as a function of the subjects who are doing the judging. It is apparent, however, that the nature of the judgment process studied is determined in part by the particular methods used. The use of more unstructured response measures should allow for a fuller analysis of cognitive strategies used in resolving contradictory information.

We are particularly interested in extending this work in relation to the analyses of the cognitive processes involved in clinical judgment. Here the need to formulate judgments based upon partial or contradictory evidence is apparent. In this regard, it should be pointed out that we have been concerned here in an essentially cross-sectional time dimension; i.e., all behavioral information is available to the judge at a given time. Such a time relationship is found most nearly in one-shot diagnostic evaluations and in forming first impressions. It would be important to extend our analyses of the cognitive processes of judgments to include the acquisition of information over time, and to study changes in judgments as subsequent inconsistent information became available. Such a process would be analogous to a more longitudinal diagnostic formulation, as in psychotherapy. It would seem reasonable that in this work the use of methods developed to study the processes of attitude change should prove helpful. This could represent yet another approach, to borrow a phrase from Rokeach (1960), to the study of the unity of thought and belief.

15 | Robert P. Abelson
Yale University

Commentary:
Situational Variables
in Personality Research

Personality research in the past ten years has brought
an enormous accumulation of little bits of evidence. There
seems to be some dismay among us that these bits do not add
up to much solid information, but on the other hand there is
considerable optimism and exhilaration over the variety of
problem areas that it now seems possible to attack. Two
lines of progress are heavily responsible for the feeling of
optimism: the large number of new types of personality
assessment devices together with the new computerized ease
of performing multivariate analyses; and the extension of
laboratory manipulations so that a wide range of social situations can be created in a controlled environment.

We are on a plateau eager to scramble on up to higher
peaks. In our haste thus far there are a few things that we
have neglected to bring with us. In particular, there has
been a rather serious neglect of situational variables. I
would like to discuss some sins of commission and omission
in our thinking about situational variables. I will address
myself in particular to the two areas mentioned above: multivariate methods and laboratory manipulations. The main
burden of my message will not be new. You will recognize
in some of my remarks the promptings and warnings of Cronbach (1957) and Cattell (1961, p. 164), among others. Never-

241

theless, I hope that these points will gain force because of their specific relevance to studies reported in this volume.

First let us turn to the clever and resourceful study reported by Jones in the present volume. Some ambiguity of interpretation attaches to the results, and several alternatives might flow from possible response-set artifacts of the Mach scale. I would like to emphasize another source of artifact lurking in experimental studies of this kind. Forgive me if my analysis is gratuitous in some of its particulars, for rhetorical purposes.

We all know that correlation does not imply causation. We all try to be careful in interpreting strictly correlational data. However, when we do an experiment and have a personality scale that was given beforehand, we tend unwittingly to forfeit our caution on the correlation-causation question. We are somehow drawn into the presumption that the personality score must determine the experimental result, overlooking the possibility that a third variable causes both.

Let us examine the Jones experiment with such a possibility in mind. The subjects are undergraduate women. The potentially powerful and unscrupulous person in the experimental situation is not the subject, but the experimenter. It is he who might be the real Machiavellian. The subjects have the opportunity to deceive the interviewers in the situation, but nothing of importance is really at stake in the interview. It is a mock interview. The girls may well be most concerned with the influence they can exert on the experimenter.

The subject, I presume, feels that the experimenter is probing her personality in some way. Overdramatizing somewhat, we may suppose that some of the subjects respond to this situation with awe, dependence and helplessness--they are looking for clues as to how to behave, and are quite responsive to such clues. They do what the experimenter tells them to do; in particular, they "obey" the set instruction. Further, they take more seriously everything that happens, so that the feedback from the interviewer exerts a stronger influence. This group of subjects, we are supposing, is the Low Mach group. Opposed to this pattern, we have a group of girls who are not awed by the experiment, who are more sophisticated, more self-possessed, and not really committed to or threatened by the situation. Such a group would be much more likely to indulge themselves in the cynical responses required to obtain high Mach scores.

In effect, then, the Machiavellianism variable may conceivably be nothing more than a sophistication variable, or a dependency variable, or something a lot more superficial than we would desire. Perhaps it could be argued that the interesting variable, Machiavellianism, includes these surface manifestations, so that we come full circle and end up free of artifact after all. Nevertheless, it is clear that we have here a hornet's nest full of annoyances (not unrelated to the social desirability family) which must be dealt with before we achieve any clarity of interpretation. Our experiments need debugging fully as much as our personality questionnaires do.

The chief bug is situational. The experimenter can objectively manipulate certain conditions, but he cannot easily control the total situation as the subject defines it for himself. The personality scale, in this case the Mach scale, can readily take on a meaning in terms of the subjective experimental situation different from the one it has for the objective experimental situation. An artifact in the scale can find its counterpart in the subjective situation; together they can falsely suggest a real relationship.

There is another way in which insufficient attention to situational variables can inhibit progress in the personality field. Because of an overdependence on static conceptions of personality, situational variables may sometimes be ignored entirely. Wallach in this volume has argued cogently for greater attention to moderator variables. He confines his examples to moderator variables characteristic of persons, however, but one should equally well keep in mind that situational or context variables may serve as moderators. For example, Janis (1958) recently noted a correlation across persons between pre-operative fear and post-operative resentment among patients undergoing major surgery. This relationship is <u>not</u> a general predispositional or characterological relationship; apparently it is moderated by the amount of information available to the patients about the post-operative deprivations to be expected. The relation holds only under low information conditions.

Countless other examples could be given, but the one that intrigues me most is the example which aroused such discussion following Bieri's excellent paper (Chapter 14). Bieri in his research kept frequency and intensity conceptually separate as trait indicators, e.g., as aspects of aggressiveness. In the discussion, it was argued by some participants that the two could not be separated. Campbell pointed out that on the basis of the Guttman or single-factor models one would expect frequency and intensity of aggressive behaviors to be redundant indices of the same trait. But Tomkins and others raised various examples of relative independence of frequency and intensity of aggressive behavior. Although Bieri was concerned with beliefs about frequency and intensity as indices of aggression, the discussion got round to the question of their independence as a matter of empirical fact. On the face of it, this disagreement would not appear to be serious. The single-factor model is either appropriate or not; the way to find out is to collect some data and see what happens.

However, I think that the matter goes deeper than this. Conceivably <u>both</u> points of view were correct--the two indices, frequency and intensity, may be conceptually both independent and cosymptomatic. After all, many instances of nonredundancy of the two can be pointed out, yet we feel intuitively that "aggressiveness" has quite a unitary character.

Having proposed this paradox, I wish to suggest a resolution by referring to a different behavioral example. Consider two responses indicative of <u>thirst</u>: quantity of water consumed, and bitterness of water that will be tolerated before the organism would prefer not to drink. I do not intend here an exact parallel with frequency and intensity. Let us say simply that we have these two alternative indices. Now, if we were interested in whether thirst were a single-factor entity, we might try to investigate this by correlating the above two measures over a set of individual organisms. However, this would be an unnatural approach. Rather, we should vary the drive states of groups or organisms experimentally, say by manipulating hours of deprivation differentially for different groups. Then we would correlate the two response variables on a between-groups basis. The between-groups and within-groups results might well come out differently. The reason for preferring the between-groups procedure might not be immediately apparent. It derives from the type of example. If thirst were indeed properly considered a single-factor state, this factor would be coordinated not to differential individual response patterns, but rather to differential environmental conditions governing the general level of response emergence.

The thirst example forces our thinking away from the traditional individual-differences framework of factor analysis. It ought to force us to rethink our measures of variables involving human motivational systems, viz., much of the personality measurement area. The following general point may be made. To the extent that response variables are controlled by motivational systems which in turn are subject to environmental arousal, the locus of appropriate factorial investigation should shift from the individual-difference level to the environmental-situations level. There is no reason why factor-analytic techniques should be applied at one level but not at the other. However, the greater complexity of a two-level approach might require more complex techniques, such as the generalized discriminant analysis I have outlined elsewhere (Abelson, 1960).

If we are aware of the double level of discourse, much of the confusion and paradox in our discussion of aggressive behavior is abated. Aggressive behavior belongs both to "trait psychology" and to "situations psychology." The occurrence of aggressive responses may be attributed to forces in the person, or in his environment, or in both. Many other responses in the personality measurement area have this

character as well. One must hope that our assessment procedures and psychometric techniques will be broadened so
that they will countenance the important role played by situational variables interacting with person variables in the
personality area. Such interactions are not nearly so critical
in the mental ability area, and it is perhaps because of this
that we have unthinkingly transferred the traditional factor
model from one area to the other.

PART V

Research Strategies

in the Study of Personality

16

Raymond B. Cattell
University of Illinois

Personality Measurement Functionally Related to Source Trait Structure

The particular approach I wish to describe in the present paper is flanked on one side by psychometry and on the other side by clinical psychology. Like any attempt to integrate, it is regarded with suspicion by those on both flanks. Indeed, I suspect that our neighbors regard it properly as a "no man's land," which should be kept wild and barren in order to separate them peacefully one from the other. The cultivation and development of this area in such a way that it requires them to adjust their ideas about one another in a more than verbal and superficial fashion could, indeed, be regarded as a kind of threat. Certainly there is a very real problem of communication here, which should be frankly discussed for the benefit of research, and I propose to do so later in this paper.

The psychometrists, on the one hand, have generally been concerned with the properties of items and the construction of scales, with relatively little interest in substantive personality theories as such. Elsewhere, I have suggested that this is not the whole of psychometrics and that it would best be named item-metrics, the science which deals with the particular properties of response to individual items and with the scaling laws that can be found from them. I did not intend this term to be in any way

249

derogatory, for this is quite a fascinating game, as intel-
lectually challenging as non-Euclidean geometry, and has
attracted some of the best minds of our generation. But I
do want to distinguish between the procedures, on the one
hand, of making a scale with certain desirable properties
in the items and, on the other, of first looking for structure
in the personality, in its biological and sociological aspects,
and then constructing a measurement which is functional in
the sense of being quite specifically oriented to aspects of
visible structure and substructure.

By functional measurement, therefore, I mean the examination of a personality and of the social distributions of
personality in such a way as to discover and recognize the
existence of particular types, of gradients of change in
measurements, and of independent traits which operate in
what may be called broadly the dynamic sense, develop-
mentally and in action.

On our other hand, we have the clinical psychologists,
who have attempted to build up ideas of personality structure from personal observation and through the operations
of their own memories upon the cases they have seen go
through their consulting rooms. It is unfortunately true
that clinicians include among their number a very high percentage who feel restricted relatively little by experimental
methodology, or even by logic; consequently, the whole
region is an immense jungle of conflicting theories, about
which perhaps the best that can be said is that they are
generally entertaining.

One of the problems of scientific cooperation in this
area, about which I shall speak later, rises from the
clinicians' not realizing that the factor analyst and the
multivariate experimentalist is, in fact, setting out with
essentially the same aims as they are. In scientific aims
and philosophical assumptions, there is actually more difference between the classical brass-instrument univariate
experimentalist and the multivariate experimentalist than
there is between the latter and the clinician. Both the
clinician and the multivariate experimentalist are inter-

ested in global influences, which usually express themselves in complex patterns, and are concerned with the integration of these influences in the total personality rather
than with isolated processes, neurological, reflexological,
or such as occur in simple learning. The only difference
is that the multivariate experimentalist proceeds by measuring a great number of experimental variables, followed
by a complex statistical analysis to find the patterns and the
independent influences; whereas the clinician has tried to
do this by virtue of his own memory. Whereas the multivariate experimentalist finds a factor of super-ego strength,
indicating a functional unity which he can demonstrate as a
certain pattern of influence on behavior, the clinician in-
tuits the same unity from a succession of cases. I am not
suggesting that the memory of the clinician is in any way
inferior to that of the best experimentalists, but we must
admit that a fact taken down in a notebook and, in addition,
rendered quantitative is better than one noted through the
corner of one's eye, and that a sample of 20 clinical cases
is not as good a basis for generalization as the 300 to 500
cases that typically enter the studies of the multivariate
experimentalist. The multivariate experimentalist is not
interested only in the clinical field, but insofar as he works
there, he differs principally by quantitative experimental
treatment of data and by using more explicit mathematical
models in putting the results together. The only compen-
sating argument which I can see on the side of the clinician
is that his subjects usually pay him, whereas the experimentalist often has to pay his subjects.

Nevertheless, the fact that the clinician and the multivariate experimentalist are, scientifically speaking,
"brothers under the skin" has not avoided the curse of an
almost complete lack of communication. When a clinician's
conscience finally urges him to become experimental,
indeed, he seems to think only of the traditional, brass-
instrument, "difference of means" design, instead of em-
bracing newer designs that are really closer to the spirit
of his own specialty. The main reason for this lack of

cooperation is that the training of these two specialists is
poles apart. The multivariate experimentalist has to have
a general background of mathematical and statistical training decidedly greater than that which the univariate, traditional experimenter uses; whereas the clinician, by reason
of all that he has to learn for clinical practice, is almost
completely uninterested in mathematical models and similar questions. This has caused the clinician to conlude, at
a superficial glance, that what the multivariate experimentalist is doing cannot have any possible relevance to
him. The paradox is that it does, indeed, have a great deal
to do with him and that some method must in consequence be
found whereby the results and notions of the multivariate
experimentalist can be put at his disposal for that enrich-
ment which would follow if the clinician gave them full play
in his case-work.

Actually, the position in multivariate experimental research in personality has changed a good deal in the last
two or three years. Whereas the first 10 or 15 years of
work in this field bristled with technical issues and grappled
with relatively recondite concepts, this line of development,
in passing from the chaos of its infancy into a certain ma-
turity, has been able to return to concepts and practical
situations important to the clinician, the counselor, and the
educational psychologist. It is this outcropping of the results of new methods in old areas that I particularly want
to discuss in the present paper.

Let us begin by glancing briefly at the history and
methods of research in this area. Although the study of
the structure of abilities is still going forward actively
through the work of such people as Guilford, Meili in
Switzerland, Hofstaetter in Germany, and the many workers
at Educational Testing Service, yet an essential confidence
about the structure in that field had already been achieved
in the 10 years after Thurstone introduced multiple factor
analysis, say by 1940. On the other hand, although personality structure was fairly systematically investigated by
factor analysis during that period and up to 1945, the syste-

matic factor-analytic study of objective measures of personality did not begin until somewhere between 1945 and 1950. The work of Eysenck's laboratory and our own at Illinois, as well as the contributions from smaller centers, such as Sydney in Australia, and individual studies by members of Educational Testing Service, are essentially matters of the last 12 years. By contrast with Eysenck's approach, which clung closely to existing clinical concepts in taking variables for factor analysis, our own approach was that of representative experiment, aiming to take as stratified a sample as possible of general behavior in normal people and to find any factor dimensions existing therein.

The general research strategy is first to discover factor patterns which replicate satisfactorily in two or three different samples, then to form hypotheses about the nature of each of these factors, and to continue the experiment with new tests which are expected, according to the hypothesis, to load high on one of the factors and zero on another factor, and so on. Thus, the first concepts are reached not by an armchair approach but by observing the patterns which gradually emerge from a search for simple structure in a great array of variables. After that, one proceeds by the usual hypothetical-deductive cycle in which the hypothesis suggests an experiment, and the experiment suggests an amendment of the hypothesis. Thus, one proceeds by just the same generalized sequence as in a univariate experiment, the differences being, first, that a factor pattern is decidedly more directive in shaping the necessary hypothesis than is a change on the single variable and, second, that the check by replication of a factor pattern is decidedly more exacting than checking that the score on a single variable differs from its score on another occasion. There are now some 20 reasonably well replicated patterns known in objective personality measurements, and these have been given both fixed index numbers, in order not to prejudice their interpretation irrevocably, and tentative names which represent the stage of precision to which the corresponding hypotheses have been checked at a given time.

If these new patterns are found to agree with existing
clinical concepts, it is a matter of considerable psychological interest and also an occasion for some rejoicing.
However, the rejoicing is not on account of any supposed
confirmation which the existence of the clinical concept
gives to the factor pattern. Psychoanalysis may go in for
an apostolic succession of authority concerning concepts,
but in science we cannot judge the new by the old--we do not
attempt to graduate a modern electrical or pressure ther-
mometer by means of an old mercury Fahrenheit thermom-
eter, nor do we check the proof of time on an electrical
clock by the original medieval water clock. This does not
mean that one seeks deliberately to break with historical
concepts. Indeed, it happens that we do find factors, both
by R- and P-techniques, which correspond to the clinical
notions of an ego-structure and a super ego-structure, and
we also find a second-order anxiety factor which fits very
closely indeed the Freudian conception of anxiety and its
manifestations (Cattell, 1957). The rejoicing over this
arises, however, not from any belief that the clinical evidence can confirm the factor-analytical, but rather from
the facts that a junction has been made between investigators tunneling from two sides of a formidable mountain and
that clinical speculations or theories offer some suggestions
for experimental work with the factors which may extend
their utility in many directions.

With this general introduction, I should now like to look
more closely at the actual mental processes and experimental sequences involved in the emergence of meaning for
a factor, for it is the guidance from these interpretations
which assists the construction of new personality tests.
Some of our earliest experiments in 1947 and 1948 revealed
a factor which had the following pattern: a large loading
for mean galvanic skin deflection in response to threat
stimuli; a loading on a paper-and-pencil test called "absence
of questionable reading preferences," which showed a tendency to choose safe rather than blood-and-thunder titles;
a third loading for much slowing of reaction time by com-

plex instructions (we measured the subject's reaction time in a simple situation and then put him in a situation with complex instructions and measured the lengthening of his reaction time); and a fourth loading for slow speed of closure in Gestalt completion, which had been used to mark one of Thurstone's perceptual factors. Now to proceed to a factor concept one begins by looking at two tests which load the factor and asking what they could have in common. One usually finds several possibilities, which are duly noted. One then turns to a third test which loads the factor and asks what each of the first two tests could have in common with the third one, thus usually reducing the number of possibilities that existed merely in the relation of one to two. For example, when we take absence of questionable reading preferences and much slowing of reaction time by complex instructions, we might say that these reflect some sort of "character" factor, marked by high aspirations. The individual presumably does not want to make errors in the complex reaction time situation and slows down a good deal in order to be sure that he won't make errors. In the reading preference he has an aspiration to better types of reading and wishes to avoid the cheap and sensational. A second hypothesis from these two tests is that this pattern, which incidentally we had indexed as U. I. 17, represents a tendency toward timidity, for it can be said that the avoidance of sensational literature is really due to an emotional timidity and that the slowing down of reaction time is also an inhibition through a timid disposition. If now we add consideration of a third variable, namely, the large mean GSR deflection, we begin to shift our concept even more toward that of timidity, for the size of deflection to threat stimuli might be considered an indication of the magnitude of the fear response. Similarly, the slower closure on the Gestalt completion test might well be interpreted as a greater caution. This individual wants to be very sure that he has the right answer before he ventures to give any response.

Accordingly, we entered the next series of experiments in 1950 with an intention to distinguish between some hypotheses about U. I. 17: first, that it was high aspiration level; second, that it was dispositional timidity; and third, that it was high general inhibition from sources other than timidity. As a test of the aspiration-level hypothesis, we inserted a variety of measures having to do with aspiration and tenacity in reaching goals. As a test of the general inhibition hypothesis, we introduced a number of measures of carefulness of procedure, such as a maze test in which the individual was scored on the number of times he cut across lines and a copying test in which he was measured on the exactness with which he reproduced figures. As a test of the timidity hypothesis, we added a finger-maze test in which the individual first ran his finger, behind a screen, as far as he could through the grooves of a maze, and then did the same thing under conditions in which he would be liable to receive an electric shock for excessive activity. We also introduced a test of the time required to name an object becoming visible through a process of dark adaptation of the eye. We argued that if the slow speed of closure arose from caution rather than from any disability in perceptual skill as such, it would also show up in another sensory test in which the same kind of perceptual ability is not involved. The outcome of the next factorization (Cattell, 1951) was a good crucial experiment in that it distinguished pretty sharply between these hypotheses and indicated that the general inhibition hypothesis was the nearest: The factor proved to load quite substantially the reduction of finger-maze activity by shock; it also loaded a measure of carefulness of procedure and a new test of the tendency to see threatening objects in unstructured pictures. The concept of general inhibition has moved forward a good deal since these 1948 and 1951 publications, for U. I. 17 has now been replicated in at least eight separate factor-analytic experiments--nine, if we count the recent research by Damarin and Warburton which has not yet been published.

Let us look at another factor which has proved to be one of rather wide theoretical interest. In a study based on 500 airmen (Cattell, 1955), we found a factor which loaded high annoyability, tendency to acquiesce (that is, to give the agree rather than the disagree response in a random set of opinionnaire items), and a test of modesty or lack of confidence in untried performances. Since this factor, indexed as U. I. 24, also loaded higher achievement in school (higher verbal achievement, specifically), one possibility was that we were dealing with an ambition or a need for achievement, the irritability and other features being a characteristic of the greater frustration which naturally arises with stronger drive. On the other hand, there were some features which suggested that we were dealing with anxiety. The indications lie in a test of high emotionality of comment; in the above-mentioned irritability, which is commonly regarded clinically as a sign of anxiety; and in the test of modesty in untried performances, which perhaps would now be reinterpreted in the light of this context as a lack of confidence in what one could do in a new situation. Actually, for publication purposes, we compromised at that time with the title "Anxiety to Achieve" and persisted with crucial tests for both hypotheses. The cycle of deduction from hypothesis and experiment, which Scheier went through intensively on this factor in the succeeding five years and which is included in our recent book, The Meaning and Measurement of Neuroticism and Anxiety (Cattell and Scheier, 1961), clearly indicated that this factor was identical with the clinical concept of anxiety. For example, we included later such measures as low electrical skin resistance, tremor, and physiological measures of anxiety such as excretion of hippuric acid, ketosteroid excretion, etc., as well as clinical ratings on anxiety. Moreover at this juncture, between 1955 and 1958, a new source of evidence came into the picture, namely the agreement of objective personality factors with the second-order questionnaire factors, about which I shall speak in more detail shortly. Examination of correlations with the reference vector showed clearly that the objective test factor aligns itself closely with the anxiety factor in questionnaires, and we have also shown that it aligns itself with the anxiety pattern in psychiatrists' ratings.

Another factor pattern which has had a lively conceptual history and is at the present moment highly relevant to a good deal of experimental work is the pattern of U. I. 22, which we call Corticalertia. This factor received major loadings for fast irregularly-warned reaction time, high oscillation of performance, high speed of alternating perspective, high reading speed, and various measures of tendencies to overreact. The first impression might be that it is a general speed factor, but it will quickly be noticed that there are indeed several other factors which have speed measures in them and, conversely, that this factor is a measure of only a particular kind of speed. It is not speed in intellectual performances, such as would arise from high general ability, nor is it speed in complex performances of any kind; it is, rather, speed at a simple, neurological level. In pursuit of a hypothesis of high cortical alertness (which we soon indicated by its title, Corticalertia) as opposed to functioning at a more hypothalamic level, we introduced measures of flicker fusion and of various kinds of reaction time requiring special alertness. We also used the instrument we have called the figitometer, which gives the number of minor adjustive movements which the person is constantly making. This factor has now been replicated in no fewer than 10 independent studies extending from 1948 to 1960. All of these studies seem to indicate that the concepts which are floating around in different fields of psychology under such titles as arousal in the work of Lindsley (1957) or activation in neurological areas are essentially perceptions of this Corticalertia factor. We hypothesize that it is primarily the degree of awakeness of the subject and represents the degree of activity in various reverberatory circuits, especially the degree of cortical innervation and stimulation occurring through the reticular system.

In this connection, the question arises whether in these factors we are always dealing with traits or whether sometimes we are dealing with states. It seems to be true that P-technique and incremental R-technique factor analyses, which should reveal states, generally reveal the same factors as those which are discovered by static R-technique, i.e., individual difference measures. This is an important and gratifying proof that what we call functional unities are functional unities in some further sense than that they merely occur in the individual difference context. But at the same time it does create the necessity for an analysis-of-variance study which will show how much of the existing variance is due to state differences and how much to trait differences. The indications are that although decided differences exist within one individual in the state of alertness or awakeness at a given moment, there are also systematic differences for individuals averaged over a day. That is to say, some people live at a higher level of arousal than others. We find, for example, that this factor differentiates good air pilots from poorer ones, in the sense that the good pilots are at a higher level of alertness, and it also differentiates neurotics from normals at the P = .001 level, the normals being at a higher activation level.

There are psychologically fascinating things to be said about all 20 of the factors which we now know, and it is regrettable to have to confine comments to only two or three. Particularly interesting are those factors, like U. I. 22, which have never appeared before in clinical or general discussions of personality and which are evidently among the more subtle patterns that can only be unearthed by systematic multivariate research.

Let me now turn to a brief overview of the methodological situation. First, I would point out that, in general, these functional unities are proven by something beyond the ordinary R-technique of individual difference study. In the absence of any really adequate, statistical test of the significance of a loading, we are compelled, as Tucker has said, to base our convictions about a factor on the existence of several replications with blind rotation. For this reason, we have usually replicated a factor at least four times, and sometimes up to 10 times, before looking at it from these other aspects of P-technique and incremental R-technique analysis, or any other experimental approach that could check the functional unity, e.g., seeing whether the pattern responds as a whole to a stimulus. But I do want to stress that our approach differs from that of many psychometrists in that we have looked at the functional unity in terms of process and P-technique as well as in terms of individual differences and R-technique. Secondly, I want to make this point: the methodology of hypothesis testing by entering a new factor analysis with variables which should load the factor more highly if a given hypothesis is correct does not reveal the whole story. In work on the meaning of a factor it is most important to include in the experiment, if possible, the whole set of known factors simultaneously. For although it is important to know whether a certain factor is loaded with certain variables, it is also important to know what variables do not load the factor. Again, as illustrated by the example of U. I. 22, one might easily be misled into supposing that a certain factor is, say, a general speed factor, if one did not also have the company of other factors which, in the very same factor analysis, also contained speed variables.

Finally, in this methodological discussion I would like to emphasize the very decided difference in meaning brought about through a multivariate as opposed to a univariate approach. There is now in the laboratory compendium of objective personality tests a total of some 500 different miniature situations--stylistic, projective, and other types of tests, most of them new, but some markers from studies before 1945 and others representing variables studied by other investigators using univariate methods; e.g., measures of rigidity, aspiration level, acquiescence, etc. It is interesting to see how much more quickly one gets to the psychological sources of variance in these single variables by having included them in a multivariate approach. Thus, in experiments done in 1946 and 1947, we included a number of formal behavior scores obtainable from opinionnaire-type tests. We were not interested in the opinions or questionnaires as such, but we were interested, first, in the tendency to fluctuate in response from occasion to occasion;

second, in the tendency to use extreme categories rather than middle categories; third, in the tendency to acquiesce, i.e., to check more agree than disagree responses; and so on through half a dozen formal types of measurement, including social desirability of response. The relations of the tendency toward extreme response, acquiescence, and the tendency to make socially preferred responses were reported in 1951 (Cattell, 1951) and were repeated in several studies in the next five years. It soon became evident that the tendency to agree, i.e., acquiescence, was divided pretty evenly in its variance between the anxiety factor and U. I. 20, the tendency to conform to conventional standards, which we have called Comention. On looking at this behavior from a dynamic viewpoint, one can well appreciate that two principles at work in determining acquiescent responses might be willingness to conform and fit in with social authority, on the one hand, and a timidity or anxiety which undermines the individual's confidence in disagreeing, on the other. Similarly, in another single test, such as the perceptual motor rigidity test, it is noticeable that the variance is divided pretty evenly, in this case among three factors: the neurotic, ergic regression factor, U. I. 23; a factor, U. I. 26, seemingly concerned with deficiency of the self-sentiment; and a factor, U. I. 29, which looks like ordinary fatigue. Surely it should not surprise us that the great majority of specific behaviors divide their variance among different sources of this kind, and it does show the futility of trying to represent a single concept of any general importance by a single variable. It is also an interesting historical commentary on the difference in emphasis of research in the testing field. For whereas many who have worked with questionnaires and opinionnaires have tended to regard these responses as intrusive nuisances in the questionnaire mode of measuring personality (Cronbach, 1950), we have treated these formal behaviors from the beginning as important pieces of real behavior that should be understood through, and can contribute to, the total setting of objective personality tests.

In this survey I can comment only very briefly on the complex and much debated relationship of factors discovered in one medium, such as the rating or the questionnaire medium, to those found in another, such as the objective test medium of experiment and observation. The early studies by Saunders and myself (Cattell and Saunders, 1950) seem to point to a complex, not to say chaotic, picture of interrelationships across media. But around 1955 we had a slight break in the clouds which threw very hopeful illumination on at least one paired relationship, that between questionnaire factors and objective test factors. We then found two instances where a second-order factor in the questionnaire medium aligned with a first-order factor in objective tests. We measured the same subjects on both objective tests and questionnaires and when we factored what had been primaries in the 16 PF into second-order factors, we came upon an almost perfect alignment between the second-order anxiety factor in the 16 PF and the first-order objective-test factor labeled U. I. 24, which has just been described above as anxiety. We also found an alignment between the second-order factor of extraversion-intraversion in the 16 PF and U. I. 32, which we had already hypothesized to be an extraversion factor. Since then there have been two more instances, namely with U. I. 19 and U. I. 22, in which a clearly replicated second-order questionnaire factor has aligned itself with the objective-test factor. In operational terms, the correlation of the reference vector for the objective-test primary with the questionnaire primaries is the same as that of the correlation of the questionnaire primaries with the second-order factor independently found in their midst by questionnaire factoring. How far this relationship will go is not certain. I suspect that a lot of the space spanned by objective tests simply does not exist in questionnaires, but the important thing is that where the space overlaps, we are getting the same kind of structure. This is an added source of confidence in the reality of the personality concepts with which, for the last 10 years, we have been directing our search for objective personality measurements.

From the standpoint of test development, there are two clearly distinct procedures in the approach we have taken: First, establish the concept that one is dealing with in a given factor, and second, establish the construct validity or, as I would prefer to call it, the concept validity of a particular measurement. This is quite different from either trying to validate a test against some concept which cannot be tied down by its author in quantitative terms or attempting to validate a test against specific life criteria with no intermediary between the test and the criterion in the applied field. It might not be necessary to comment on the value of concept validity were it not that some theoretical psychometrists, as well as some highly practical industrial psychologists, seem quite content to proceed from the validation of an ad hoc test to a highly particularized criterion. The value of the concept-validity approach is surely that we are enabled to do something more than make a merely actuarial prediction. The meaning of the factor includes such information as that its variance in a particular group might be expected to be less than in some other group; that it has more (or less) constitutional than environmental determination; that its typical age curve in our society is of such and such a kind; that it might respond to a traumatic situation in such and such a way, etc. Surely if we are to be more than "psychological accountants," all this extra information is of considerable value and enables us to apply psychological laws, so that in fact our predictions from a test today to behavior a year hence are decidedly better than could be made on purely statistical grounds.

An important motive, therefore, in the search for the meaning of factors is to be able to extend predictions by the application of psychological as well as statistical laws. It was for this reason that our research immediately after the factor definition tackled a problem which should be one of the first to guide further hypotheses, namely the nature-nurture ratio for the principal objective test factors. This was done by Stice, Blewett, Beloff and others in extensive studies of various relational groups in Chicago, New York, and Boston a few years ago (Cattell, Stice, and Kristy, 1957; Cattell, Blewett, and Beloff, 1955). The evidence showed that U. I. 22, the Corticalertia factor, for example, is about 90% environmentally determined; whereas U. I. 20 and U. I. 19 come much nearer to intelligence in being largely constitutionally determined. It is for this reason also that we have made studies of the life course of various factors, so that we know, for example, that anxiety (U. I. 24) tends to run high through adolescence and then drop thereafter, or that ego-strength tends to rise through most of the life period, or that surgency tends to decline through much of the life period, and so on. The recent work of Scheier (cf. Cattell and Scheier, 1961) on stress situations has also shown the effect of examinations and other stresses upon levels of certain of these factors. One can barely do more than mention this work in progress, but I think we can confidently anticipate that in the next two or three years there will be a very great development in the meaning of personality factors, increasing their utility for all types of test users. For example, Professor John Butcher of the University of Manchester, England, has recently concluded an extensive series of surveys of urban and rural children, investigating the prediction of school achievement when personality factors and also dynamic factors are measured as such, in addition to the ability factors. The evidence indicates that the prediction of school achievement is just about doubled by adding the personality factor variance to the ability variance. Moreover, the way in which particular factors operate makes very good psychological sense. For example, other things, such as intelligence, being equal, the child with greater ego-strength makes the greater progress, and the more schizo-thyme child, who is happier with books than with people, makes greater progress in verbal ability.

Perhaps, like most researchers, we are impatient, but it seems to us that the feedback since 1955, when most of these personality measures were first made available, should have been decidedly greater than it has been. The use of replicated personality factors in education, industry, the clinical field, etc., would obviously result in an increase in the meaning of the factors far greater than could be achieved by work in the laboratory alone. Moreover, in the second of the above tasks--namely, the production of good batteries through the invention of new objective tests to measure a given factor even better--it seems that a vast realm of creativity remains untapped. The number of people who have a flair for inventing good objective tests must be considerable, judging by the output of isolated procedures. One cannot help feeling that if more of this ingenuity had been turned to constructing concept-valid tests in terms of the known factors, the progress towards batteries with respectable validity would have been much faster.

There is some problem here of communication between the clinically oriented people who invent test measures and the statistically trained people who can follow the more intricate factor-analytic researches on personality structure. I would estimate, moreover, that there is about a five-year lag between basic research and its effective application. Batteries for the replicated objective tests, especially the objective analytic test battery, were first made available in 1955. Admittedly, they were cumbersome batteries, because one had to utilize a dozen or more subtests in order to achieve a reasonably acceptable estimate of each factor, but they were no more complicated to administer than most of the laboratory measures any good psychologist handles. Of course, if one looks in other areas, one sees a similar lag. Captain Lancaster discovered the cause and cure of scurvy at sea in 1605, but sailors died of scurvy for two hundred years more before naval surgeons acted on the discovery. In our time 13 years elapsed between Fleming's discovery of penicillin and its availability for use in clinical medicine. Perhaps psychologists should not grumble at a delay of five years. In fact, there has been a most encouraging acceleration in feedback from the applied fields during the last two years. For example, there are studies by Hutchinson and White at the University of Toronto on neurotic and normal groups, by Swenson in Tennessee on alcoholics and others, by Butcher on educational prediction, by Migliorino and Meschieri in Italy on clinical and industrial predictions, by Saul Sells in pilot selection, by Dubin and Scheier on psychotics, by Spreen in Germany on the affect of drugs upon personality, by Robert Knapp on response to stress in submarine crews, and many other pioneer undertakings from which we should soon have much more systematic knowledge about the predictive situations in which these personality dimensions are important. It should be emphasized that not a single such experiment yet reported has failed to uncover some significant relationship between a personality factor so measured and the real-life criterion involved in the study. Nevertheless, this work now going on still leaves large areas unexplored, and people from our own laboratory have gone out themselves to obtain data where conspicuous neglects appeared. This is very interesting to us, for in a sense the payoff of all this work is the significance of the criterion predictions. Yet from the standpoint of scientific strategy this is an uneconomic and poor arrangement; people who have the unusual, complex training in structural analysis are spending their time in work which could be done by clinicians, who do not need to know the factor-analytic techniques but only how to use the tests and who have, moreover, far better skills in clinical and measurement situations.

Let us not delude ourselves that work in this area will go ahead automatically. It is only by a very fortunate concatenation of circumstances that a research center of this kind for the investigation of personality structure can be brought effectively into being. One needs a laboratory team composed of experts in statistical and especially factor-analytic research, and of clinicians and others with good intuitions about the behavior to be expected from factors and, therefore, about the kinds of test situations that might be useful measures of such factors. One needs, moreover, the installation of a really good electronic computer and

the creation of computing programs. All this takes years
to bring about. One needs, also, opportunities for full-
time concentration on research and a guarantee of continuity to pursue the hypothetico-deductive spiral over many
years. All this is only obtainable with difficulty by the
average member of a university faculty. It is not surprising, then, that out of the hundreds of psychological laboratories in this country and abroad, the laboratories making
systematic contributions in this field can be counted upon
the fingers of one hand. Good research planning would,
obviously, conserve these teams to work specifically on
the basic structural problems themselves. At the same
time it would coordinate such a laboratory team with prac-
ticing clinicians and educators, as well as with theorists
working with controlled experiments. The latter should be
able to avail themselves of the instruments without having
to go through all the work required to produce factor measures as such, just as it is desirable that those skilled in
refined factor work should not have to spend too much time
in criterion validation in the field. Only by such social
organization of research can we obtain in a reasonable
time an understanding of the meaning of many of these
personality factors, and such understanding of functionally
meaningful measurement is the necessary basis for inte-
grating psychometrics with general psychological principles
and laws.

17 Robert R. Holt
New York University

A Clinical-Experimental Strategy
for Research in Personality

I have been asked to state an alternative position to Dr. Cattell's on the strategy of research and theory-building in the field of personality. He has presented some unorthodox proposals, so I find myself cast in a novel and somewhat uncomfortable role: the proponent of the status quo, the voice of conservatism. In these matters, I lay no claim to originality; therefore, I can only summarize here my version of an approach that seems to me quite widely accepted.

Conservatism connotes dogmatism to me; therefore, let me start by arbitrarily enunciating ten principles of faith.

1. The subject matter of personology (Murray's term for the psychology of personality) is human lives in all their multitudinousness and in all their aspects, whether secret and shameful or trivial and banal.

2. To save itself from being choked by the abundance of its subject-matter, personology must concentrate its best efforts on those aspects of lives that appear crucial or critical to the understanding and the prediction, ultimately,

Written during a fellowship at the Center for Advanced Study in the Behavioral Sciences, 1960-61. I am grateful to my friends, Silvan Tomkins and David Wallace, for critical readings of the first draft of this paper.

269

of the important events of life. This statement is of course
riddled with value judgments like "crucial" and "important."
So:

   3. Some general theoretical orientation is vital to the
study of personality to give guidance and orientation through
the bewildering thickets of phenomena, and to help decide
what is important. Everyone, of course, has his theoretical
orientation; most people today would agree that it is desirable to make it explicit. Mine is Freudian with an ego-psy-
chological slant derived largely from Rapaport (1960).

   4. From this vantage-point, among the critical variables to be dealt with are (a) motivations--especially unconscious ones; (b) inward, implicit and reluctantly revealed
behaviors like fantasies, dreams, aversions, fears, and
hopes; (c) ego-structural parameters of most behavior such
as enter into the best diagnostic formulations (e.g., defenses), but including also such conflict-free matters as
coping resources (Murphy, 1960) and style of cognitive
control (Gardner, Holzman, Klein, Linton, and Spence,
1959); (d) pathological tendencies, whether the subject be
explicitly a patient or not; and (e) the subject's view of and
feelings about himself in all their social and somatic embeddedness, which I prefer to call identity, following Erikson
(1959), but which is less comprehensively conceptualized as
self-concept or body-image.

   5. The fact that many of these critical variables cannot
today be measured with highly satisfactory reliability does
not mean that they should be neglected; personology must
forge ahead as best it can, muddling through if necessary
but never taking its eye off the main chance.

   6. Since many of the crucial phenomena of lives are
kept secret and can be elicited neither by a researcher's
bland smile and assurance that all data will be kept strictly
confidential, nor by the apparent anonymity of an objective
test, personality research cannot do without the two highly
suspect types of data provided by projective tests and by the
psychotherapeutic interview--the first a technique to circum-
vent the subject's wariness, the second to meet it head on

and offer it a good reason for being abandoned. But breadth requires eclecticism, and the contributions of objective testing methods must not be eschewed, either.

7. The explorations of psychotherapists and psychoanalysts incidental to their therapeutic practice are a vital source of discoveries about personality.

8. In the total program of personology, such exploratory research must be followed up by more formalized investigations aimed at the verification of precisely formulated propositions. The latter type of research must have a design that is essentially experimental, though it need not take place in a laboratory.

9. Even when an experiment has been set up to test a specific proposition as rigorously as possible, it is essential that the experimenter take every advantage of his opportunities to learn something new, to form new hypotheses, to observe unexpected parameters, and to ascertain the embeddedness of the phenomena under scrutiny in the personalities of his subjects by means of multiform assessment of them.

10. Finally, the attempt must be made continually to confront the guiding theory with experimental fact, to develop small-scale theories that may be consistent with the larger model, and to modify or reject concepts repeatedly found wanting.

Here is a decalogue, a draft of an investigatory credo. There remains little but to expand, expound, examine, and exemplify these statements.

Let me go back to the beginning, then. Clearly, I follow Murray (1938) and White (1952) in defining the subject matter of personology as human lives. Personology is scientific biography, and the genetic method can hardly be dispensed with even when the aim is just to understand a contemporary cross-section of a man. From this perspective, even the carefully standardized biographical inventory (which strives to make life-history data objectively measurable and which can be highly useful) obviously cannot provide all the necessary data for the illumination of the

unique life: at a minimum, the autobiography and structured interview must be added.

It is obvious that the student of personality runs a
danger of becoming overwhelmed by the quantity of data
that can be obtained on a single case, let alone on a sample.
A moderately exhibitionistic, deferent, abasive, or verbally
fluent subject can easily fill a file drawer with material for
any experimenter who has anything of the collector's bent.
Faced with this embarrassment of riches, many a personologist makes simplifying assumptions to prevent drowning
in data. Some decide that a single test (typically the Rorschach, but sometimes the MMPI or TAT) measures the
total personality, and they concentrate on that. Others exclude all data that are not measured with specifiable and
respectable reliability and validity, which cuts the task
down enormously. Still others decide that only the patient's
own words, uttered from a horizontal position and filtered
through a trained therapist, really mean anything. It might
be fruitful to look at the problem from the standpoint of
J. G. Miller's (1960) list of strategies for coping with an
overload of informational inputs; I am sure they would all
be exemplified in the working practices of the various students of personality.

My own Guide for the Perplexed is psychoanalytic
theory. Whatever its faults--and it has them in generous
supply--it has the great virtue of having been based on pro-
longed contact with people who were willing to talk about
many sides of themselves for many hours, nay, years.
Such a quantity of direct contact with its subject matter,
human lives, is unparalleled in this field, and gives psychoanalysis the same kind of advantage that the diagnosing
internist of today has over his pre-Victorian antecedent who
never got a chance to take an unobstructed look at the suf-
fering body. Psychoanalytic theory, as modified and extended by such workers as Rapaport, Hartmann, and Erikson, has the additional advantage of being broader in scope
than almost any other approach to personality, providing
at least a rough scaffolding into which may be fitted specific

partial models for the explanation of a limited class of phenomena.

Under my fourth point, I have listed or alluded to the principal classes of variables with which I think person-ologists must deal. The list is intended to indicate a mini-mum, not to exclude other variables from consideration, and is more miscellaneous than it should be, containing concepts on all levels of abstraction. Likewise, when it comes to specifying the particular variables to be assessed under each of my five major headings, there are no guide-lines that enable us to list coordinate and cleanly differen-tiated concepts. We must work with a variety of uneasy compromises: variables that overlap, that approach be-havior on different conceptual levels, and that differ in degree of specificity. Some of the ones we use at the NYU Research Center for Mental Health are derived rather di-rectly from theory (e.g., primary and secondary process and their components); others are frankly empirical and commonsensical (e.g., breadth of interests, hostility towards the opposite sex); still others derive from psy-chologists' common heritage (e.g., vividness of imagery, social sensitivity); some own to a few factor analysts on their family trees (e.g., variables of ability and of cogni-tive control; we also work with the constructs purportedly measured by factored tests).

Am I setting up a perfect target for Dr. Cattell's shoot-ing-iron? No, because of my fifth commandment. It would be unwise and hardly feasible to factor the variables we work with because so many of them are necessarily meas-ured with such poor reliability and on such small samples. If you make intensive studies of personality, you are re-stricted to small samples with few degrees of freedom. All the more reason for a stern psychometric purification? I don't think so. Factor analysis and the other tools of the psychometrician are splendid for certain purposes, but not for all. When ratings of personality have been factored, they have sometimes yielded variables with so little intui-tive meaning that they could not be rated directly, and not measured in any other way either.

It is good to know something about the redundancy in
your conceptual equipment, but not to eliminate all of it.
Measuring personality is in part a communicative process,
and it is by now well established that a certain amount of
redundancy is vital to efficient communication. When the
only way we can get hold of an aspect of personality quanti-
tatively is to rate it, I believe that we ought to do our best
to rate it well. Raters are seldom able to make much use
of a set of factor loadings as the definition of something to
be extracted from a mass of rich, qualitative data. What
is to be rated has to be defined in such a way as to make
rating possible and to make it as reliable as is feasible.
With the proper conceptual and practical training, raters
can perform prodigies, but there is a question of diminish-
ing returns: For any given research, is it worth the enormous investment of time to train raters to quantify something that doesn't make intuitive sense, or something that
can't be rather directly inferred from the data available?
Such practical issues have a lot to do with the particular
set of variables you actually end up with.

As I hope I have made amply clear, theoretical issues
require the retention of some variables that cannot be
quantified with any elegance whatsoever. Doubtless there
are many who will disapprove of the determination to keep
up the struggle to use such refractory concepts. Let them
reflect on the history of medicine: If physicians of the 19th
century--an era when on the whole the medical profession
did more harm than good--had given up the attempt to cure
diseases they could do nothing for, and if instead they had
stuck to what they did have demonstrable success with,
their patients would have undoubtedly been happier and
healthier in the short run, but we wouldn't be today.
Modern scientific medicine developed only because the old,
primitive medical men stuck at it and kept plugging as best
they could. Similarly, if we in psychology turn away from
the attempt to measure unconscious motives, for example,
because of the fact that this can't be done today with demonstrable reliability or validity, this vitally important area

of personality will be neglected. The psychoanalysts can't be expected to provide such measures, and the factor analysts working with pencil-and-paper tests, objective performances, or physiological measures, surely won't. As our science progresses, we should hope to see ratings progressively supplanted by tests or other objective techniques, but for the immediately foreseeable future, the personality researcher will have to cope with many variables as best he can by means of rating scales.

The dangers of this position are not to be denied or ignored. The personologist must not forget that many of his conceptual tools are in constant need of replacement or overhauling; he runs the danger of fooling himself that he is really measuring something like the superego or the sense of identity just because he is making the effort to do so. We have to be constantly on the lookout for unwanted consequences of conceptual redundancy (as in getting too excited by a string of significant findings involving a group of variables that essentially measure the same thing), and must at least try to measure that redundancy so that we can be aware of it and allow for it (and here I welcome the aid of factor analysis). In general, my formula for tolerating the ambiguity and disrespectability of concepts and measuring devices is to be as fully aware of their defects as possible--preferably by means of measurement--and to avoid self-deception in their use.

Coming now to the sixth point of faith, the necessity to use such questionably quantifiable data as are provided by projective tests, personal documents, and interviews, much of what I have just said is applicable. Psychologists working with these slippery instruments need to know psychometrics and the standards of good test construction, even if they don't always put it all into practice. If the APA Test Standards were rigorously applied to the Rorschach and TAT, these indispensable diagnostic tools would have to be abandoned; but the alternative is not to say that such standards are wholly inappropriate to projective techniques and to go our merry way without restraint or responsibility.

No, I think that any user of these tests who is not content to be a mere technician, doing what he was taught in a routine way, ought to be continually aware of the test standards and to strive towards them. Likewise for personality measurement generally: It needs a set of rigorous ideals, not to plunge its practitioners into despair but to guide them onto higher, firmer ground from which they will be able to get better leverage for their work.

Another aspect of the sixth point is a metric catholicism, which in itself is a safeguard. Here is another fruit of redundancy--using many simultaneous methods of measuring personality, one gains security from the overlap of findings. Thus, for example, in a study on reality deprivation Holt and Goldberger (1959) found a pattern of positive adaptation to the unusual experimental demands (mostly, to perceive and do nothing for eight hours) and proceeded to look for its personological correlates. It was correlated with clinical ratings of effeminacy and with questionnaire measures of it (feminine identification scale of Grygier's DPI); this experimental measure correlated with esthetic sensitivity as measured in three different ways: by pencil-and-paper instruments like the Allport-Vernon-Lindzey Study of Values, by an objective technique like the Barron-Welsh Art Scale (of the Welsh Figure Preference Test), and by the clinical ratings. Such comforting consensus increases one's faith that the clinical ratings based on qualitative data have some reliability and that the objective instruments have some validity.

When we come to the seventh point, about the necessity of exploratory research, we approach the most exciting and creative aspect of work in personology. I cannot think of a single major discovery or hypothesis in this field that did not come out of exploratory and often quite informal investigation, rather than from rigorous verification of propositions. By the very nature of the scientific process, it is hard to lay down rules about how insights and researchable hunches are to be obtained; one can only expose a prepared and curious mind to an extended opportunity to observe

important phenomena. Statistical inquiry is as unpromising
a context of discovery as clinical work is a context of verification. The statistical manipulation of a set of data, such
as a factor analysis, can disclose unsuspected unities within
an area that has already been staked out for measurement,
but that is all. By contrast, it would be hard to improve on
the intensive study of individual cases in diagnostic or therapeutic practice as a source of ideas about how people are
put together, fall apart, or manage to function. Such study
brings the clinician into intimate contact with the emotionally
central facts of existence, many of which are so thoroughly
concealed that we non-therapists are likely to overlook or
forget about them.

Psychoanalysts and other clinicians have been mining
these rich lodes for many years and have not been loath to
speculate freely in print about what they have observed.
We are very far from exhausting the suggestions for more
systematic inquiry in the writings of even one man, Sigmund
Freud. Yet many important discoveries remain to be made
by the clinical method. One has only to reflect that Erikson's clinical observations and theorizing in his exploratory research on identity (cf. Erikson, 1959) date from the
recent past to realize that testable new insights will continue to issue from the consulting room for years to come.

I stress testability to usher in point 8, the necessity to
make the transition from the clinic to the laboratory or to
its equivalent in carefully designed research. It seems
obvious that the psychoanalyst's form of clinical research,
done as an incident to therapeutic practice, can hardly be
used to verify or disprove propositions. But there are various ways in which the laboratory researcher can draw on
the results of exploratory research. Obviously, one is the
execution of experiments that test propositions ready-made
by the clinician. A simpler way is for the experimenter to
borrow concepts from the clinician (e.g., separation
anxiety, narcissism) and apply them directly to the assessment of personality via ratings. Or clinical concepts may
suggest an area, which the laboratory researcher proceeds

to explore with his own methods; an example would be the recent work of Fisher (1954), Luborsky and Shevrin (1956) and our own group (cf. Klein and Holt, 1960) in the area of preconscious cognitive phenomena. When we carried out our first study of this sort (Klein, Spence, Holt, and Goure-vitch, 1958), we wanted to use the masking phenomenon, or metacontrast as it is sometimes called, as a way of seeing what happens to a cognitive process when it goes on without awareness, so that we might learn about the preconscious. Since then, we have worked our way into a number of prob-lems in the subliminal field that have no direct contact with the concept of preconscious mental processes, a term we don't even use any longer in conceptualizing these experi-ments.

Another major focus of our work illustrates a third way in which concepts deriving from exploratory clinical re-search may be put to work in more formalized investiga-tions which are not yet true tests of propositions. This method is to take a psychoanalytic concept with empirical referents, make those explicit (that is, given them opera-tional definitions), and then explore the phenomena con-cerned in new contexts or with methods different from the ones used in the work that generated the concept.

One such concept Freud (1953) called the primary process; from his clinical studies of his own and his pa-tients' dreams, he found he had to postulate an intervening variable, the primary process, to account for the trans-formations of the latent dream thoughts into the manifest, reported dream. After a study of his theoretical writings on dreams and those of other, more recent ego-psychologists (particularly Hartmann, 1950), I arrived at an operational definition of a two-fold character: (a) Primary process ideation is drive-dominated--the images or ideas contain palpable signs of unneutralized drives; and (b) it has formal characteristics that result from its operating with free rather than bound cathexis--condensation, displacement, symbolization, fragmentation, tolerated contradiction, autistic logic, and the other formal properties Freud described for the dream and dream work. Armed with this definition, I set up a system of scoring categories to pick up manifestations of the primary process in Rorschach responses (Holt, 1960). We are also using the definition in direct rating of primary process in TAT stories, free verbalizations of subjects kept in perceptual isolation (deprivation of meanings), and the productions of subjects who had been given LSD-25 (lysergic acid diethylamide), in addition to dream protocols. It has made possible the exploratory study of thinking that shows the hallmarks of the primary process in a variety of circumstances that tend to distort and disorder thinking. We have also been able to do some modest testing of hypotheses, although those tested so far have had more of the earmarks of empirically derived hunches than of propositions rigorously derived from psychoanalytic theory.

Which brings me to another point about the testing of psychoanalytic propositions: It is difficult to make this theory yield testable propositions, and a lot of theoretical work must go on before anything like a critical test of the theory is possible. Why? First, because psychoanalytic theory has never been fully formalized or systematized and does not exist in neat, propositional form. You have to dig to find anything that sounds like such a proposition. Once you have found it, the chances are that it is not what it seems; it may not be a theoretical statement at all, but an empirical generalization. Thus, for example, Freud has been quoted as saying that the Oedipus complex is universal. Fine, that can be tested; a single exception will disprove it. But it is merely a rash empirical generalization, with no theoretical content, and may be disproved without touching the fabric of the theory. Or if the statement you propose to work with is not such a generalization, it is almost certain to be hard to understand out of context. This means that it must be carefully rephrased by someone who knows the corpus of psychoanalytic theory and its historical development.

Let me exemplify again. Consider the following quotation from <u>An Outline of Psychoanalysis</u> (Freud, 1949), which is pretty clearly a theoretical proposition:

> ...we speak of cathexes and hypercathexes of
> the material of the mind and even venture to sup-
> pose that a hypercathexis brings about a sort of
> synthesis of different processes--a synthesis in
> the course of which free energy is transformed
> into bound energy.

I recently had occasion to make a close study of this and related passages in Freud's writings (Holt, 1962) and can assure you that here he is asserting a relation between the degree of consciousness and the degree to which thinking is rational, i.e., follows the rules of the secondary rather than the primary process. The key to the translation is that hypercathexis, which does the binding, is the construct Freud coordinated to attention and consciousness, and free and bound energy characterize the primary and secondary processes. You will grant me that this last proposition in my rewording is not obvious in what Freud wrote, but that it sounds more testable. It can be quite rigorously tested, in fact, and a study from our laboratory has verified it in a limited way. The specific proposition tested in this experiment by Sheldon Bach (1960) was that when subjects were asked to look at a card with a word written on it and then to write down a list of words (i.e., to associate), their associations would be logically related (according to the secondary process) to the meaning of the word on the card when the latter was clearly visible (in Freud's language, hypercathected), but that associations would be related by means of symbolic transformations when the word was too faint to be visible (could not be hypercathected). The findings with a small sample tentatively verified the predictions.

Even in this last case, which looks like a direct test of a theoretically derived proposition, I have to confess that the theoretical derivation was supplied only after the experiment was completed, the problem having been arrived at by a rather different route. Clearly, it is not easy to extract a good theoretical proposition and to test it by experiment, but when you do, you feel you are getting somewhere. One reason you are getting somewhere is that if the proposition is verified, you can start making parametric studies, you can close in on and define the specific conditions (parameters) under which the relation in question holds.

Now to cover my last two points. The ninth is just a reminder that to test a hypothesis is not to make discoveries, but that any piece of research offers opportunities for discovery, for the formation of hunches and the obtaining of insights, if you keep your eyes open to everything that is going on and not just to whether the statement tested was confirmed or disconfirmed. A valuable adjunct to experimental research, emphasized by Murray, is to study the personality of each subject, quantify it in ratings, and then statistically explore the relations between laboratory findings and assessments, or make qualitative comparisons of extreme cases. In the study on reality deprivation (Holt and Goldberger, 1959) cited above, for example, we got valuable leads about the role of the passivity required by the experiment from the assessment data on our subjects.

Some final comments on theory-building in relation to research in personology will elucidate my final summary statement of the desirable relation between theory and experiment. In relation to the complexity of its subject matter, the field is too young to expect of it any highly sophisticated, rigorous, over-all theory. It is not necessary to derive testable propositions from such a theory for models and experiments to stimulate and fructify each other; the much looser relationship that is possible in personology is still most useful. With Marquis (1948), I consider the times right for small-package theories dealing with a limited range of phenomena, though it seems desirable to frame these sub-theories so that they fit into the general framework provided by some overarching theory.

But how should we arrive at variables to be quantified and woven into the fabric of theory? I have suggested above that we should exploit existing models and the suggestions of exploratory research, and also that we should go ahead and quantify whatever we can. We then have concepts of every stripe jostling each other without any perceptible order. I have been preoccupied for 20 years with the problem of how some order can be introduced, or how a self-consistent set of concepts might be generated, but so far in vain. I am not convinced that factor analysis will always do it, even though at times it is very useful, for the following reasons:

A. Factor analysis would perform a great service if it could come up with basic dimensions in psychology comparable to the centimeter-gram-second system in physics that makes possible dimensional analysis, since these dimensions are involved in all classical physical equations. But it hasn't yet done so.

B. Factor analysis can digest only sets of data that can be measured in comparable ways and correlated; it must omit aspects of personality that are not yet so measurable. It cannot go beyond the limitations of the data that are fed it; if an aspect of personality is not implicit in the data supplied, it won't be found.

C. At best, factor analysis can provide only a set of variables; it can tell us nothing about the equations into which they are to be entered to make a model of functional dependencies in nature.

D. The concepts that result may be intuitively unintelligible, and thus unusable.

E. The relations among the resulting factors, whether orthogonal or oblique and correlated, are predetermined by the choice of factor-analytic method.

F. One of the strongest criticisms that can be levelled against factor analysis does not take issue with it on principle, but in terms of practice. With the advent of high-speed computers and factor-analytic programs for them, it has become too easy to toss into this seductive hopper any miscellaneous batch of data and to subject it to the Procrustean program that happens to be available, usually an orthogonal one. I am essentially coming out against sin at this point; one of the seven deadly sins is Sloth--here manifested in the lazy habit of using an easy analytic method instead of the one most appropriate to the problem and the data.

As an alternative, then, I propose experimental use and refinement of concepts. Put them to work! Let them prove themselves in suggesting new research and ordering new phenomena. If the propositions they generate consistently fail to be verified, let them expire gracefully.

Finally: I am sure that it is not accidental (after all, I am a clinical psychologist) that in the first draft of this paper I omitted one of the most important of all principles of psychological research. Few people will quarrel with it, but almost everyone forgets to give it more than lip-service. It may be summarized in three words: Replicate! Replicate! Replicate!

18 | Silvan S. Tomkins
Princeton University

Commentary:
The Ideology
of Research Strategies

The two preceding papers by Cattell (Chapter 16) and Holt (Chapter 17) appear to have generated a discussion of one part illumination to two parts heat. As I listened to the enthusiastic recrimination between the rigorous, objective, psychometric multivariate experimentalists and the deep, sensitive clinicians I cannot escape the impression that we are host to an old familiar friend, the mote-beam mechanism. That we are united in our dissatisfaction with our present knowledge of the field of personality is abundantly clear. We differ only in our diagnosis of who shall be blamed, and how best each might atone and make restitution for his past sins and errors. It is not the first time that men have found it easier to tolerate their own failures when viewed, from a comfortable distance, in the behavior of others.

Our field is admittedly a difficult one, and our progress to date is somewhat less than the heart desires. Despite the revolutionary insights of Freud and the promise of factor analytic methods, there is an enduring, gnawing discontent which generates the flamboyant, inflated self-assertion of the clinician and factor analyst alike, and which also generates their mutually extrapunitive posture. To these somewhat jaded eyes and ears, the score is even, and lower than we would like it to be. It may well be that it will always so

appear at the growing edge of our science or of any science.
In knowledge as in virtue, there is no royal road. But it is
just this suspicion which I think prompts the over-inflation,
now of the value of free association in psychoanalytic space
and, again, of the value of free rotation in factor analytic
space. Neither method appears to me to have opened the
royal road though both have opened exciting vistas. I will
defend the pre-Freudian, pre-Thurstonean dogma that
science begins and ends in an active brain enclosed in a
body comfortably supported in an arm chair. In between
these reflective moments are interposed a variety of fact
findings, hypothesis testings, and statistical analyses designed to illuminate the cognition before and after. Which
methods of fact finding, which methods of statistical analysis, appear to me to be of secondary importance so long as
one has been bright enough, or persistent enough, or lucky
enough, or all of these, to stumble onto something important. It seems highly improbable that any method will ever
guarantee the discovery of truth. Nor should we forget that
radical discovery is a rare event and that there are necessarily many more failures than successes. The whole spirit
of the advocates of free association and of the protagonists
of factor rotation belies to the investigator the fundamental
recalcitrance of nature. The two methods have more in
common than has been supposed. Each assumes that there
are critical linkages between responses which will appear
when the circumstances are made more favorable. Psychoanalysis assumes that the removal of the noise due to cen-
sorship and conscious control will lay bare these fundamental
linkages, and factor analysis also assumes that co-variation
of responses is the key to the underlying unities. Insofar
as either of these methods does lay hold of co-variations,
either in associations or other types of responses, we should
be grateful for favors received. To suppose, however, that
either method qua method has radically increased the probability either of discovery or of verification betrays an overweening optimism. It is as reasonable as the expectation
that the invention of the correlation coefficient would surely

produce laws, since one could now say how much co-variation there was between phenomena.

Personality appears to me to be organized as a language is organized, with elements of varying degrees of complexity--from letters, words, phrases, and sentences to styles-- and with a set of rules of combination which enable the generation of both endless novelty and the very high order of redundancy which we call style. If we had to be blind about one or the other of these types of components, one should sacrifice the elements for the rules. Factor analysis appears to have made the opposite decision. It would tell what letters, or words, or phrases, or even styles were invariant and characteristic of a personality or of a number of personalities. I have not yet seen it generate the rules of combination which together with the elements constitute personality.

It is more than a matter of the linearity or non-linearity of relationships which the dynamic rules of combination generate. It is the sensitive variation of the dynamic relationships themselves which guarantee the complexity of the human being and at the same time complicate the problem for the theorist. If the human being is a computer, he has numerous programs and combinations of programs. So it frequently becomes more important to know whether the traits revealed by a factor analysis are themselves constant or labile, general or specific, or whether they vary in generality according to circumstance and if so why. I am supposing that a factor analysis of various measures of an operating automobile might reveal its components at the level of steering wheel, carburetor, brakes, and so on without yielding a model of the automobile as an integrated system. I would suppose that a factor analysis of a computer which never twice used the same program might be even less revealing. In short, it is my prejudice that factor analysis is as appropriate for the unravelling of a dynamic system as complex as man as a centrifuge might be, though the latter rotation would also yield some real and independent components of man's basic stuff.

It is no secret that my own orientation is closer to that of Holt than to Cattell. Holt's catholicism, his willingness to suspend judgment, his psychoanalytic orientation, his tolerance for variables which cannot yet be measured, his insistence on vigilance for the main chance, all of these recommend themselves to me, not as ends in themselves but as reasonable strategies of the logic of discovery.

This is probably because I was trained as a philosopher and am still a philosopher, my own tragic destiny. When I could no longer tolerate the conceptual weightlessness of being orbited indefinitely in free-floating philosophic space, I descended, first to earth, and then into the underground, in Cambridge, Massachusetts, at the Harvard Psychological Clinic. Here, happily, for over a decade we observed, studied, and argued about human beings. The focus, as the title of Murray's first book (1938) suggested, was Explorations of Personality. Difficult and unrewarding as any voyages of intended discovery can be, it never lacked excitement. Beyond the horizon was the truth about human nature, and if we failed to find the prize on one voyage we would surely capture it when we tried again. If this, was a fool's paradise, it was at the least a paradise. After the war we were ultimately to be expelled from the Garden of Eden not for having tasted the fruit of the tree of knowledge, but for having been tempted by overweening pride and premature identification with God. The question changed from "Do I dare to eat an apple?" to "How can one be sure it really is an apple?" to "What do you mean by eating?", and finally to "Couldn't an automatic apple picker really do the thing more reliably?" My experience with philosophers had come full circle. I now found myself once again in the company of philosophers disguised as methodologists of psychology. Lest you think my dismay at this turn of events was entirely extrapunitive let me reassure you that there had been some return of the repressed in my own case too. I was busy showing that Mill's canons of inference could indeed be applied to the TAT (Tomkins, 1947), and then that this essential logic could be built into any projective test, and

in particular into my own PAT (Tomkins and Miner, 1957),
in such a way that a computer program could be written to
do quite complex profile analyses which compared favorably
with the analyses of the experienced clinician.

It would appear then, on the surface, that there is a
very real consensus among the contributors to the present
volume that reason, mathematics, logic, programming, and
all the apparatus of objectivity is here to stay and that we
are all on the side of the angels. There may nonetheless
be a suspicion among you that Professor Holt and myself
are only nouveau celestial and that we are conflicted and
somewhat unreliable defenders of the power of reason and
light, and consort from time to time with the Prince of
Darkness. And in this suspicion you would be right. Why
are we such reluctant angels? Basically, I think, because
we cannot surrender our overweening pride and our secret
hope that we are more than fallen angels and that some day
we may no longer toil by the sweat of our logical and mathematical brows but eat of the fruit of the tree of knowledge
and so be able to achieve the divine "aha" experience.

More seriously, I wish to defend the proposition that
in any science the probability of information gain is directly
proportional to the risk one is prepared to tolerate and that
those who prefer verification over discovery and who prefer
objectivity over subjectivity will necessarily enjoy limited
gains in information.

All sciences range over a wide spectrum of complexity
of affirmation and inference. Consider the differences between tests or measures, laws, and theoretical systems.
Any measuring instrument or test, whether it be a ruler,
a voltmeter, or a test for pregnancy, has essentially very
modest aims. It purports to give a reliable answer to a
very limited set of questions. Either the woman is pregnant or she is not; either the object measures one inch, two
inches, three, four inches--up to 12 inches in the case of a
ruler; either the object weighs one pound, two pounds--up
to 30 pounds in the case of a baby scale; either the automobile is going 10, 20, or 100 miles an hour--such measures

characteristically test simple variables and their power for
any science is a derivative of the frequency of their use.
Although a ruler or a scale will not per se generate laws or
systems it will over and over again give some limited information about an unlimited number of test objects. It will
tell that these 100,000 women are pregnant and those 100,000
are not. The instrument is usually designed for repeated
use. Such a method, whether used in physics or psychology,
is a highly specialized one, and a great price is paid for its
undoubted virtues. That price is that it will never tell you
more than that some aspect of a test object has one of a
limited number of characteristics. There is a real question
in my mind whether we possess one test in clinical psychology. We have characteristically wished to develop measuring instruments which permitted a bonus in the collection of
information, frequently as an auxiliary type of further observation. The Rorschach and the TAT are clearly not
tests in this sense, or at best they are sets of tests. My
own very self-conscious attempt to devise such a simple-
minded personality test has characteristically elicited the
response that it doesn't give "enough" information to be
very exciting--but neither does any test.

A law, in contrast to a test, is a much more pretentious
affirmation. It says, at the very least, that if one aspect
of a domain has one value, some other aspect of that domain
also has a particular value. Such a law can ordinarily be
expressed in a compressed form, mathematical or otherwise, so that the empirical determination of one variable
specifies the value of another variable, with sufficient precision so that we need not in fact test the other variable.
In contrast to a test, which is expected to keep on working
until the end of time, a law lives on borrowed time. It is
continually being subjected to experimental scrutiny to see
whether it is a better law than one suspected, or what its
boundary conditions are; as soon as exceptions to the law
are found and a more general law formulated, the old law
becomes a special case. In contrast to the test method,
which is designed for continual repetition of the same pro-

cedure, no one ever repeats exactly the experiment by which a law is established, or at most it is replicated once or twice to make sure that what appeared to happen did in fact happen and is generally replicable. There would, however, be no point in repeating any of the classical experiments in any science except for pedagogical purposes. As soon as the finding has been established, the limits of the matter begin to be explored and variations of the conditions under which the law holds or breaks down are further probed.

Finally, a theoretical system is a still more pretentious set of affirmations. It may, as in the case of the Newtonian scheme, be based on a number of laws which together give a coherent account of a large domain or, as in the case of psychoanalytic theory, be based on a number of sub-theories.

As we go from tests, to laws, to theoretical systems, we increase the complexity of what is affirmed, and ordinarily also at the same time suffer certain paradoxical consequences. While the number of theoretical alternatives continues to increase as complexity increases, the resistance to change also increases. A new scale, or voltmeter, or ruler, is relatively easily introduced into a science. A new law is established with more difficulty and a theoretical system is surrendered only once in a while, because it explains too much and because it becomes increasingly difficult to construct an alternative which is better. The types of evidence, inference, and cognitive activity necessary to construct a test, a law, and a theoretical system are at the least of a quite different order of complexity.

The second distinction I would make in types of cognition and inference cuts across the foregoing distinction. I refer to the radical difference between discovery and proof. The cognitive process and types of inference which are necessary to demonstrate that a law is really a law seem to me quite distinct from those exciting, frustrating pursuits after will-o-the-wisps, 99 percent of which prove to be blind alleys. The latter knowledge is born only in pain and error and there is no royal course through the vast uncharted sea of risk--and in the nature of the case there can be

no royal road. This is not to say that the complexities of
very high-order thinking may not be objectified. They can
be and indeed are being objectified, in such attemps as
the general program solving program of Newell, Shaw, and
Simon (1958). My argument is rather that such inference
is as distinct from formal logical inference as a test is distinct from a theoretical system.

The spectrum of complexity which would be generalized
by these two criteria, therefore, would range from the relatively simple demonstration, via the correlation coefficient,
that a test did in fact test what it purported to test (that a
scale, for example, gave honest weight under the average
variation in temperature of the room in which it was used)
to the attempt of a theorist to produce a theoretical system
which would account for all the phenomena accounted for by
the best present theoretical system, and then some. In the
first attempt there are very few ways of failing, with reasonable intelligence and diligence, and in the latter attempt
there are very few ways of succeeding, given the highest
intelligence and the most passionate commitment to the
enterprise.

If science is, as I think, a many-splendored thing, why
do some of us choose to break our intellectual necks or to
drown in a whirlpool of risk, and others of us insist on
doing something in which both the probability of success is
higher and in which the ease of demonstrating that we have
succeeded is also guaranteed by reliance on the power of
logic or mathematics?

I have for the past five years been studying this question in a variety of fields ranging from mathematics through
philosophy, theories of education, jurisprudence, theology,
and psychology. In every field there appear controversies
which have been sustained over hundreds of years, evoking
highly polarized and articulate positions and producing
passionate commitment to one position and hostility to the
other, and which appear to be supported by minimal empirical evidence. Further, it is the same argument which
appears to be equally debated in mathematics, as in philosophy, jurisprudence, and psychology. The argument is

whether a human being is the most real and valuable entity
in nature, an end in himself--or whether that which is most
real and valuable is some norm, some ideal essence quite
independent of the human being. In philosophy it is, on the
one hand, the extreme idealistic posture which holds that
the world is created by man and, on the other hand, the extreme Platonic view that neither the world nor man is real
or valuable, but that there exists an ideal set of essences,
of which the world and man are imitations. In the humanistic view it is what the individual wants that defines what is
good, true, and beautiful. In the normative view the individual must struggle to attain value and reality by conformity to the ideal norm. These two postures are generated,
I believe, by socializations which stress either that the
child is an end in himself, that he is loved for what he is,
or which say that if he wishes to grow up to be a good human
being he must conform to a norm administered by parents,
whether he feels like it or not. Such initial self-evaluations
then generate a resonance for one or another of the following types of ideologies in science. In mathematics one is
impressed either by its correctness or its freedom. Thus
Courant says of the "game" interpretation of mathematics,
"If mathematics were only a game...no adult could be seriously interested in it...it would make of mathematics...a
capricious...childish game." Poincaré on the same subject says, "Mathematics is a wonderful game. In it man
achieves his highest reach...his greatest freedom...be-
cause in mathematics man is completely free to construct
an infinite number of mathematical systems." The attitudes
toward the word "game" appear to be diagnostic of a very
general attitude toward childhood--toward affect and ideation--
as ends in themselves which represent man's highest function, or else as childish impulses in the sense that they are
capricious and to be outgrown. In art we see a recurrent
polarity of classicism and romanticism, and in literary
criticism a recurrent polarity of the image of the lamp
versus the mirror. In theories of government there is a
polarity between theories of the state as the major instrument through which men attain such limited freedom as is

possible, versus theories of the state as of the people, for the people, and by the people.

In aesthetics there is a recurrent polarity between beauty as in the object, or in the mind of the beholder. In theories of education a recurrent polarity, now intensified, between education as the learning of information versus a stimulation of the potential of the individual. In theories of perception in psychology we see this polarity between those who would account for perception by an analysis of the stimulus, against those who regard the percept as a personal construct. Within the Rorschach we are confronted with the insistence on norms by Beck, and the more free-wheeling cognition of Klopfer.

Those who have insisted on the objective, whether in science or in art, have derogated man and insisted on certainty. Those who have insisted on the subjective have glorified man and stressed the value of both play and risk. It is our conviction that the humanistic ideology, in the long run, will yield both the greater and the surer payoff.

Bibliography

Abelson, R. P. Scales derived by consideration of variance
    components in multi-way tables. In H. Gulliksen and
    S. Messick (Eds.), Psychological scaling: Theory and
    applications. New York: Wiley, 1960. Pp. 169-186.
Adams, Georgia S. Techniques of minimizing or capitaliz-
    ing upon response tendencies in structured self-report
    inventories. Paper read at Int. Congr. Psychol.,
    Bonn, Germany, August, 1960.
Adams, H. E., and Berg, I. A. Affective tone of test option
    choice as a deviant response. Psychol. Rep., 1961, 8,
    79-85. (a)
Adams, H. E., and Berg, I. A. Schizophrenia and deviant
    response sets produced by auditory and visual test con-
    tent. J. Psychol., 1961, 51, 393-398. (b)
Allport, G. W. Personality. New York: Holt, 1937.
Allport, G. W., and Vernon, P. E. Studies in expressive
    movement. New York: Macmillan, 1933.
Asch, S. E. Forming impressions of personality. J. ab-
    norm. soc. Psychol., 1946, 41, 258-290.
Bach, S. Symbolic associations to stimulus words in sub-
    liminal, supraliminal and incidental presentation.
    Unpublished doctoral dissertation, New York Univer.,
    1960.

Barker, R. G., Schoggen, M. F., and Barker, L. S. Hemerography of Mary Ennis. In H. Burton and R. E. Harris (Eds.), Case histories in clinical and abnormal psychology. Vol. 2. Clinical studies of personality. New York: Harper, 1955. Pp. 768-808.

Barnes, E. H. The relationship of biased test responses to psychopathology. J. abnorm. soc. Psychol., 1955, 51, 286-290.

Barnes, E. H. Response bias and the MMPI. J. consult. Psychol., 1956, 20, 371-374. (a)

Barnes, E. H. Factors, response bias, and the MMPI. J. consult. Psychol., 1956, 20, 419-421. (b)

Barron, F. An ego-strength scale which predicts response to psychotherapy. J. consult. Psychol., 1953, 17, 327-333.

Bass, B. M. Authoritarianism or acquiescence? J. abnorm. soc. Psychol., 1955, 51, 616-623.

Bass, B. M. Development and evaluation of a scale for measuring social acquiescence. J. abnorm. soc. Psychol., 1956, 53, 296-299.

Beech, H. R., and Maxwell, A. E. Differentiation of clinical groups using canonical variates. J. consult. Psychol., 1958, 22, 113-121.

Benton, A. L. The interpretation of questionnaire items in a personality schedule. Arch. Psychol., N. Y., 1935, No. 190.

Berg, I. A. Response bias and personality: The deviation hypothesis. J. Psychol., 1955, 40, 61-72.

Berg, I. A. The unimportance of test item content. In B. M. Bass and I. A. Berg (Eds.), Objective approaches to personality assessment. Princeton, N. J.: Van Nostrand, 1959. Pp. 83-99.

Block, J. The development of an MMPI-based scale to measure ego control. Berkeley, Calif.: Institute of Personality Assessment and Research, Univer. of California, 1953, unpublished manuscript.

Briggs, D. A. The Stern Activities Index as a means of predicting social acceptability and improvement in reading skills. Unpublished doctoral dissertation, Syracuse Univer., 1958.

Bruner, J. S. The process of education. Cambridge, Mass.: Harvard Univer. Press, 1960.

Bruner, J., Shapiro, D., and Tagiuri, R. The meaning of traits in isolation and in combination. In R. Tagiuri and L. Petrullo (Eds.), Person perception and interpersonal behavior. Stanford, Calif.: Stanford Univer. Press, 1958.

Burt, C. L. The factors of the mind. New York: Macmillan, 1941.

Buss, A. H. The effect of item style on social desirability and frequency of endorsement. J. consult. Psychol., 1959, 23, 510-513.

Campbell, D. T., and Fiske, D. W. Convergent and discriminant validation by the multitrait-multimethod matrix. Psychol. Bull., 1959, 56, 81-105.

Cattell, R. B. Primary personality factors in the realm of objective tests. J. Pers., 1948, 16, 459-487.

Cattell, R. B. A factorization of tests of personality source traits. Brit. J. Psychol., Statist. Sect., 1951, 4, 165-178.

Cattell, R. B. Psychiatric screening of flying personnel. I. Personality structure in objective tests. Report No. 9. Randolph AF Base, Texas: USAF School of Aviation Medicine, 1955, 1-50.

Cattell, R. B. Personality and motivation structure and measurement. Yonkers-on-Hudson, N. Y.: World Book, 1957.

Cattell, R. B. Extracting the correct number of factors in factor analysis. Educ. psychol. Measmt, 1958, 18, 791-838.

Cattell, R. B. Theory of situational, instrument, second order, and refraction factors in personality structure research. Psychol. Bull., 1961, 58, 160-174.

Cattell, R. B., Blewett, D. B., and Beloff, J. R. The inheritance of personality. Amer. J. hum. Genet., 1955, 7, 122-146.

Cattell, R. B., and Saunders, D. R. Inter-relation and matching of personality factors from behavior rating, questionnaire and objective test data. J. soc. Psychol., 1950, 31, 243-260.

Cattell, R. B., and Scheier, I. H. The meaning and
measurement of neuroticism and anxiety. New York:
Ronald Press, 1961.

Cattell, R. B., Stice, G. F., and Kristy, N. F. A first
approximation to nature-nurture ratios for eleven primary personality factors in objective tests. J. abnorm.
soc. Psychol., 1957, 54, 143-159.

Chapman, L. J., and Bock, R. D. Components of variance
due to acquiescence and content in the F scale measure
of authoritarianism. Psychol. Bull., 1958, 55, 328-333.

Chilman, C. S. A comparative study of measured personality needs and self-perceived problems of ninth and
tenth grade students: Half of the group possessing
characteristics associated with early school leaving
and the other half not possessing such characteristics.
Unpublished doctoral dissertation, Syracuse Univer.,
1959.

Christie, R., and Merton, R. K. Procedures for the sociological study of the values climate of medical schools.
J. med. Educ., 1958, 33, Part 2, 125-153.

Clayton, Martha B., and Jackson, D. N. Equivalence range,
acquiescence, and overgeneralization. Educ. psychol.
Measmt, 1961, 21, 371-382.

Cofer, C. N., Chance, June, and Judson, A. J. A study of
malingering on the Minnesota Multiphasic Personality
Inventory. J. Psychol., 1949, 27, 491-499.

Cohen, J. The factorial structure of the WISC at ages 7-6,
10-6, and 13-6. J. consult. Psychol., 1959, 23, 285-
299.

Cole, D. Some emotional factors in couples presenting a
pattern of habitual abortion. Unpublished doctoral
dissertation, Syracuse Univer., 1958.

Comrey, A. L. A factor analysis of items on the MMPI
depression scale. Educ. psychol. Measmt, 1957, 17,
578-585. (a)

Comrey, A. L. A factor analysis of items on the MMPI
hypochondriasis scale. Educ. psychol. Measmt, 1957,
17, 568-577. (b)

Comrey, A. L. A factor analysis of items on the MMPI
    hysteria scale. Educ. psychol. Measmt, 1957, 17,
    586-592. (c)
Comrey, A. L. A factor analysis of items on the F scale
    of the MMPI. Educ. psychol. Measmt, 1958, 18,
    621-632. (a)
Comrey, A. L. A factor analysis of items on the K scale
    of the MMPI. Educ. psychol. Measmt, 1958, 18, 633-
    639. (b)
Comrey, A. L. A factor analysis of items on the MMPI
    hypomania scale. Educ. psychol. Measmt, 1958, 18,
    313-323. (c)
Comrey, A. L. A factor analysis of items on the MMPI
    paranoia scale. Educ. psychol. Measmt, 1958, 18,
    99-107. (d)
Comrey, A. L. A factor analysis of items on the MMPI
    psychasthenia scale. Educ. psychol. Measmt, 1958,
    18, 293-300. (e)
Comrey, A. L. A factor analysis of items on the MMPI
    psychopathic deviate scale. Educ. psychol. Measmt,
    1958, 18, 91-98. (f)
Comrey, A. L. Comparison of two analytic rotation pro-
    cedures. Psychol. Rep., 1959, 5, 201-209.
Comrey, A. L., and Levonian, E. A comparison of three
    point coefficients in factor analyses of MMPI items.
    Educ. psychol. Measmt, 1958, 18, 739-755.
Comrey, A. L., and Marggraff, W. M. A factor analysis
    of items on the MMPI schizophrenia scale. Educ.
    psychol. Measmt, 1958, 18, 301-311.
Comrey, A. L., and Soufi, A. Further investigation of
    some factors found in MMPI items. Educ. psychol.
    Measmt, 1960, 20, 777-786.
Comrey, A. L., and Soufi, A. Attempted verification of
    certain personality factors. Educ. psychol. Measmt,
    1961, 21, 113-127.
Couch, A., and Keniston, K. Yeasayers and naysayers:
    Agreeing response set as a personality variable.
    J. abnorm soc. Psychol., 1960, 60, 151-174.

Cowen, E. L., and Tongas, P. The social desirability of trait descriptive terms: Applications to a self-concept inventory. J. consult. Psychol., 1959, 23, 361-365.

Cronbach, L. J. Response sets and test validity. Educ. psychol. Measmt, 1946, 6, 475-494.

Cronbach, L. J. Further evidence on response sets and test design. Educ. psychol. Measmt, 1950, 10, 3-31.

Cronbach, L. J. Coefficient alpha and the internal structure of tests. Psychometrika, 1951, 16, 297-334.

Cronbach, L. J. The two disciplines of scientific psychology. Amer. Psychologist, 1957, 12, 671-684.

Cronbach, L. J. Review of "Basic readings on the MMPI in psychology and medicine" (G. S. Welsh and W. G. Dahlstrom, Eds.). Psychometrika, 1958, 23, 385-386.

Cronbach, L. J., and Gleser, Goldine, C. Psychological tests and personnel decisions. Urbana, Ill.: Univer. Illinois Press, 1957.

Cronbach, L. J., and Meehl, P. E. Construct validity in psychological tests. Psychol. Bull., 1955, 52, 281-302.

Cuadra, C. A. A scale for control in psychological adjustment. In G. S. Welsh and W. G. Dahlstrom (Eds.), Basic readings on the MMPI in psychology and medicine. Minneapolis: Univer. Minnesota Press, 1956.

Dahlstrom, W. G., and Welsh, G. S. An MMPI handbook: A guide to use in clinical practice and research. Minneapolis: Univer. Minnesota Press, 1960.

Damarin, F. L., and Messick, S. Response styles as personality variables: Evidence from published multivariate research. Princeton, N. J.: Educational Testing Service Research Bulletin, 1962, in preparation.

Davidson, D., Suppes, P., and Siegel, S. Decision making: An experimental approach. Stanford, Calif.: Stanford Univer. Press, 1957.

Edwards, A. L. The relationship between the judged desirability of a trait and the probability that the trait will be endorsed. J. appl. Psychol., 1953, 37, 90-93. (a)

Edwards, A. L. Manual for the Edwards Personal Preference Schedule. New York: Psychological Corporation, 1953. (b)

Edwards, A. L. Social desirability and Q sorts. J. consult. Psychol., 1955, 19, 462.

Edwards, A. L. The social desirability variable in personality assessment and research. New York: Dryden, 1957. (a)

Edwards, A. L. Social desirability and probability of endorsement of items in the Interpersonal Check List. J. abnorm. soc. Psychol., 1957, 55, 394-396. (b)

Edwards, A. L. Social desirability and the description of others. J. abnorm. soc. Psychol., 1959, 59, 434-436.

Edwards, A. L. Social desirability or acquiescence in the MMPI? A case study with the SD scale. J. abnorm. soc. Psychol., 1961, 63, 351-359.

Edwards, A. L., Heathers, Louise B., and Fordyce, W. E. Correlations of new MMPI scales with Edwards SD scale. J. clin. Psychol., 1960, 16, 26-29.

Elliott, Lois L. Effects of item construction and respondent aptitude on response acquiescence. Educ. psychol. Measmt, 1961, 21, 405-415.

English, H. B., and English, A. C. A comprehensive dictionary of psychological and psychoanalytical terms: A guide to usage. New York: Longmans, Green, 1958.

Epstein, L. The relationship of certain aspects of the body image to the perception of the upright. Unpublished doctoral dissertation, New York Univer., 1957.

Erikson, E. H. Identity and the life cycle; selected papers. Psychol. Issues, 1959, 1, No. 1.

Exline, R., Thibaut, J., Brannon, Carole, and Gumpert, P. Visual interaction in relation to Machiavellianism and an unethical act. Amer. Psychologist, 1961, 16, 396. (Abstract)

Faterson, Hanna F. Articulateness of experience: An extension of the field-dependence-independence concept. In S. Messick and J. Ross (Eds.), Measurement in personality and cognition. New York: Wiley, 1962. Pp. 171-181.

Fillenbaum, S. Some stylistic aspects of categorizing behavior. J. Pers., 1959, 27, 187-195.

Fisher, C. Dreams and perception: The role of precon-
    scious and primary modes of perception in dream for-
    mation. J. Amer. psychoanal. Ass., 1954, 2, 389-445.

Fordyce, W. E. Social desirability in the MMPI. J. con-
    sult. Psychol., 1956, 20, 171-175.

Frederiksen, N., and Messick, S. Response set as a meas-
    ure of personality. Educ. psychol. Measmt, 1959, 19,
    137-157.

French, J. W. The description of personality measurements
    in terms of rotated factors. Princeton, N. J.: Educa-
    tional Testing Service, 1953.

Freud, Anna. The ego and the mechanisms of defense.
    New York: International Univer. Press, 1946.

Freud, S. Collected papers. Vol. IV. London: Hogarth
    Press, 1925.

Freud, S. An outline of psychoanalysis. New York: Norton,
    1949.

Freud, S. Analysis terminable and interminable. In Col-
    lected papers. Vol. V. London: Hogarth Press, 1950.

Freud, S. The interpretation of dreams (standard ed.).
    Vols. 4 and 5. London: Hogarth Press, 1953.

Fricke, B. G. Response set as a suppressor variable in
    the OAIS and MMPI. J. consult. Psychol., 1956, 20,
    161-169.

Fricke, B. G. A response bias (B) scale for the MMPI.
    J counsel. Psychol., 1957, 4, 149-153.

Fruchter, B. Introduction to factor analysis. New York:
    Van Nostrand, 1954.

Fulkerson, S. C. An acquiescence key for the MMPI.
    Report No. 58-71. Randolph AF Base, Texas: USAF
    School of Aviation Medicine, July 1958.

Gage, N. L., and Chatterjee, B. B. The psychological
    meaning of acquiescence set: Further evidence.
    J. abnorm. soc. Psychol., 1960, 60, 280-283.

Gage, N. L., Leavitt, G. S., and Stone, G. C. The psycho-
    logical meaning of acquiescence set for authoritarian-
    ism. J. abnorm. soc. Psychol., 1957, 55, 98-103.

Gardner, R. W. Cognitive styles in categorizing behavior.
    J. Pers., 1953, 22, 214-233.

Gardner, R. W. Cognitive controls of attention deployment as determinants of visual illusions. J. abnorm. soc. Psychol., 1961, 62, 120-127.

Gardner, R. W. Cognitive controls in adaptation: Research and measurement. In S. Messick and J. Ross (Eds.), Measurement in personality and cognition. New York: Wiley, 1962. Pp. 183-198.

Gardner, R., Holzman, P. S., Klein, G. S., Linton, Harriet, and Spence, D. P. Cognitive control; a study of individual consistencies in cognitive behavior. Psychol. Issues, 1959, 1, No. 4.

Gardner, R. W., Jackson, D. N., and Messick, S. Personality organization in cognitive controls and intellectual abilities. Psychol. Issues, 1960, 2, No. 4.

Gardner, R. W., and Lohrenz, L. J. Leveling-sharpening and serial reproduction of a story. Bull. Menninger Clin., in press.

Gardner, R. W., and Long, R. I. Errors of the standard and illusion effects with the inverted-T. Percept. mot. Skills, 1960, 10, 47-54. (a)

Gardner, R. W., and Long, R. I. Error of the standard and illusion effects with L-shaped figures. Percept. mot. Skills, 1960, 10, 107-109. (b)

Gardner, R. W., and Long, R. I. Leveling-sharpening and serial learning. Percept. mot. Skills, 1960, 10, 179-185. (c)

Gladstein, G. A. The relationship between study behavior and personality for academically successful students. Unpublished doctoral dissertation, Univer. of Chicago, 1957.

Goodenough, D. R., and Karp, S. A. Field dependence and intellectual functioning. J. abnorm. soc. Psychol., 1961, 63, 241-246.

Gough, H. G. Some common misconceptions about neuroticism. J. consult. Psychol., 1954, 18, 287-292.

Gough, H. G. California Psychological Inventory Manual. Palo Alto, Calif.: Consulting Psychologists Press, 1957.

Guilford, J. P. Personality. New York: McGraw-Hill, 1959.

Guilford, J. P., Frick, J. W., Christensen, P. R., and
    Merrifield, P. R. A factor-analytic study of flexibility
    in thinking. Rep. Psychol. Lab. Univer. So. Calif.,
    1957, 18.
Gulliksen, H. Mathematical solutions for psychological
    problems. Amer. Scientist, 1959, 47, 178-201.
Guttman, L. A new approach to factor analysis: The radex.
    In P. F. Lazarsfeld (Ed.), Mathematical thinking in the
    social sciences. Glencoe, Ill.: Free Press, 1954. Pp.
    258-348.
Hadamard, J. The psychology of invention in the mathe-
    matical field. Princeton, N. J.: Princeton Univer.
    Press, 1945.
Hanley, C. Social desirability and responses to items from
    three MMPI scales: D, Sc, and K. J. appl. Psychol.,
    1956, 40, 324-328.
Hanley, C. Deriving a measure of test-taking defensive-
    ness. J. consult. Psychol., 1957, 21, 391-397.
Hanley, C. Responses to the wording of personality test
    items. J. consult. Psychol., 1959, 23, 261-265.
Hanley, C. Social desirability and response bias in the
    MMPI. J. consult. Psychol., 1961, 25, 13-20.
Haring, N. G., Stern, G. G., and Cruickshank, W. M.
    Attitudes of educators toward exceptional children.
    Syracuse, N. Y.: Syracuse Univer. Press, 1958.
Hartmann, H. Comments on the psychoanalytic theory of
    the ego. Psychoanal. stud. Child., 1950, 5, 74-96.
Hartmann, H. Ego psychology and the problem of adapta-
    tion. New York: International Univer. Press, 1958.
Hathaway, S. R., and Briggs, P. F. Some normative data
    on new MMPI scales. J. clin. Psychol., 1957, 13,
    364-368.
Hathaway, S. R., and McKinley, J. C. The MMPI manual.
    Revised. New York: Psychological Corporation, 1951.
Heider, F. The psychology of interpersonal relations.
    New York: Wiley, 1958.
Heilbrun, A. B., and Goodstein, L. D. Social desirability
    response set: Error or predictor variable. J. Psychol.,
    1961, 51, 321-329.

Heineman, C. E. A forced-choice form of the Taylor
    Anxiety Scale. Unpublished doctoral dissertation,
    State Univer. of Iowa, 1952.

Heineman, C. E. A forced-choice form of the Taylor
    Anxiety Scale. J. consult. Psychol., 1953, 17, 447-
    454.

Hempel, C. G. Fundamentals of concept formation in
    empirical science. In O. Neurath et al. (Eds.),
    International encyclopedia of unified science. Vol. 2,
    No. 7. Chicago: Univer. Chicago Press, 1955.

Hillmer, M. L., Jr. Social desirability in a two-choice
    personality scale. Unpublished master's thesis,
    Univer. of Washington, 1958.

Hollingshead, A. B., and Redlich, F. C. Social class and
    mental illness: A community study. New York: Wiley,
    1958.

Holt, E. B. The Freudian wish and its place in ethics.
    New York: Henry Holt, 1915.

Holt, R. R. Manual for the scoring of primary process
    manifestations in Rorschach responses (8th rev.).
    New York: Research Center for Mental Health, 1960.
    (Dittoed)

Holt, R. R. A critical examination of Freud's concept of
    bound vs. free cathexis. J. Amer. psychoanal. Ass.,
    1962, in press.

Holt, R. R., and Goldberger, L. Personological correlates
    of reactions to perceptual isolation. WADC Technical
    Report 59-735. Wright-Patterson AF Base, Ohio, 1959.

Holzman, P. S. The relation of assimilation tendencies in
    visual, auditory, and kinesthetic time-error to cogni-
    tive attitudes of leveling and sharpening. J. Pers.,
    1954, 22, 375-394.

Holzman, P. S., and Gardner, R. W. Leveling and repres-
    sion. J. abnorm. soc. Psychol., 1959, 59, 151-155.

Holzman, P. S., and Klein, G. S. Cognitive system-
    principles of leveling and sharpening: Individual dif-
    ferences in assimilation effects in visual time-error.
    J. Psychol., 1954, 37, 105-122.

Jackson, D. N. Cognitive energy level, acquiescence, and
    authoritarianism. J. soc. Psychol., 1959, 49, 65-69.

Jackson, D. N., and Messick, S. A note on "ethnocentrism" and acquiescent response sets. J. abnorm soc. Psychol., 1957, 54, 132-134.

Jackson, D. N., and Messick, S. Content and style in personality assessment. Psychol. Bull., 1958, 55, 243-252.

Jackson, D. N., and Messick, S. Acquiescence and desirability as response determinants on the MMPI. Educ. psychol. Measmt, 1961, 21, 771-790.

Jackson, D. N., and Messick, S. Response styles on the MMPI: Comparison of clinical and normal samples. J. abnorm. soc. Psychol., 1962, in press.

Jackson, D. N., Messick, S., and Solley, C. M. How "rigid" is the "authoritarian"? J. abnorm. soc. Psychol., 1957, 54, 137-140.

Jackson, D. N., and Pacine, L. Response styles and academic achievement. Educ. psychol. Measmt, 1961, 21, 1015-1028.

Janis, I. L. Psychological stress. New York: Wiley, 1958.

Jones, E. E., Gergen, K. J., and Davis, K. E. Some determinants of reactions to being approved or disapproved as a person. Psychol. Monogr., 1962, 76, No. 2 (Whole No. 521).

Jones, E. E., and Thibaut, J. W. Interaction goals as bases of inference in interpersonal perception. In R. Tagiuri and L. Petrullo (Eds.), Person perception and interpersonal behavior. Stanford, Calif.: Stanford Univer. Press, 1958.

Jung, C. G. Psychological types. New York: Pantheon, 1959.

Kagan, J., and Moss, H. A. Styles of conceptualization. Paper read at Amer. Psychol. Ass., Chicago, 1960.

Kagan, J., Moss, H. A., and Sigel, I. The psychological significance of styles of conceptualization. Paper read at conference sponsored by Social Science Research Council, Minneapolis, 1961.

Kaiser, H. F. The varimax criterion for analytic rotation in factor analysis. Psychometrika, 1958, 23, 187-200.

Kelly, G. A. The psychology of personal constructs. New York: Norton, 1955.

Kenny, D. T. The influence of social desirability on discrepancy measures between real self and ideal self. J. consult. Psychol., 1956, 20, 315-318.

Klein, G. S. Need and regulation. In M. R. Jones (Ed.), Nebraska symposium on motivation. Vol. 2. Lincoln, Nebr.: Univer. Nebraska Press, 1954. Pp. 224-280.

Klein, G. S. Cognitive control and motivation. In G. Lindzey (Ed.), Assessment of human motives. New York: Rinehart, 1958.

Klein, G. S. Tolerance for unrealistic experiences: A generality study. (In preparation.)

Klein, G. S., and Holt, R. R. Problems and issues in current studies of subliminal activation. In J. G. Peatman and E. L. Hartley (Eds.), Festschrift for Gardner Murphy. New York: Harper, 1960.

Klein, G. S., and Schlesinger, H. J. Perceptual attitudes toward instability: I. Prediction of apparent movement experiences from Rorschach responses. J. Pers., 1951, 19, 289-302.

Klein, G. S., Spence, D. P., Holt, R. R., and Gourevitch, S. R. Cognition without awareness: Subliminal influences upon conscious thought. J. abnorm. soc. Psychol., 1958, 57, 255-266.

Kogan, N., and Wallach, M. A. The effect of anxiety on relations between subjective age and caution in an older sample. In P. H. Hoch and J. Zubin (Eds.), Psychopathology of aging. New York: Grune and Stratton, 1961. Pp. 123-135.

Lachman, R. The model in theory construction. Psychol. Rev., 1960, 67, 113-129.

Leary, T. Interpersonal diagnosis of personality. New York: Ronald Press, 1957.

Lentz, T. F. Acquiescence as a factor in the measurement of personality. Psychol. Bull., 1938, 35, 659.

Levonian, E., Comrey, A., Levy, W., and Procter, D. A statistical evaluation of the Edwards Personal Preference Schedule. J. appl. Psychol., 1959, 43, 355-359.

Lindsley, D. B. Psychophysiology and motivation. In M. R. Jones (Ed.), Nebraska symposium on motivation. Vol. 5. Lincoln, Nebr.: Univer. Nebraska Press, 1957. Pp. 36-40.

Little, K. B., and Fisher, J. Two new experimental scales of the MMPI. J. consult. Psychol., 1958, 22, 305-306.

Loevinger, Jane. Objective tests as instruments of psychological theory. Psychol. Rep., 1957, 3, 635-694.

Luborsky, L., and Shevrin, H. Dreams and day-residues: A study of the Poetzl observation. Bull. Menninger Clin., 1956, 20, 135-147.

Luce, R. D. On the possible psychophysical laws. Psychol. Rev., 1959, 66, 81-95.

Marlowe, D., and Crowne, D. P. Social desirability and response to perceived situational demands. J. consult. Psychol., 1961, 25, 109-115.

Marquis, D. Research planning at the frontiers of science. Amer. Psychologist, 1948, 3, 430-438.

McCarter, R. E. Emotional components of early recollections. ONR Technical Report and doctoral dissertation, Princeton Univer. Princeton, N. J.: Educational Testing Service, 1961.

McFee, A. The relation of students' needs to their perceptions of a college environment. J. educ. Psychol., 1961, 52, 25-29.

McGee, R. K. Response style as a personality variable: By what criterion? Psychol. Bull., 1962, in press.

Meehl, P. E. Wanted--a good cookbook. Amer. Psychologist, 1956, 11, 263-272.

Meehl, P. E., and Hathaway, S. R. The K factor as a suppressor variable in the MMPI. J. appl. Psychol., 1946, 30, 525-564.

Merrill, R. M., and Heathers, Louise B. The relation of the MMPI to the Edwards Personal Preference Schedule on a college counseling center sample. J. consult. Psychol., 1956, 20, 310-314.

Messick, S. Dimensions of social desirability. J. consult. Psychol., 1960, 24, 279-287.

Messick, S. Personality structure. Annu. Rev. Psychol., 1961, 12, 93-128.

Messick, S. Response style and content measures from personality inventories. Educ. psychol. Measmt, 1962, 22, in press.

Messick, S., and Frederiksen, N. Ability, acquiescence, and "authoritarianism." Psychol. Rep., 1958, 4, 687-697.

Messick, S., and Jackson, D. N. The measurement of authoritarian attitudes. Educ. psychol. Measmt, 1958, 18, 241-253.

Messick, S., and Jackson, D. N. Desirability scale values and dispersions for MMPI items. Psychol. Rep., 1961, 8, 409-414. (a)

Messick, S., and Jackson, D. N. Acquiescence and the factorial interpretation of the MMPI. Psychol. Bull., 1961, 58, 299-304. (b)

Miller, J. G. Information input overload and psychopathology. Amer. J. Psychiat., 1960, 116, 695-704.

Murphy, Lois B. Coping devices and defense mechanisms in relation to autonomous ego functions. Bull. Menninger Clin., 1960, 24, 144-153.

Murray, H. A. Explorations in personality. New York: Oxford Univer. Press, 1938.

Murray, H. A. Toward a classification of interactions. In T. Parsons and E. A. Shils (Eds.), Toward a general theory of action. Cambridge, Mass.: Harvard Univer. Press, 1952. Pp. 434-464.

Newell, A., Shaw, J. C., and Simon, H. A. Elements of a theory of human problem solving. Psychol. Rev., 1958, 65, 151-166.

Nunnally, J., and Husek, T. R. The phony language examination: An approach to the measurement of response bias. Educ. psychol. Measmt, 1958, 18, 275-282.

OSS Assessment Staff. Assessment of men. New York: Rinehart, 1948.

Pace, C. R. Five college environments. Coll. Bd. Rev., 1960, 41, 24-28.

Pace, C. R., and Stern, G. G. An approach to the measurement of psychological characteristics of college environments. J. educ. Psychol., 1958, 49, 269-277.

Paul, I. H. Studies in remembering; the reproduction of connected and extended verbal materials. Psychol. Issues, 1959, 1, No. 2.

Pettigrew, T. F. The measurement and correlates of category width as a cognitive variable. J. Pers., 1958, 26, 532-544.

Piaget, J. The psychology of intelligence. New York: Harcourt, Brace, 1950.

Piaget, J., Vinh-Bang, and Matalon, B. Note on the law of the temporal maximum of some optico-geometric illusions. Amer. J. Psychol., 1958, 71, 277-282.

Rao, C. R., and Slater, P. Multivariate analysis applied to differences between neurotic groups. Brit. J. Psychol., Statist. Sect., 1949, 2, 17-29.

Rapaport, D. The autonomy of the ego. Bull. Menninger Clin., 1951, 15, 113-123.

Rapaport, D. Cognitive structures. In Contemporary approaches to cognition. Cambridge, Mass.: Harvard Univer. Press, 1957. Pp. 157-200.

Rapaport, D. The theory of ego autonomy: A generalization. Bull. Menninger Clin., 1958, 22, 13-35.

Rapaport, D. The structure of psychoanalytic theory: A systematizing attempt. In S. Koch (Ed.), Psychology: A study of a science. Vol. III. Formulation of the person and the social context. New York: McGraw-Hill, 1959.

Rapaport, D. The structure of psychoanalytic theory. Psychol. Issues, 1960, 2, No. 2.

Rapaport, D., Gill, M., and Schafer, R. Diagnostic psychological testing. Vol. I. Chicago: Year Book, 1945.

Rogers, C. R. A theory of therapy, personality, and interpersonal relationships, as developed in the client-centered framework. In S. Koch (Ed.), Psychology: A study of a science. Vol. III. Formulation of the person and the social context. New York: McGraw-Hill, 1959. Pp. 184-256. (a)

Rogers, C. R. Toward a theory of creativity. In H. H. Anderson (Ed.), Creativity and its cultivation. New York: Harper, 1959. Pp. 69-82. (b)

Rokeach, M. A method for studying individual differences
    in "narrow-mindedness." J. Pers., 1951, 20, 219-233.
Rokeach, M. The open and closed mind. New York: Basic
    Books, 1960.
Rudin, S. A., and Stagner, R. Figure-ground phenomena
    in the perception of physical and social stimuli.
    J. Psychol., 1958, 45, 213-225.
Ryle, G. The concept of mind. New York: Barnes and
    Noble, 1950.
Saunders, D. R. Moderator variables in prediction. Educ.
    psychol. Measmt, 1956, 16, 209-222.
Saunders, D. R. A computer program to find the best-
    fitting orthogonal factors for a given hypothesis.
    Psychometrika, 1960, 25, 199-205.
Scanlon, J. The Activities Index: An inquiry into validity.
    Unpublished doctoral dissertation, Syracuse Univer.,
    1958.
Schaefer, E. S. A circumplex model for maternal behavior.
    J. abnorm. soc. Psychol., 1959, 59, 226-235.
Schultz, D. Simulation by college students of prescribed
    patterns in the Activities Index. Unpublished master's
    thesis, Syracuse Univer., 1955.
Sechrest, L. B., and Jackson, D. N. Deviant response
    tendencies: Their measurement and interpretation.
    University Park, Penna.: Pennsylvania State Univer.
    Research Bulletin No. 19, 1961.
Siegal, R. S. The leveling-sharpening system principle,
    serial learning and retroactive interference. Unpub-
    lished doctoral dissertation, Univer. of Kansas, 1957.
Siegelman, M., and Peck, R. F. Personality patterns re-
    lated to occupational roles. Genet. psychol. Monogr.,
    1960, 61, 291-349.
Stern, G. G. Assessing theological student personality
    structure. J. pastoral Care, 1954, 18, 76-83.
Stern, G. G. Preliminary manual: Activities Index--College
    Characteristics Index. Syracuse, N. Y.: Syracuse Uni-
    ver. Psychological Research Center, 1958. (a)
Stern, G. G. Some reflections on delinquency research.
    Syracuse, N. Y.: Syracuse Univer. Youth Development
    Center, 1958. (b)

Stern, G. G.   Congruence and dissonance in the ecology of
    college students. Student Med., 1960, 8, 304-339. (a)
Stern, G. G.   Student values and their relationship to the
    college environment. In H. T. Sprague (Ed.), Re-
    search on college students. Boulder, Colo.: Western
    Interstate Commission for Higher Education, 1960.
    Pp. 67-104. (b)
Stern, G. G.   Continuity and contrast in the transition from
    high school to college. In N. F. Brown (Ed.), Intro-
    ducing entering students to the idea of learning.
    Washington, D. C.: American Council on Education,
    1961. Pp. 33-58.
Stern, G. G.   Environments for learning. In R. N. Sanford
    (Ed.), The American college: A psychological and
    social interpretation of higher learning. New York:
    Wiley, 1962. Pp. 690-730.
Stern, G. G., and Scanlon, J. C. Pediatric lions and gyne-
    cological lambs. J. med. Educ., 1958, 33, Part 2,
    12-18.
Stern, G. G., Stein, M. I., and Bloom, B. S. Methods in
    personality assessment. Glencoe, Ill.: Free Press,
    1956.
Stevens, S. S. Mathematics, measurement, and psycho-
    physics. In S. S. Stevens (Ed.), Handbook of experi-
    mental psychology. New York: Wiley, 1951. Pp. 1-49.
Stricker, L. Some item characteristics that evoke acqui-
    escent and social desirability response sets on psycho-
    logical scales. Princeton, N. J.: Educational Testing
    Service Research Bulletin, 1962, in preparation.
Suppes, P. Introduction to logic. Princeton, N. J.: Van
    Nostrand, 1957.
Taylor, Janet A. A personality scale of manifest anxiety.
    J. abnorm. soc. Psychol., 1953, 48, 285-290.
Taylor, J. B. Social desirability and MMPI performance:
    The individual case. J. consult. Psychol., 1959, 23,
    514-517.
Thistlethwaite, D. L. College environments and the de-
    velopment of talent. Science, 1959, 130, No. 3367,
    71-76. (a)

Thistlethwaite, D. L. College press and student achievement. J. educ. Psychol., 1959, 50, 183-191. (b)

Thurstone, L. L. Multiple factor analysis. Chicago: Univer. Chicago Press, 1947.

Tomkins, S. S. Thematic Apperception Test. New York: Grune, 1947.

Tomkins, S. S., and Miner, J. B. Tomkins-Horn Picture Arrangement Test. New York: Springer, 1957.

Torgerson, W. S. Theory and methods of scaling. New York: Wiley, 1958.

Toulmin, S. E. Notes on the logical status of psychoanalysis. Proc. Tenth Int. Congr. Phil., 1948-49. Pp. 925-927.

Voas, R. B. Relationships among three types of response sets. Report No. 15. Pensacola, Fla.: Naval School of Aviation Medicine, 1958.

Wallach, M. A., and Gahm, R. C. Personality functions of graphic constriction and expansiveness. J. Pers., 1960, 28, 73-88.

Wallach, M. A., Green, L. R., Lipsitt, P. D., and Minehart, J. B. Contradiction between overt and projective personality indicators as a function of defensiveness. Psychol. Monogr., 1962, 76, No. 1 (Whole No. 520).

Wallach, M. A., and Greenberg, C. Personality functions of symbolic sexual arousal to music. Psychol. Monogr., 1960, 74, No. 7 (Whole No. 494).

Wassertheil, S. M. A study of the need patterns of negative and positive individuals. Unpublished master's thesis, Syracuse Univer., 1955.

Watson, R. I. Historical review of objective personality testing: The search for objectivity. In B. M. Bass and I. A. Berg (Eds.), Objective approaches to personality assessment. Princeton, N. J.: Van Nostrand, 1959. Pp. 1-23.

Webster, H. Correcting personality scales for response sets or suppression effects. Psychol. Bull., 1958, 55, 62-64.

Webster, H. A note on "Correcting personality scales for response sets or suppression effects." Psychol. Bull., 1959, 56, 240.

Wechsler, D. Manual for the Wechsler Intelligence Scale for Children. New York: Psychological Corporation, 1949, V, 113 pp.

Wechsler, D. Manual for the Wechsler Adult Intelligence Scale. New York: Psychological Corporation, 1955, VI, 110 pp.

Welsh, G. S. Factor dimensions A and R. In G. S. Welsh and W. G. Dahlstrom (Eds.), Basic readings on the MMPI in psychology and medicine. Minneapolis: Univer. Minnesota Press, 1956. Pp. 264-281.

White, R. W. Lives in progress. New York: Dryden, 1952.

White, R. W. The abnormal personality. New York: Ronald Press, 1956.

Wiggins, J. S. Interrelationships among MMPI measures of dissimulation under standard and social desirability instructions. J. consult. Psychol., 1959, 23, 419-427.

Wiggins, J. S. Definitions of social desirability and acquiescence in personality inventories. In S. Messick and J. Ross (Eds.), Measurement in personality and cognition. New York: Wiley, 1962. Pp. 109-127. (a)

Wiggins, J. S. Strategic, method, and stylistic variance in the MMPI. Psychol. Bull., 1962, 59, 224-242. (b)

Wiggins, J. S., and Rumrill, C. Social desirability in the MMPI and Welsh's factor scales A and R. J. consult. Psychol., 1959, 23, 100-106.

Williams, H. L. The development of a caudality scale for the MMPI. J. clin. Psychol., 1952, 8, 293-297.

Witkin, H. A. The perception of the upright. Scient. Amer., 1959, 200, 50-70.

Witkin, H. A., Dyk, Ruth B., Faterson, Hanna F., Goodenough, D. R., and Karp, S. A. Psychological differentiation. New York: Wiley, 1962.

Witkin, H. A., Karp, S. A., and Goodenough, D. R. Dependence in alcoholics. Quart. J. stud. Alcohol, 1959, 20, 493-504.

Witkin, H. A., Lewis, Helen B., Hertzman, M., Machover, Karen, Meissner, Pearl B., and Wapner, S. Personality through perception. New York: Harper, 1954.

Woerner, Margaret, and Levine, T.   A preliminary study
   of the relation between perception and thinking in
   children.   Unpublished study, 1950.
Wright, C. E.   Relations between normative and ipsative
   measures of personality.   Unpublished doctoral dissertation, Univer. of Washington, 1957.

Name Index

317

Subject Index